Walter Lippmann's
Philosophy of International
Politics

FOREIGN POLICY RESEARCH INSTITUTE: UNIVERSITY OF PENNSYLVANIA

Walter Lippmann's Philosophy of International Politics

by Anwar Hussain Syed

University of Massachusetts

Philadelphia
University of Pennsylvania Press

Foreword

I wish to express my deep gratitude to Professors Robert Strausz-Hupé, Norman D. Palmer and Howard C. Perkins of the University of Pennsylvania for their encouragement and advice during the preparation of this work. I wish to thank Mr. Robert C. Herber, Managing Editor of *Orbis,* for his many excellent editorial suggestions. I must acknowledge also my debt to the Foreign Policy Research Institute, University of Pennsylvania, for their interest and assistance in the publication of this work.

Amherst, Massachusetts   A.H.S.
September 1963

To my Father and Mother
in love and gratitude

Introduction

IN RECENT YEARS STUDENTS OF INTERNATIONAL RELATIONS
have increasingly turned to an investigation and analysis
of the forces and drives which shape and mold the behavior
of nation-states and underlie their foreign policies. The
action of these basic forces is twofold. Men may be moved
by them unconsciously. But they are also moved in one way
rather than another by their ideas and estimates of the ethical
as well as the actual nature of these forces and drives. They
make their decisions and judgments not in an intellectual
vacuum but within a certain frame of reference and according to certain criteria of judgment, provided by their positive
and normative theories, interpretations and images of the external reality. As these images change, ways of looking at
foreign affairs, the content and direction of foreign policy
change along with them.

The following work is an attempt to discover and state
the philosophy of international politics of Walter Lippmann,
who has been writing on the subject for a half century. That
in the course of these years he has influenced American
public and official opinion on foreign affairs cannot be
doubted. He is the author of more than twenty books—some
of them "best sellers"—scores of essays published in popular
magazines and learned journals, and countless newspaper
editorials, articles and columns. His syndicated column "To-

7

day and Tomorrow" has regularly appeared in the New York *Herald Tribune* since September 8, 1931. Some years ago, Dr. David Weingast placed his *minimum* readership in the United States at one and a half million.[1] In spite of the fact that Lippmann does not direct his column to the "masses," he is one of the most popular syndicated columnists. As one of his fellow journalists has put it, there was perhaps as much truth as humor in a *New Yorker* cartoon which showed two dowagers in a dining car, one of whom, buried in the *Tribune,* was saying: "Of course, I only take a cup of coffee in the morning. A cup of coffee and Walter Lippmann is all I need."[2]

Lippmann's influence and popularity are also indicated by the fact that he is a highly controversial figure. To some he is the "Man with the Flashlight Mind," the "Great Elucidator," the "Pundit."[3] In 1933, Professor James Truslow Adams went so far as to describe him as "one of the most potent political forces in the nation," as "the American phenomenon." He observed:

[Lippmann] is the only national leader who has appeared in these postwar years. . . . This phenomenon of Walter Lippmann is, it seems to me, a fact of possibly deep significance, and the remainder of his career will teach us not a little as to what sort of a world we are living into. . . . What happens to Lippmann in the next

[1] David E. Weingast, *Walter Lippmann: A Study in Personal Journalism* (New Brunswick: Rutgers University Press, 1949), p. 31. Dr. Weingast notes that the newspapers which carry Lippmann's column have a total circulation of well over 12 million. Lippmann's syndicate estimates that he may have as many as 48 million weekday readers in the United States and abroad.

[2] John Mason Brown, "A Preface to Lippmann," *Saturday Review,* Vol. 37, No. 17 (April 24, 1954), p. 10.

[3] Beverly Smith, "A Man with a Flashlight Mind," *American Magazine,* Vol. 114, No. 3 (September 1932), pp. 16, 86–92.

decade may be of greater interest than what happens to any other single figure now on the American scene.[4]

Others, such as Amos Pinchot, have maintained that Walter Lippmann is an "obfuscator" who drugs "lazy minds" with "pompous nonsense," an "equivocator" who "can be quoted on either side of almost any question," "an ambassador of goodwill to the philistines," a "salesman of plutocracy" whose attacks on democracy leave it "little more than a bleeding stump," a disciple of Alexander Hamilton who was "the first strong advocate of plutocratic fascism in America."[5] Professor Fred Rodell has objected to Lippmann's "uncanny knack of using words in such an impressive way as to appear to be sapient and lucid and even liberal," and to his "temerity to state the disputed as though it were obvious and to intone the obvious as though it were profound.[6]

Much to the annoyance of some of his colleagues, Lippmann's connections with the "high and the mighty" in the officialdom at home and abroad have always been extensive. Though he himself admits to no more than a few interviews with President Wilson, such as "any journalist" would have had, certain quarters suggest that the two men "were much closer than Lippmann admitted. Some careful observers maintain that Wilson used Lippmann's ideas and even, occasionally, his language."[7] In 1917 Lippmann became the Secretary to The Inquiry—a research organization established by President Wilson to collect geographic, ethnic and political data for

[4] James T. Adams, "Walter Lippmann," *Saturday Review of Literature*, Vol. 9, No. 25 (January 7, 1933), p. 362.

[5] Amos Pinchot made these charges in a series of articles in 1933 in *The Nation*: "The Great Elucidator," Vol. 137, No. 3548 (July 5, 1933), pp. 7–10; "The New Tammany," No. 3549 (July 12, 1933), pp. 36–38; "Obfuscator de Luxe," No. 3550 (July 19, 1933), pp. 67–70; "On Democracy," No. 3552 (August 2, 1933), pp. 126–131.

[6] Fred Rodell, "Walter Lippmann," *American Mercury*, Vol. 60, No. 3 (March 1945), pp. 263–273.

[7] Weingast, *op. cit.*, p. 14.

use at the Peace Conference. The Inquiry drafted the memo-
randa which eventually became the territorial sections of the
Fourteen Points. In September 1918, Lippmann was attached
to Colonel House's staff in Paris. When the Germans agreed
to surrender on the basis of the Fourteen Points, the British
and Italian statesmen asked House what Wilson's declaration
meant. The task of explaining the Fourteen Points was en-
trusted to Lippmann. He wrote the "official commentary,"
which was then cabled to Wilson and received his approval.[8]
Lippmann is known to have been on very friendly terms with
the late Cordell Hull and with former Under Secretary of
State Sumner Welles. As a rule, he makes it his business to
cultivate the leaders in business, government and diplomacy.
The latter, on their part, are eager "for his friendly notice as
a matter of good public relations. His stature in the world
of journalism makes him a person to be cultivated."[9]

   Walter Lippmann is undoubtedly in a position to influence
popular and official opinion on foreign affairs. It would then
be appropriate, and perhaps also fruitful, to identify his basic
assumptions and premises, to inquire into the nature of the
philosophy which he urges men in private and public life to
accept as the basis of their thinking on international politics.
More specifically, we should ask: what is his concept of the
nature of man and society; what is his view of the functions,
responsibilities and qualifications of the rulers of men; what
in his opinion is the significance of the division of the world
into sovereign nation-states; what positions does he take on
such controversial subjects as the national interest, the rivalry
of nations, the role of force and of power in international relations, collective security, world government, and the balance

---

[8] Charles Seymour (ed.), *The Intimate Papers of Colonel House* (Boston: Houghton Mifflin Company, 1938), Vol. III, pp. 319–322, Vol. IV,
pp. 152–158.
   [9] Weingast, *op. cit.*, p. 26.

of power; where does he stand in the great debate between political realism and political idealism; what, if any, is his image of the "good society"?

Contents

Walter Lippmann's
Philosophy of International
Politics

I

The Nature of Man and the International Society

On Human Nature

IN *A Preface to Politics,* WALTER LIPPMANN OBSERVES THAT each of the political philosophers of the past, from Plato down to Bentham and Mill, had his own view of human nature which formed the basis of his deliberations on politics. Since the time of Bentham, whose utilitarianism was killed by the refusal of the common man to believe that human actions were solely motivated by calculations of pleasure and pain, political scientists have tended to discuss political institutions without an accompanying analysis of man who makes them and lives under them. Yet when one probes their theories,

there is no escaping the conclusion that they are based on some notion of what man is like. The student of politics must consciously or unconsciously form a conception of human nature, and the less conscious he is of his conception the more likely he is to be dominated by it.[1]

In other words, the student of political science today con-

[1] Graham Wallas, *Human Nature in Politics* (New York: Alfred A. Knopf, 1910), p. 38, cited by Lippmann in *A Preface to Politics.*

structs his system of theory on assumptions which he not only fails to examine and analyze but of which he is hardly aware. Lippmann condemns this indifference to the study of human nature, asserting that observations on this subject are the only part of the thought of the past and present which can claim lasting merit. For whereas the social environment, of which political institutions are but a part, constantly changes, human nature in all its profounder aspects remains constant over an extensive period of time. There is no such thing as a perfect theory embodying the final truth, for the truth which it is supposed to embody is in fact a thousand truths which constantly grow and change. The value of Plato's work, for instance, lies not in the details of his system but in his insight into human nature. This insight, partial though it be,

is what constitutes the abiding monument of Plato's genius. . . . If [a] thinker sees at all deeply into the life of his own time, his theoretical system will rest on observation of human nature. That remains as a residue of wisdom long after his reasoning and his concrete program have passed into limbo.[2]

Lippmann himself has written on the subject in some detail, and it would seem appropriate to begin a study of his political philosophy with an examination of his views on human nature.

Moral and political philosophers have debated the question whether man is inherently "good" or "bad." Lippmann is not a party to this controversy, but his comments on the two schools indicate a possible leaning. He criticizes those liberals who maintain that all the mischief and misery in the world is finally attributable to social environment, since man himself is naturally good and innocent. These people never

[2] Walter Lippmann, *A Preface to Politics* (New York: Mitchell Kennerley, 1913), p. 210.

stop to think that in taking this position they challenge the testimony not merely of their "maiden aunts, but of all the greatest teachers of wisdom."[3] They create an image of man, and then frown at reality which does not answer to it. They are bound to be frustrated because human nature is a shocking affair if one approaches it with romantic optimism.

The one thing that no democrat may assume is that the people are dear good souls, fully competent for their task. The most valuable leaders never assume that. No one, for example, would accuse Karl Marx of disloyalty to working men. Yet his "contempt for popular opinion was one of his most strongly developed characteristics."[4]

On the other hand, some people have thought that the natural impulses of man are lecherous, greedy and cruel. They assume that each impulse has a certain typical expression, and that if the particular expression is evil the impulse itself must be evil. Their way to deal with these impulses is to outlaw them, and to taboo their satisfaction. We know a little better today! We know that there can be many avenues for the satisfaction of desire. And if one of them is evil, it does not follow that the desire itself is evil.

In *A Preface to Politics* Lippmann observes that the controversy is futile, for nothing is intrinsically good or evil. Theories of morality are meaningful only in so far as they help find a mode of living which men who live it will instinctively find to be good. The criteria of moral judgment are subjective, residing in the mind of the agent of the act. "Plato may describe the objects which men rejoice over, he may guide them to good experiences, but each man in his inward life is a last judgment on all his values."[5] The goal

---

[3] Walter Lippmann, *A Preface to Morals* (New York: The Macmillan Company, 1929), p. 152.
[4] *A Preface to Politics*, pp. 302–303.
[5] *Ibid.*, p. 200.

of all action is, in the final analysis, aesthetic and not moral. But the futility of the controversy points to another channel into which we may direct our study. We may take a positive rather than a normative approach to the study of human nature and ask how men act, what moves them to do the things they do. Some writers, such as the classical economists and even some modern political scientists and statesmen, have argued that human action is guided and determined by the laws of reason, that a man consciously desires something, thinks out a plan of action and then acts. Inspired by the writings of Graham Wallas, William McDougal and Sigmund Freud, and supported by some psychologists, Lippmann rejects this thesis.[6] He submits that men quite often desire first and reason afterwards. The great philosophers from Machiavelli to Marx employed their knowledge of history, logic and science to support and strengthen their deepest desires. "The original genius sees the dynamic purpose first, finds reasons afterwards. This amounts to saying that man when he is most creative is not a rational, but a wilful animal."[7]

Is it deplorable that man is not always a rational, reasoning being? Should we try to make him more rational and subject his impulses to reason? In *A Preface to Politics*, Lippmann is not at all unhappy about the irrationality of man. He approv-

---

[6] Graham Wallas warns against the tendency to exaggerate the "intellectuality of mankind and to ignore the pre-rational bases of human behavior." *Human Nature in Politics*, pp. 45–72. He maintains further that it is not possible for man to be rational all the time. "A man may be convinced by a long train of cogent reasoning that he will go to hell if he visits a certain house; and yet he will do so in satisfaction of a half-conscious craving whose existence he is ashamed to recognize." *Ibid.*, pp. 63–64.

[7] *A Preface to Politics*, p. 213. Disraeli made a remarkably similar statement in *Coningsby*: "We are not indebted to the reason of man for any of the greatest achievements which are the landmark of human action and human progress. . . . Man is only truly great when he acts from the passions; never irresistible but when he appeals to imagination." Quoted in Graham Wallas, *op. cit.*, p. 192.

ingly quotes Hume as having said that reason itself is an irrational impulse, and agrees with George Santayana, who contended that

the ideal of rationality is itself as arbitrary, as much dependent on the needs of a finite organization, as any other ideal. Only as ultimately securing tranquillity of mind, which the philosopher instinctively pursues, has it for him any necessity. . . . What really demands rationality, what makes it a good and indispensable thing, is not its own nature, but our need of it both in safe and economical action and in the pleasures of comprehension.[8]

Reason is then not an end in itself, but only an instrument for providing tranquillity of mind and pleasures of comprehension to those who seek the truth of things. But not all men may seek the truth; for not only is it a thousand truths which constantly grow and change, but it has no intrinsic value. The pursuit of truth is not the *summum bonum*.

The falseness of an opinion is not for us any objection to it: it is here, perhaps, that our new language sounds most strangely. The question is how far an opinion is life-furthering, life-preserving, species-preserving, perhaps species-rearing.[9]

Not everything that seems irrational, unreasonable or untrue is valueless. Lippmann points to the usefulness of social myths, which, he says, are to be judged by their ability to express human aspirations. As the embodiment of a nation's desires, they may represent its finest energy. It is precisely because they are expressions of will rather than descriptions of facts that they leave their mark on the course of history.[10]

[8] Quoted in *A Preface to Politics*, p. 216.

[9] Friedrich W. Nietzsche, *Beyond Good and Evil*, quoted in *A Preface to Politics*, pp. 233–234.

[10] *A Preface to Politics*, pp. 231–232. Several writers have defended social and political myths as being essential to the satisfaction of vital emotional needs of the individual. The mythical "sovereign" authority of the British monarch is a case in point. "We must not let in daylight upon magic. . . . The existence of this secret power is, according to abstract

The tranquillity of mind for the individual, the satisfaction of his desires, is the end of human effort. Reason is a means to that end. "It seems like topsy-turvyland," says Lippmann, "to make reason serve the irrational. Yet this is just what it has always done, and ought always to do."[11] A human impulse is more important than any existing theory. We cannot ignore human impulses. Neither good nor bad, they are the motive power of behavior. "They are the energies of the soul. . . . Like dynamite they are capable of all sorts of uses. . . . All that is dynamic in human character is in these rooted lusts."[12]

We have noted above that in *A Preface to Politics*, Lippmann denies the efficacy of moral codes and maintains that each individual is himself the final arbiter of the ethics of his thought and behavior. Men do and should live by impulse. But then do we not face the prospect of society sinking into sheer anarchy under the stress and strain of the conflicting and ever-changing standards of judgment of innumerable individuals? Having discarded his ethical heritage, and hav-

---

theory, a defect in our constitutional polity, but it is a defect incident to a civilization, such as ours, where august and therefore unknown powers are needed, as well as known and serviceable powers." Walter Bagehot, *The English Constitution*. (London: Oxford University Press, 1952 impression), p. 53.

[11] *A Preface to Politics*, p. 235. At this point the psychologist parts company with Lippmann. He supports Lippmann in the view that reason does often serve the irrational, but would not say that such should be the case. That is evidently a norm and, therefore, outside his field. As a matter of fact, Professor Wallas, who was both a psychologist and a political scientist, takes the opposite position, as we shall see in the following pages. Lippmann's stand is akin to that implicit in the statements of Disraeli and Santayana quoted above, and also to that of Hume, who maintained that reason is the guide of conduct only in the sense that it indicates the means to the desired end, but that the desirability of the end itself is neither reasonable nor unreasonable. "Reason is and ought only to be the slave of the passions and can never pretend to any other office than to serve and obey them." Quoted in George H. Sabine, *A History of Political Theory* (New York: Henry Holt and Co., 1950), p. 600.

[12] *A Preface to Politics*, p. 50.

ing received in turn the dictum that he should rely, as a guide to behavior, on an aesthetic sense which he may or may not possess, is not the individual now altogether without a standard, groping in the dark, acting arbitrarily on his impulses like his counterpart in Hobbes's state of nature? Apart from being a menace to his fellow man, has he not lost whatever little of that supreme good—the tranquillity of mind—he had under the rule, tyrannical perhaps, of moral codes?

Lippmann is not oblivious to the dangers inherent in an unqualified reliance on impulses. The point of his argument seems to lie in the advocacy of a new approach to the problems created by the non-rational and irrational self of man, to the impulses which motivate his action perhaps more often than does reason. The way to deal with the evil expressions of desire is not to taboo the desire, but to give it new interests. Instead of trying to crush it, we should turn the energy behind it into new channels, remembering all the time that every lust is capable of some civilized expression. History shows that while the impulses of man have not changed over the centuries, the modes of their expression have changed enormously from epoch to epoch.[13]

---

[13] *A Preface to Politics*, pp. 49–50, 300.

This seems to be a point at issue among psychologists. Some of them maintain that the observable behavior of the individual is socially determined, for what is fixed in his nature is only unchanneled energy. As the complex whole of innate capacities and acquired abilities, human nature is infinitely malleable. See Hadley Cantril, "Don't Blame It On Human Nature," *New York Times Magazine*, July 6, 1947, p. 32.

Graham Wallas makes the same point in *Human Nature in Politics* (pp. 59–60). He offers it as his "provisional opinion" that new expressions can be given to the instincts of possession and pugnacity so as to render their indulgence completely harmless.

On the other hand, some experts maintain that the view of our innate capacities as pure energy can be exaggerated. They incline to the view that inherent qualities determine, to some extent, the channels into which they will be directed. See John Bowlby, "Psychology and Democracy," *The Political Quarterly*, Vol. 17, No. 1 (January–March 1946), p. 62.

Again, Professor Durbin holds that "as far as aggressiveness and fighting is concerned, there is no noticeable improvement in the behavior of adults

Shifting the focus of attention from ethics to psychology does not mean that we accept human nature in its present character. Lippmann concedes that in their uncivilized or partially civilized state, our impulses cannot be relied upon to create the beautiful life. We cannot obey every impulse or desire, for the result would be anarchy. But neither can we distrust and curb every impulse, for the result then would be suicide. We should understand that each desire and each object as such, taken separately, is as innocent and as neutral as the forces that move the planets. The quality of good and evil lies not in the impulses as such, or in the objects as such, but in the relation between impulses and objects. The making of inventories of good and bad impulses is, therefore, fundamentally misleading. It is likewise misleading to make lists of human impulses, for if we consider them closely, we must realize that they do not move all persons alike, nor any one person the same way at all times and under all circumstances. Again, at any given time, we desire only those objects which we are capable of desiring. Desires change, and the desirability of the objects around us changes too. Each moment of behavior is then to be regarded not as the isolated manifestation of some fixed elements in human nature, but as a stage in its evolution.

The conception of human nature as developing behavior is indeed heartening to those who seek to reconstruct it in order to create the good society, to make man's life more worth living, pleasant and beautiful. But the builders of the new man must have some terms of reference, certain criteria

---

compared with that of the most savage animals and children. If anything, it is more ruthless. . . . Men will die like flies for theories and exterminate each other with every instrument of destruction for abstractions." He concludes that "the character of the *id*—or complex of instinctive impulses —does not change materially as the individual grows older." *The Politics of Democratic Socialism* (London: Routledge and Kegan Paul Ltd., 1940), pp. 49–50, 53.

for determining the channels into which developing behavior is to be directed and for measuring the progress of their mission. Lippmann believes that the goal of their reconstructive endeavor, which would also be the standard of judgment and the measure of progress, must be the creation of "right relationships" between the individual and his environment. Right relationships are those in which there is a harmonious adjustment between desires and the objects of desires, where men are moved not by considerations of good and evil but by their sense of beauty and by the desire to create beauty, order, harmony and neighborliness. The model of this harmonious adjustment is Chuck Connors' "gentleman," who "is 'a bloke as can do whatever he wants to do.' . . . He is not the battlefield of wants and prohibitions; in him impulses flow freely through beneficent channels."[14] When a man becomes civilized, when his aesthetic sense is perfected, when he becomes a true artist, morality becomes irrelevant to his conduct. He does the right thing not because he thinks that that is what he should do, but because he cannot do otherwise.

Let someone throw the energies of his soul into the making of something and the instinct of workmanship will take care of his honesty. . . . A genuine craftsman will not adulterate his product: the reason isn't because duty says he shouldn't, but because passion says he couldn't.[15]

In *A Preface to Politics,* the ideal world is inhabited by artists and craftsmen, who are moved to action by their sense of beauty, and live in the enjoyment of their desires in peace and harmony. Lippmann admits that not all men have the same creative abilities, nor do they have similar tastes. Half-protestingly, he says, one accepts Bernard Shaw's amendment to the golden rule: "Do not do unto others as you would that

[14] *A Preface to Politics,* p. 147.
[15] *Ibid.,* pp. 59–60.

they should do unto you. Their tastes may not be the same."[16]
But Lippmann seems to believe that these individual variations only make for the richness of life in society.

Living as one likes and following one's impulses as they
come, without the restraints of traditional morality, may be a
safe and ideal way of life for Plato's guardians, Chuck Connors' gentlemen and Lippmann's artists. But surely the so-
called common man cannot rely on his impulses, which are
by hypothesis uncivilized, to provide him with a guide to
conduct. Lippmann implies that the agents of human reconstruction, such as his gentlemen-artists, will, in the course of
their own pursuit of beauty and the pleasures of comprehension, set standards of judgment and guides to behavior which
the common man can follow. He can accept them with
sympathy and understanding if he is artistic and spiritual
enough. If he is not—as is more likely—he must accept them
unquestioningly and follow them blindly. The shift of emphasis from ethics to aesthetics has then no intellectual significance for him. Formerly, he had a code of morality which he
understood dimly and practiced half-heartedly. He now has
a guide to action which he understands perhaps even more
imperfectly and, therefore, follows still more reluctantly.

Lippmann must be cognizant of these difficulties, for he
is exceedingly pessimistic about the possibility of re-creating
man. The politics of reconstruction, he says, can bear fruit
only among people who are educated and who are willing to
subject their prejudices and established ways of thinking to
critical examination.[17] But usually men do not like to change;
they tend to fall into a routine which has all the appearances
of activity with few of its responsibilities.

To do what has always been done, to think in well-cut channels,
to give up "the intolerable disease of thought," is an almost con-

---

[16] Quoted in *A Preface to Politics*, p. 147.
[17] *A Preface to Politics*, p. 305.

stant demand of our natures. . . . Confronted with a novelty, the first impulse is to snub it, and send it into exile. . . . But if the problem is more heavily charged with power, the taboo irritates the force until it explodes. . . . At this point, the whole routineer scheme of things collapses, there is a period of convulsion and Caesarian births, and men weary of excitement sink back into a newer routine. Thus the cycle of futility is completed.[18]

At the end of *A Preface to Politics*, Lippmann leans to the view that a final state of blessedness will never materialize, and that the world of harmony and beauty will remain an ever-receding goal of human endeavor.

The student of Lippmann's political philosophy can draw the following conclusions from the argument in *A Preface to Politics*. In spite of his criticism of the school of thought which regards human nature as inherently base and mischievous, Lippmann's own position is not radically different. Men may not be naturally greedy, cruel and brutish. But they certainly are uneducated, foolish and obstinate. It is true that they can become wise, sensitive and creative through education. But the process is so long and difficult, and the standards of accomplishment so high, that the aforementioned weaknesses constitute a condition of mankind given and unalterable in the foreseeable future.

Secondly, it seems that Lippmann's argument is not addressed to the common man, purporting to give him a new standard of judgment, but to practical politicians and statesmen. He exhorts them to shift the point of emphasis from what they think human nature should be to what human nature actually is, to turn from doctrine and dogma to reality. It is they who have to become guardians and gentlemen-artists. They have to guide and lead the common man, rather than be guided and led by him.

A word may be said here about the genesis of Lippmann's

[18] *Ibid.*, pp. 298–300.

statement on human nature in *A Preface to Politics*. We have indicated above that his psychology was heavily influenced by the leading contemporary men in the field. The picture becomes somewhat blurred when we try to identify the philosophic sources of his inspiration. He himself writes that the ideal of human reconstruction together with its model—the civilized man—is a thoroughly Greek concept.[19] This is true, so far as it goes. But it is clear that the main body of his argument is not Greek in origin. On the contrary, it is a product of the rebellion, as Bertrand Russell would put it, of the modern man of action against the authority of Greece, and more particularly of Plato. It bears the unmistakable mark of the nineteenth-century romanticist revolt against reason. In *A Preface to Politics*, Lippmann is more concerned with "the tree of life" than with knowledge, and in that respect is closer to Byron than to Plato.[20]

Lippmann came into close personal contact with William James, George Santayana and Graham Wallas at Harvard, and was considerably influenced by them.[21] But it would be difficult to name any one of the great molders of opinion from Rousseau and Hume down to James and Dewey as the principal source of Lippmann's views. In *A Preface to Poli-*

[19] *Ibid.*, p. 147.
[20] One may contrast Plato's "Virtue is knowledge" with Byron's
      Sorrow is knowledge: they who know the most
      Must mourn the deepest o'er the fatal truth
      The tree of knowledge is not that of Life.
Quoted in Bertrand Russell, *A History of Western Philosophy* (New York: Simon and Schuster, 1945), p. 750.
[21] Lippmann was not formally a student of James, but met him from time to time. Santayana regarded Lippmann and T. S. Eliot as his most promising pupils. He chose Lippmann, when the latter was in his fourth year at Harvard, as his assistant in a course on the history of philosophy. The extent of Lippmann's relations with Graham Wallas is indicated by the fact that Professor Wallas dedicated his famous book, *The Great Society*, to him. See David Elliot Weingast, *Walter Lippmann: A Study in Personal Journalism* (New Brunswick: Rutgers University Press, 1949), p. 6.

tics, there is at work a whole cluster of influences, emanating from men who in some instances were diametrically opposed to each other. Lippmann takes from Schopenhauer and Nietzsche the idea of the primacy of the will but replaces their pessimism with the warmth and benevolence of William James. His gentleman-artist bears little resemblance to Nietzsche's "artist-tyrant," who is a cruel, cunning and ruthless aristocrat, ready to sacrifice the majority of men—"the bungled and botched"—to promote his selfish interests. Lippmann's Roosevelt, on the other hand, is principally concerned with the happiness and well-being of the masses. Again, he takes from Bergson and James his preference for action over contemplation, but gives it the foundation of art and beauty which he takes from Santayana and Hume.

In *A Preface to Morals* Lippmann emphatically denounces the thesis that man can rely on his impulses to lead the good life. Now he is more concerned with the need to discipline them than with the task of finding fine expressions for them. It is highly significant, he says, that in one form or another Socrates and Buddha, Jesus and Saint Paul, Plotinus and Spinoza have all taught that the good life is impossible without asceticism. "They cannot all have been so foolish as Anthony Comstock. They must have had some insight into experience which led them to that conclusion."[22] Asceticism should not be confused with self-mutilation. There is a sane and civilized asceticism, for instance that of Plato's guardians, whom their discipline has taught to abandon all private aims and to find happiness in an appreciation of a perfectly ordered commonwealth.[23]

The philosophers' emphasis on asceticism is easily understood when we look at human nature as developing behavior. The moral goal of this development is maturity, which is the

[22] *A Preface to Morals*, p. 156.
[23] *Ibid.*, pp. 159–160.

stage at which the individual, having grown up to understand the reality of things, adjusts his wishes to the world around him. The mature man is at peace with himself, and in harmony with the facts of human existence. He has virtue, and he is happy. His desire receives from its object a complex stimulus which evokes a complex response. He discovers that there are more things in heaven and earth than he had imagined in his earlier, immature life, that

there are many choices and that none is absolute, that beyond the mountains, as the Chinese say, there are people also. The obviously pleasant and unpleasant become less obviously so. Delight is perhaps not so intense nor pain so poignant as youth and the romantics would have them.[24]

In order to reach maturity, man has to break with the child's attachment to persons and things. He has to learn that he cannot possess whatever his heart may desire, and therefore he has to teach and train his heart to desire only that which is attainable. He has to reconcile himself to the hard fact that he cannot possess things forever, because they change and slip away. He has to modify his sense of possession and learn to hold things not by grabbing and grasping them but by understanding and remembering them. Then he is wholly an adult.

Then he has conquered mortality in the only way mortal men can conquer it. For he has ceased to expect anything of the world which it cannot give, and he has learned to love it under the only aspect in which it is eternal.[25]

The asceticism which the philosophers have preached is another name for the career in conquering immaturity. When maturity is attained, the pangs of renunciation, the ascetic discipline become unnecessary. Then man does not face the problem of whether to yield to impulse or whether to curb

[24] *Ibid.*, p. 183.
[25] *Ibid.*, p. 191.

it, and how much to curb it and how much to yield. "A mature desire is innocent. This, I think, is the final teaching of the great sages."[26]

The immature man is a lost soul. Lippmann warns, however, that the road to maturity is long and arduous. No wonder then that the world is full of these lost souls. We should also remember that the human character is a complicated thing, that its elements do not march in step and develop evenly. A man may be a sage in some things and a child in others. That explains why so many people are only partially matured and civilized. We learn to do things, get information, and "become intelligent more easily than we learn what to like and what to reject. In a word, we learn the arts and sciences long before we learn philosophy."[27] The essence of maturity lies in acquiring a different outlook on life, and not in gathering information about names and dates.

The immature cannot believe that so much in the universe is completely indifferent to them and to their purposes and ambitions, that in the nature of things there is much fumbling and trial and error, that frustration and defeat are just as normal in human experience as are victory and glory. They never face the fact that ". . . there is evil which is as genuine as goodness, that there is ugliness and violence which are no less real than joy and love."[28] With the immature, says Lippmann, the belief that evil is unreal becomes a deep preference for not knowing the truth, a habitual desire to live in a utopia. "Out of this rebellion against truth, out of this determination that facts shall conform to our wishes, are born all manner of bigotry and uncharitableness."[29]

The final stage in the development of human behavior in

26 *Ibid.*, p. 192.
27 *Ibid.*, p. 186.
28 *Ibid.*, p. 188.
29 *Ibid.*, p. 190.

both *A Preface to Politics* and *A Preface to Morals* is maturity. But the gentleman-artist has now become a philosopher. Formerly he was in harmony with the objects of his desire because he was a creative artist with a sharp intuition and a keen aesthetic sense. Now that he is a philosopher, the source of his contentment is not his sense of beauty but knowledge. He is essentially rational, and his tool is reason, which is no longer the handmaid of impulse. Good and evil are still subjective qualities but nonetheless real. Truth is perhaps still a thousand truths, but its pursuit is indispensable to the attainment of maturity. The essence of virtue lies not in the creation of beauty, but in acquiring knowledge and discovering the reality of things. Lippmann has retained his ideal of human reconstruction, but its hue and color are now distinctly classical. He has likewise retained his pessimism about the final outcome of the endeavor to reconstruct human nature. Men are childish, immature and unwise; they muddle their way into more muddles.

The argument of *A Preface to Morals* is further developed and refined in *The Public Philosophy*. Reason is now clearly the master, and not the servant, of the impulse. Lippmann now rejects the position of Hume and Nietzsche, Santayana, Shaw and McDougal that reason is an instrument for the fulfillment of impulses, which determine the ends of action and provide the criteria of judgment. He complains that "when reason no longer represents society within the human psyche, then it becomes the instrument of appetite, desire and passion."[30] He no longer regards the natural impulses of man, which constitute his first nature, as pure, innocent and neutral like the forces which move the planets. They are now barbaric, "ever insurgent against reason."[31] In the

[30] Walter Lippmann, *The Public Philosophy* (Boston: Little, Brown and Co., 1955), p. 77.
[31] *Ibid.*, p. 138.

traditions of civility, they must be subordinated to man's second, acquired and more rational nature.

In recounting the death of Socrates, says Lippmann, Plato provides a perfect illustration of the distinction between our first and second natures. Refusing to escape from the prison, Socrates argues:

The Athenians have thought it fit to condemn me, and accordingly I have thought it better and more right to remain here and undergo my sentence; for I am inclined to think that these muscles and bones of mine would have gone off long ago to Megara or Boeotia . . . if they had been moved only by their own idea of what was best, and if I had not chosen as the better and the nobler part, instead of playing truant and running away, to undergo any punishment which the state inflicts. There is surely a strange confusion of causes and conditions in all this. It may be said, indeed, that without bones and muscles and the other parts of the body I cannot execute my purposes. But to say that I do as I do because of them, and that this is the way in which mind acts, and not from the choice of the best, is a very careless and idle mode of thinking.[32]

It will be seen that in spite of the radical changes which Lippmann's view of human nature underwent from 1913 to 1955, his estimate of the common man's moral and intellectual abilities has remained practically unchanged. Except in the rare case when they are civilized, men cannot comprehend the reality of complex things; they are ever insurgent against reason, and their natural impulses cannot be trusted to create the good life.

[32] Plato, *Phaedo*, in *The Dialogues of Plato*, Jowett translation, (New York: Random House, 1937), p. 483. Quoted in *The Public Philosophy*, p. 138.

A World of Nation-States

The operative unit in international affairs is the sovereign nation-state. It is true, says Lippmann, that international commerce and contact have been corroding frontiers, making supra-national groupings, and intermingling the populations, but it would be a mistake to think that this process has gone far or deep. On the whole, nations still live behind their frontiers, over which few people ever look. When they deal with one another, "they are dealing with foreigners, each focussed into a sovereignty. . . . They settle differences by negotiation or war."[33] Writing in 1943, Lippmann observed that this condition was given and unalterable for practical purposes, at least in the foreseeable future.[34]

"Nation" is one of those vague and elusive terms in political thought which are difficult to define. Religion, language, ethnic composition, history, geography, customs and mores, all enter into its realization. According to the *Nation*,

a nation exists where its component atoms believe it to be a nation; where they are willing to live for and to die for a mystical entity whose life includes the lives of all the individuals but whose life transcends the lives of those individuals.[35]

What is the magic in this mystical entity that men live for it and die for it? Lippmann's answer is significant in that it reveals his distaste for nationalism. Discussing the subject at some length in *The Stakes of Diplomacy*, he traces the feel-

[33] Walter Lippmann, *The Stakes of Diplomacy* (New York: Henry Holt and Co., 1915), p. 45.

[34] Walter Lippmann, *U.S. Foreign Policy: Shield of the Republic* (Boston: Little, Brown and Co., 1943), p. 106. This should not be taken to mean that he regards the condition as desirable. As we shall see in the following pages, Lippmann condemns the nation-state as the unit of human political organization.

[35] *Nation* (London), June 26, 1915; quoted in *The Stakes of Diplomacy*, p. 58.

ing of nationality to the impressions, associations and loyalties which we form in our infancy and early childhood.
Basically, it is a cluster of primitive feelings which a man
absorbs long before his conscious education begins.

The house, the street, the meadow and hill upon which he first
opened his eyes, the reactions to family and strangers which remain as the types of his loves and hates, the earliest sounds which
brought fear and pleasure—these are the stuff out of which nationality is made.[36]

This conglomeration of early impressions and attitudes constitutes the ultimate background of the mind, its first culture.
It modifies and is modified by later experiences. It may be
present only in the subconscious, forgotten beyond easy recall. But it does not perish. In times of peace and prosperity
we are hardly aware of it. But in periods of stress and strain
we quickly retreat into our origins. The mental images of
things long past are revived, re-created and enlivened. Once
again, our first culture returns to dominate our conscious
mind.

We become intensely aware of the earliest things with which we
were associated. . . . We huddle to the people with whom we
played as children. . . . The alleys and the rookeries where we first
met the world are transfigured in memory. They are us, more
poignant than recent attachments, deeper than all later theories.
Whatever conflicts with them breaks down. We cannot imagine
anything to be right or worthy which these dumb affections do
not sanction.[37]

This first culture, this ultimate background of the mind,
performs an indispensable function in that it serves as the
foundation on which the personality structure of later years
is built. It is a source of inspiration to the artist, it imparts

[36] *The Stakes of Diplomacy*, p. 60.
[37] *The Stakes of Diplomacy*, p. 61.

color and beauty to his product, and at the same time it is the raw material with which his talent, acquired in later life, must work. Life would be dry, thin and colorless without it. To the average man, who may not be an artist, it gives self-confidence and keeps him going. Like the pride of race, nationalism is the sense that our origins are worthy of respect. A man without it is a man without the ground under his feet. If he is ashamed of his origins, they will haunt him forever, "they will rob him of the basis of his assurance, leave him an interloper in the world."[38] When we speak of a thwarted nationality like that of the Irish or the Jews, we mean something deeper than apparent political subjection. We mean a kind of homelessness in the wide, wide world which houses of brick can hide but not remedy. In this sense, nationalism is the pride in that essence of our being which gives us standing and distinction vis-à-vis other peoples. "If the nationality to which we belong is honored, we feel honored; we swell up perceptibly at hearing a name that is great in the world."[39] The greatness and glory of the nation, its strength, its triumphs and its honor mitigate the pain of our individual failures, the shame of our personal weaknesses. Like a magnet the nation attracts that vast fund of loyalty which men desire to shower on an entity more permanent and extensive than their personal lives.[40]

This union with our origins is an exceedingly powerful factor in all politics. It may appear as a desire to civilize the heathen, as a passion to defend the American ice-cream soda, or as a readiness to be maimed, starved and frozen to death in defense of the nation's honor.

National patriotism, where it is directed against foreign powers, unites men otherwise divided by religion, by party, by class and

[38] *The Stakes of Diplomacy*, p. 61.
[39] *Ibid.*, p. 68.
[40] *Ibid.*, p. 69.

occupation. Nationalism is more powerful, being rooted so profoundly in human nature, than any ideology which has recently been propounded by a party congress and is being imposed by propaganda on the top of men's heads. . . . Being so powerful, nationalism is, of course, powerful both for good or evil. But the one thing we can be sure of is this: it is too powerful to be ignored by us or repressed by the Russians.[41]

Nationalism then can be a constructive force in human affairs, but, cautions Lippmann, only so long as it lies dormant in the subconscious mind, passively suggesting, perhaps, new goals of endeavor to our creative ability, but held always in subservience to our more rational and civilized selves. When this sleeping giant is aroused—and it is most surely aroused when it is attacked—it takes on the character of an irrational desire to possess, hold and protect whatever is associated with our earliest hates and loves. It becomes primarily an offensive and defensive reaction to fear: a signal to "rush and take cover" or to "tighten up for a fight." When it dominates the minds of men, they ask to be led by someone to whom they can give supreme power. They line up behind that "mortal god," and obey. The community is turned into one super-person. The group lives; the individual is lost in its greater glory.[42] Men are moved by their first, and not their second, acquired and civilized natures.

Lippmann's analysis of the national sentiment has merit in so far as it identifies the raw materials which go into its making. But it fails to explain why the love of the "rookeries and the alleys" does not produce an equally strong national feeling in all countries and in all ages. It would appear that nationalism is more than the sum total of our primitive feelings, our early associations. One may argue that it is partly

[41] Walter Lippmann, "Today and Tomorrow" in the New York *Herald Tribune*, July 7, 1953. Hereinafter referred to as T and T.
[42] *The Stakes of Diplomacy*, pp. 69–70.

a product of the specific ideas which men have developed at a certain stage in the history of their intellectual evolution.[43] Our early loves and hates could perhaps be regarded as energy which can be directed into several channels, and inasmuch as it has been called to the service of the nation-state rather than the alley or the village, its role and significance in the affairs of men have been transformed. One may say with Professor Kohn:

Nationalism—our identification with the life and aspirations of uncounted millions whom we shall never know, with a territory which we shall never visit in its entirety—is qualitatively different from the love of family or of home surroundings. It is qualitatively akin to the love of humanity or of the whole earth. . . . In modern times it has been the power of an idea, not the call of blood that has constituted and molded nationalities.[44]

When the tide of nationalism runs high, when the pride in their heritage and origins swells up, men tend to embrace the view that they are, in some crucial way, superior to the rest of mankind, that they have the sole right to define and determine their "place in the sun," which they may occupy and hold to the exclusion of others. Lippmann calls it the doctrine of exclusive nationalism, which, he says, found expression in the conduct of Germany before and after World War I. In 1917 Lippmann wrote that Germany's acceptance and practice of this theory had been a major factor in bringing about the war. The Anglo-German agreement of June 1914 had named Asia Minor as Germany's place in the sun. But Germany decided unilaterally that she needed the exclusive and absolute control of the Balkan highway to reach and exploit the Turkish Empire. She denied that other nations had an interest or a stake in the fate of Europe. She pro-

[43] See Snyder, Richard Carlton and H. Hubert Wilson, Roots of Political Behavior (New York: American Book Company, 1949), p. 3.

[44] Hans Kohn, The Idea of Nationalism (New York: The Macmillan Company, 1951), pp. 9, 16.

ceeded to crush Serbia and, in violating the neutrality of Belgium, attacked the "public law of Europe."[45]

Germany's ruthless and reckless application of the doctrine of exclusive nationalism so horrified Lippmann that in April 1917 he was ready to denounce all nationalism. The grand alliance against Germany became in his eyes a union of peoples "determined to end forever that intriguing, adventurous nationalism which has torn the world for three centuries."[46] He observed that out of the necessity to defend themselves against the ravages of exclusive nationalism, men had gradually formulated the concept of a "cooperative nationalism." He saw a widespread movement toward the goal of a free and cooperative world.

China and India have been stirred out of their dependence. America has abandoned its isolation. Russia has become something like a republic. The British Empire is moving toward closer federation. . . . Men are crying that they must be free and that they must be united. They have learnt that they cannot be free unless they cooperate, that they cannot cooperate unless they are free.[47]

Needless to say, subsequent events did not justify Lippmann's optimism. Men who were supposedly consumed by the passion to cooperate with one another continued to quarrel and fight over "vital" interests. The tide of exclusive nationalism continued to rise.

In *The Good Society*, Lippmann observes that modern nationalism is exclusive and divisive, because its standard-bearers are protectionist, collectivist and authoritarian in their premises.[48] It is significant, he says, that the movement toward the amalgamation of small sovereignties into larger

---

[45] Walter Lippmann, "The World Conflict in its Relation to American Democracy," *Annals of the American Academy of Political and Social Science*, Vol. 72, No. 161 (July 1917), p. 4.
[46] *Ibid.*
[47] *Ibid.*
[48] Walter Lippmann, *The Good Society* (Boston: Little, Brown and Co., 1937), p. 134.

political unions should have stopped after 1870. He rejects the argument that it stopped because the peoples who had a common linguistic, cultural or ethnic background, or a common national consciousness, had united by that time. For among the unifications that were effected up to 1870, we find instances where political union preceded the appearance of a strong national feeling, where people who spoke different languages and professed different religions overcame their particularism and became politically united.

It should be remembered, says Lippmann, that the nationalism which encouraged larger political unions flourished in the interlude between the decline and revival of mercantilism.[49] The period from, say, 1776 to 1870, which saw the accomplishment of many great political unifications, was the golden age of free trade between nations and free markets at home.[50] The movement was arrested and then reversed when reaction against economic freedom set in about 1870.

Lippmann argues that the relation between economic illiberalism and divisive nationalism is not coincidental, but organic. In the nature of things, liberalism unites and authoritarianism divides.[51] Let us take, says Lippmann, a

[49] *Ibid.*, p. 135. It is possible to take a different view of the matter, to wit, that mercantilism too acted as a unifying force. It stimulated trade, and sought to break down the economic particularism which underlay the uniformity of the medieval order. It operated to make the state the economic unit and to assert its undivided authority in the sphere of trade and manufacture throughout its territory. Externally, it sought to increase the wealth and therefore the power of the state in relation to other states. The idea, as Colbert had put it, was that "trade is the source of finance, and finance is the vital nerve of war." E. F. Heckscher, *Mercantilism* (London: George Allen and Unwin Ltd., 1935), Vol. II, p. 17.

[50] *The Good Society*, p. 135.

[51] *The Good Society*, p. 135. There seem to be some important forces, other than liberalism, which make for political unification. According to W. B. Pillsbury, a common hate is one of the most frequently effective factors in making and uniting nations. See *The Psychology of Nationality and Internationalism* (New York: D. Appleton and Co., 1919), Chapter 3. In *The Stakes of Diplomacy* (pp. 174–175), Lippmann himself observed that fear was "one of the most powerful forces that unify mankind," and

simple example of authoritarianism, the protective tariff. Suppose two or more of the major industrial powers established a system of free trade as between themselves, but imposed a uniform tariff against the rest of the world. This arrangement would not satisfy the protectionists in any of these countries, who would insist that in order to make protection effective the trading area would have to be narrowed down and organized into national tariff systems. This is "the logic of the process by which the use of political power to direct human affairs forces men to segregate themselves into smaller and smaller communities."[52] Once a society accepts the authoritarian principle, there is no end to its atomization. Thus in large territories, such as the United States, the national tariff alone has never satisfied the protectionists. They have supplemented it with internal tariffs, applied through railroad rates and monopolistic agreements. The monopolist tends to retire into an exclusive stronghold, for he finds that "the larger the area the more precarious will be his monopoly, the more diluted his advantages."[53]

The inevitable goal of all collectivism is the isolated, self-

---

that it had "almost always played a large part in welding states together." In 1953, he observed that the military and political institutions which Western policy had constructed were founded on the fear of Russian aggression. T and T, June 18, 1953.

Fear, hate, conflict and war could hardly be classed with liberalism. We would also submit that the role of liberalism in the history of political unifications seems to have been somewhat modest. The unifications of France and Great Britain were chiefly the products of annexations and conquests. Liberalism seems to have played a very limited role in the unification of Germany. The German liberals were frightened out of their democratic ideals by the socialist manifestations of the revolution of 1848, and hastened to make a deal with the Prussian conservatives. In the economic sphere, the progress of Germany was more along mercantilist than liberal lines. *Nationalism: A Report by a Study Group of the Royal Institute of International Affairs* (London: Oxford University Press, 1939), Chapter 4.

[52] *The Good Society*, p. 138.
[53] *Ibid.*

contained community. "This is not because mankind is unable to fraternize: it is because the authoritarian regime has to be exclusive."[54] The overhead direction of human affairs by the sovereign state rests ultimately on its power to coerce: to command and forbid under penalty of death. This power is likely to be challenged, resisted and overthrown when the territory of the centrally administered state is large. "The more writs the king issues, the less far do they run. . . . As the state moves in the direction of more elaborate and more intense intervention, it must contract its jurisdiction."[55]

The collectivist movement has thus transformed the concept of nationalism. The former nationalists exploited the vague and latent sense of a common heritage among peoples and localities to unite them. And then as the federating or the participating units found the union beneficial, they developed a much stronger feeling of a common nationality. The advocates of modern nationalism, on the other hand, would unite only those groups into a political union which already have the distinct feeling that they are a nation.

They [the modern nationalists] have turned history upside down. The fusion of innumerable wandering tribes into nations is inexplicable except on the hypothesis that national feeling develops from the experience of living together successfully. By treating strong nationalism as the antecedent condition rather than the consequence of political union, the modern nationalists have given the world a doctrine which divides mankind into ever smaller, particularist communities.[56]

[54] *Ibid.*, p. 140.
[55] *Ibid.*, p. 141.
[56] *Ibid.*, pp. 134–135. It will be noticed that Lippmann does not distinguish between the character of the British and French unifications on the one hand, and the German and Italian unifications on the other. The unified state preceded the emergence of national consciousness in Britain and France. But this relationship was reversed in the case, say, of Germany. The German nation preceded and helped to create the modern German state. See *Nationalism, op. cit.*, p. 35.

The slogan of divisive nationalism—the principle of national self-determination—which Lippmann identified in *The Political Scene* as the ideal of "local autonomy and joint action," comes under the heavy fire of his criticism and denunciation in *U.S. War Aims*. He criticizes Wilson for having identified himself with it. "Forgetting Abraham Lincoln, forgetting the greatest constitutional issue in the history of the United States, he never paused to define the difference between the right of self-determination and the right of secession."[57] Curiously enough, Lippmann suggests that President Wilson invoked the principle of self-determination to encourage rebellion in Austria-Hungary, and that he did not believe in it.[58] He maintains that the principle is destructive of organized government. It is readily used as an instrument of disorder and anarchy, intervention and aggression. Hitler subverted and annexed the neighboring states in the name of self-determination. "He invoked it when he annexed Austria, dismembered Czechoslovakia, attacked Poland . . . infiltrated Alsace-Lorraine, conspired against Russia in the Ukraine."[59]

[57] Walter Lippmann, *U.S. War Aims* (Boston: Little, Brown and Co., 1944), p. 172. Wilson's Secretary of State, Robert Lansing, denounced self-determination in very similar terms. See Lansing, *The Peace Negotiations: A Personal Narrative* (Boston: Houghton Mifflin Company, 1921), pp. 97–101.

[58] *U.S. War Aims*, p. 173. Lippmann does not substantiate the charge of hypocrisy against Wilson, and it should perhaps be considered a conjecture on his part rather than an established fact. Professor Cobban seems to think that Wilson was steeped in the tradition of self-determination. "The key to the understanding of Wilson's conception of self-determination is the fact that for him it was entirely a corollary of democratic theory. . . . Even if he belonged to the generation that had accepted the Union, as a Virginian and a Southern democrat, he had the right of secession in his bones." Alfred Cobban, *National Self-Determination* (Chicago: The University of Chicago Press, 1947), p. 20.

Professor Cobban also notes that both House and Wilson believed in early 1918 that Austria-Hungary was a political necessity, and that it was as late as October 18, 1918 that the President definitely changed his position in this respect. *Ibid.*, pp. 13–14.

[59] *U.S. War Aims*, p. 173.

Lippmann goes on to say that the principle of self-determination is deeply reactionary in that it rejects the civilized ideal of a state in which diverse peoples enjoy liberty and find justice under equal laws. By sanctioning the right of secession, it encourages factions in a community to take uncompromising and irreconcilable positions in their dealings with one another. It makes them feel that they need not cooperate, since soon they will be aliens. Thus "there is no end to this atomization of human society. Within the minorities who have seceded there will tend to appear other minorities who in their turn will wish to secede."[60]

Lippmann's thesis that collectivism has corrupted nationalism and made it exclusive and divisive is not altogether defensible. It obscures the true relation between nationalism and collectivism. Many scholars attribute the revival of mercantilism to the rising popularity of the doctrines of national self-determination, national sovereignty, and national independence.[61] The major weakness of Lippmann's explanation seems to be that it does not relate the aggressive or passive, unifying or divisive character of nationalism to the evolution of the concept of the nation.

The concept of the nation has passed through three main stages of development. During the first period, which began with the dissolution of the medieval unity of empire and church, the nation resided wholly in the person of the king, and it is perhaps more appropriate to speak of monarchism than nationalism in relation to this period. During the second

[60] *Ibid.,* p. 174.

[61] "Planned economy is a Janus with a nationalist as well as a socialist face; if its doctrine seems socialist, its pedigree is unimpeachably nationalist." Edward H. Carr, *Nationalism and After* (New York: The Macmillan Company, 1945), p. 24. According to Sir Norman Angell, "Economic nationalism is the outcome very largely of ideas which gather about the conception of political independence." Quoted from "The New Imperialism and Old Nationalism," *International Affairs,* Vol. 10, No. 1 (January 1931).

phase, which began with the French Revolution and ended in 1914, the nation was identified with "the people." However, "the people" in this period consisted of a solid, propertied and "respectable" middle class which made up the Third Estate. Nationalism was democratised. The third period—in which we are now living and which roughly dates from 1870 —has seen the formerly excluded social and economic classes rise to full membership in the nation and to power. The nation in this period, we may say, has been socialized. Nationalism has become "jingoism," a term coined in Britain to describe a hitherto unknown phenomenon—the nationalism of the masses.[62] It is largely in this socialization of the nation that we find the explanation of the rise and popularity of collectivism and of the decline of international law, morality and cooperation in the twentieth century.

One may condemn or praise nationalism and the division of the world into sovereign nation-states. But one must confront the fact, as Lippmann does, that this division is a given and more or less permanent feature of the international society. On the relations between these sovereignties hinges the fate of mankind. The patterns of their cooperation and conflict shape and decide the issues of war and peace in the world. We now turn to examine what these patterns are and how Lippmann looks at them.

[62] Carr, *Nationalism and After*, p. 20.

II

The Foundations of International Politics

The National Interest

THE AGE OF THE SELF-CONTAINED, SELF-SUFFICIENT, ISOLATED community is past beyond recall. Nation-states have interests in the outside world which they wish to promote and protect. From the interaction of these interests emerge the patterns of cooperation and conflict, alliances and counter-alliances, peace and war between nations. This brings us to the controversial subject of the national interest. What is its nature, and what is its role in the formulation of foreign policy?

Lippmann observes that the acid test of whether a foreign interest is a vital national interest lies in whether or not the people consider it worth defending at the risk of war. The supreme national interest, he says, is survival—security of the nation in peace and war.[1] Survival, for a people, does not mean merely physical existence; it means ". . . their families and their homes, their villages and lands, their countries and their own ways, their altars, their flags and their hearths."[2] An

---

[1] *U.S. Foreign Policy*, p. 51. For a very similar view of the place of survival in the concept of the national interest, see Hans J. Morgenthau, "Another Great Debate," *American Political Science Review*, Vol. 46, No. 4 (December 1952), pp. 971–973.

[2] *U.S. War Aims*, p. 182.

interest is then a "vital national interest" to the extent that its realization may promote and fortify the nation's independence and way of life. One may object that this proposed criterion cannot be employed except when national survival is threatened. But the objection is met when we remember that no nation is ever completely and permanently secure against aggression.

Lippmann observes that when the national interest has been discovered and made the objective of foreign policy, the people tend to unite behind their leaders. Then the proposed policies are "in harmony with what the great mass of the people believe intuitively and by common sense."[3] The fundamental principle in this respect is that a policy will win general acceptance if it is sound, and it will be sound only if it reflects the national interest. For "a free people cannot and should not be asked to fight and bleed, to work and sweat, for ends which they do not hold to be so compelling that they are self-evident."[4]

A corollary of the foregoing principle would seem to be that general acceptability is the test of soundness in public policy: a policy is sound if it meets with popular approval —or, in other words, a popular policy is sound. At one point in his career, Lippmann did apply this criterion in evaluating American foreign policy. Through much of the mid-thirties, for instance, he advocated aloofness from European politics on the ground that European postwar conduct had disgusted Americans and hardened their traditional objection to participation in foreign affairs.[5] Again, he cheerfully accepted the defeat of the World Court in the Senate in January 1935, arguing that the people of the United States did not wish to be drawn into European disputes in which the Court was

[3] T and T, December 18, 1950.
[4] *U.S. Foreign Policy*, pp. 85–86.
[5] T and T, May 17, 1934.

entangled.[6] During this period, Lippmann did not believe that the executive should educate public opinion or that it should lead rather than follow the people.

In *U.S. Foreign Policy*, however, he criticizes the neutrality policy of the thirties, which at the time he had endorsed. The American people, he says, backed that policy because their leaders did not enlighten them on the nature of their vital interests. In this work he seems to take the position that sound policies are most likely to be popular, but rejects the corollary that popular policies necessarily reflect the national interest at any given time. This rejection becomes much more explicit and emphatic in *The Public Philosophy*, wherein he excludes the "public" altogether from the task of discovering and determining the national interest. Public opinion, he says, is important only insofar as it tells us what the people want. But the opinions and interests of voters

are not, as such, propositions in the public interest. The Gallup Polls are reports of what people are thinking. But that a plurality of the people sampled in the poll think one way has no bearing on whether it is sound public policy.[7]

Discovering the national interest is the task of statesmen, not of Mr. Gallup.

Some of the so-called moralists have held that ideals, rather than the national interest, should underlie foreign policy. Speaking nearly forty years ago in Mobile, Alabama, Woodrow Wilson declared:

It is a very perilous thing to determine the foreign policy of a nation in the terms of material interest. It not only is unfair to those with whom you are dealing, but it is degrading as regards your own actions.[8]

[6] T and T, February 2, 1935.
[7] *The Public Philosophy*, pp. 41–42.
[8] *Selected Literary and Political Papers and Addresses of Woodrow Wilson* (New York: Grosset and Dunlap, 1927), Vol. II, p. 41.

In 1876, William Gladstone urged the British government to declare that it would defend the Bulgarian Christians against the Turks. He decried Disraeli's policy toward the Sultan because it was motivated by the British national interest rather than by sympathy for fellow Christians. He protested, "I object to this constant system of appeal to our selfish leanings."[9]

This school of thought has been challenged by a number of scholars and statesmen. In the Federalist period of American history, we find a deep concern with safeguarding the national interest. Arguing against the fulfillment of the treaty with France and joining her in the War of the First Coalition, Hamilton observed that the "mischiefs and perils" to which the United States would be exposed as a result of war were out of proportion to the benefits that might accrue to France. He went on to say:

Indeed the rule of morality in this respect is not precisely the same between nations as between individuals. The duty of making its own welfare the guide of its actions, is much stronger upon the former than upon the latter; in proportion to the greater magnitude and importance of national compared with individual happiness, and to the greater permanency of the effects of national than of the individual conduct.[10]

At the turn of the century, men like Alfred Mahan, Theodore Roosevelt and Henry Cabot Lodge revived the Federalist tradition. Lippmann himself has almost always taken the Hamiltonian-Rooseveltian approach to the subject of the national interest. In contradistinction to the idealistic and

[9] William E. Gladstone, *Bulgarian Horrors and Russia in Turkistan* (Leipzig: Bernhard Tauchnitz, 1876), pp. 46–48. For Disraeli's view of the primacy of the national interest in foreign policy, see T. E. Kebbel (ed.), *Selected Speeches of the Late Right Honourable the Earl of Beaconsfield* (London: Longmans, Green and Co., 1882), p. 199.

[10] Quoted by Hans J. Morgenthau in *In Defense of the National Interest* (New York: Alfred A. Knopf, 1951), pp. 15–16.

utopian argument for the United States' intervention in
World War I, he argued that the country had a vital interest
in the safety of the Altantic highway.

We do not hesitate to say . . . that if the Allied fleet were in
danger of destruction, if Germany had a chance of securing
command of the seas, our navy ought to be joined to the British
in order to prevent it. . . . They [the Atlantic Powers] are today
more inextricably bound together than most even as yet realize.
But if that community were destroyed we should know what we
had lost. We should understand then the meaning of the unfortified Canadian frontier, of the common protection given
Latin America by the British and American fleets. . . . And now
that she [Germany] is seeking to cut the vital highways of our
world we can no longer stand by.[11]

Lippmann's observations on Anglo-French policy respecting the Italo-Ethiopian dispute further crystallize his position.
Commenting on the Hoare-Laval Pact, he observed that
Britain and France had found the cost of restraining Mussolini to be out of proportion to their interest in the integrity
of the Ethiopian empire. "France has done what all great
powers do: she has been unwilling to risk everything where
her vital interests were not at stake."[12] Surely the Hoare-
Laval Pact was immoral, but the moral way could well have
been the way of war against Italy. And "to incur the risks
of war without knowing that their people were ready and
their military forces adequate would have been even more immoral" for the two great powers.[13] He welcomed President
Franklin D. Roosevelt's statement on October 5, 1935 that
individual Americans would have to trade with the belligerents at their own risk. The President's action, he explained,

[11] Walter Lippmann, "The Defense of the Atlantic World," *New
Republic*, Vol. 10, No. 120 (February 17, 1917), pp. 59–61.
[12] T and T, December 17, 1935.
[13] *Ibid.*, December 24, 1935.

stemmed not from any sympathy for the League, but from an "enlightened view" of the American national interest, which was "not to become entangled in a war because of neutral rights."[14]

After the outbreak of World War II, Lippmann became even more emphatic in asserting the supremacy of the national interest as a guide to foreign policy. He recalled the example of Jefferson, who, thirteen months after he had coined the phrase "no entangling alliances," was ready to "marry ourselves to the British fleet and nation" if "impetuous and restless" France replaced the "feeble and pacific" Spain in Louisiana.[15] We must always bear in mind, urged Lippmann, that in international affairs there are at stake the well-being and, indeed, the very life of the nation. Therefore,

We must consider first and last the American national interest. If we do not, if we construct our foreign policy on some kind of abstract theory of our rights and duties, we shall build castles in the air. We shall formulate policies which in fact the nation will not support with its blood, its sweat, and its tears.[16]

In *U.S. Foreign Policy* he sought to explain America's intervention in World War I, her postwar isolation and her rejection of the League of Nations in terms of the national interest. The United States did not go to war to make the world safe for democracy or to found a League of Nations. Lippmann suggested that President Wilson was moved to declare war against Germany for the same reasons he himself had set forth in his editorial in the *New Republic* on February 17, 1917.[17] The postwar disillusionment with world

[14] *Ibid.*, December 31, 1935.

[15] Walter Lippmann, "Acquisition of the British Naval Bases," *Congressional Digest*, Vol. 20, No. 1, pp. 24–25.

[16] *U.S. Foreign Policy*, p. 137.

[17] *Ibid.*, pp. 33–34. Lippmann made the same assertion in a magazine article in 1941: "The military and diplomatic advisers of President Wilson

politics resulted from the fact that Wilson avoided the real explanation, basing his case for intervention, instead, on the legal objection to unlimited submarine warfare and on the moral objection to lawless aggression. The American people rejected the League because Wilson failed to demonstrate that it was a vital national interest—that it would perpetuate the security which the nation had won by war. They got the impression that the new responsibilities of the League flowed from the President's philanthropy, and not from the need of finding allies to help defend American commitments in the Western Hemisphere and the Pacfic.[18]

The foregoing should establish that Lippmann is convinced of the supremacy of the national interest in matters of foreign policy. At the same time, he emphasizes that the policy-makers of a nation should not close their eyes to the genuine and valid interests of other nations.[19] In a multinational world, this is a requirement of political wisdom; in the age of total war, it is also one of the conditions of survival. In the postwar period, Lippmann has published literally scores of

knew then and were moved then by the same essential estimate of America's vital interests as are Secretaries Hull, Stimson and Knox, the advisers of President Roosevelt." See "The Atlantic and America," *Life*, Vol. 10, No. 14 (April 7, 1941), p. 87.

This is a rather uncommon explanation of Wilson's reasons for going to war. We should, perhaps, confront Lippmann's testimony with that of Wilson's close advisers. Colonel House, for instance, records that in the fall of 1914 "[Wilson] did not believe that there was the slightest danger to this country from foreign invasion, even if the Germans were success-ful." Quoted in Robert E. Osgood, *Ideals and Self-Interest in America's Foreign Relations* (Chicago: The University of Chicago Press, 1953), p. 175.

Again, in the summer of 1916 Robert Lansing, Wilson's Secretary of State, found the President unable to appreciate that a German victory in Europe would eventually threaten the security of the United States. (*Ibid.*, p. 175.)

[18] *U.S. Foreign Policy*, pp. 33–39.

[19] Lippmann's position is quite close to that of Theodore Roosevelt, whom he often cites as a model President. For a statement of Roosevelt's position on this subject see Osgood, *op. cit.*, p. 89.

articles criticizing American foreign policy in Asia and Europe on the ground that it ignored the vital interests of other powers. Writing in 1950, he observed that the United States was involved in Korea not as a principal but as an agent of the United Nations. The powers which had a permanent stake in the future of Korea were her three immediate neighbors—China, Japan and the Soviet Union—whose vital interests in the Far East met in this "strategical centerpiece." Therefore, a Korean settlement which ignored the interests of these powers was bound to be short-lived. Lippmann urged the American people

to be wise enough to know that Korea, Japan and China and Russia will all still be there in the Far East when we who make speeches and write articles are dead and forgotten, and that in a long-range settlement it is the enduring interests of nations that have to be taken in to account.[20]

In January 1951, Lippmann noted that the United States was fighting a "lone struggle" in the Far East, principally because in Washington it had become customary to "go ahead and act on matters of grave concern to our allies and then consult them when they have lost the freedom to differ radically."[21] Addressing himself a few months later to the "interventionists"—the advocates of war with China—he warned that America's European allies would not stand by her if she got involved in a general Asian war which might eventually become a war with the Soviet Union. The instinct of survival, he warned, would not permit the people of Western Europe "to stake their very existence on the soundness of General MacArthur's ideas."[22]

Lippmann has repeatedly criticized the so-called containment policy pursued by both Truman and Eisenhower be-

[20] T and T, August 28, 1950; *ibid.*, July 28, 1953.
[21] *Ibid.*, January 1, 1951; also May 28, 1953.
[22] *Ibid.*, May 7, 1951.

cause it ignored the fact that Western Europe lay completely defenseless against a nuclear attack from the Soviet Union. He maintained that the possibility of such an attack had put a "fearful strain" on American alliances in Europe.[23]

In the post-World War II period, Lippmann has consistently advocated Franco-German reconciliation and unity to serve as the core of an "all-European system."[24] But he has denounced the De Gaulle-Adenauer "axis" which the two old "kings" have tried to forge for creating a Gaullist Europe in which France would have an independent nuclear striking force. By the end of 1963 France hopes to have a nuclear force capable of killing twenty million people. Her objective, says Lippmann, is twofold: if she can kill twenty million Russians, she can resist involvement in an American-Soviet nuclear war in which her own vital interests are not engaged; and secondly, if she can start a nuclear war which the United States must join to finish, because France herself cannot finish it, the ultimate decision with regard to nuclear war or peace rests with Paris and no longer with Washington.[25] This may suit French interests as De Gaulle sees them, but it endangers the vital interests of the United States.[26] De Gaulle is playing a masterly game of power politics. American statesmen should not condemn it as a "wicked plot" or fret and fume over it. They should play the same game and play it better. They do not have a divine right to keep the ultimate decisions in their hands, but they should try, in their own interest, to hold on to their present decision-making power as long as they can.[27]

The pursuit of the national interest is the primary concern of the foreign policies of all nations. But it should not mean

---

[23] *Ibid.*, April 1 and May 4, 1954.
[24] See Chapter VI, below.
[25] T and T, May 15, 1962.
[26] *Ibid.*, May 22, 1962. See *Infra*, p. 80.
[27] *Ibid.*, May 15, 1962.

grabbing. There can be no real international cooperation unless national governments take an enlightened, a long and rounded rather than a short and narrow view of their interests —unless they start with the homely fact that vital interests and not "charters, covenants, blueprints and generalities" are what men live for and will, if need be, die for.[28]

At any given time many interests may, in varying degrees, contribute to national security and qualify as national interests. But not all of them may become the official objectives of foreign policy, for it would be impossible to pursue all of them at the same time with equal vigor. A government must, therefore, limit its objectives, arrange them in the order of their importance, and work out a system of priorities. It must strike a balance between the possible and the desired. That the schedule of objectives should be in equilibrium with the schedule of available resources is a principle universal in its application. Lippmann maintains that it holds good in foreign no less than in domestic affairs.

Without the controlling principle that a nation must maintain objectives and its power in equilibrium, its purposes within its means and its means equal to its purposes, its commitments related to its resources and its resources adequate to its commitments, it is impossible to think at all about foreign affairs.[29]

He concedes that it is not easy to judge between the competing interests, to weigh them and to assign them a higher or a lower place on the schedule of objectives. In preparing such a schedule, one has to make decisions on a number of related questions. One cannot decide whether or not to make a foreign commitment without considering, say, its military requirements, the phase of the business cycle at home and abroad, the domestic political situation, and a multitude of

[28] Walter Lippmann, "The Four Policemen," *Vital Speeches of the Day*, Vol. 10, No. 5 (December 15, 1943), p. 140. Also *U.S. War Aims*, p. 182.
[29] *U.S. Foreign Policy*, p. 7.

similar questions. Each of these judgments, says Lippmann, is in itself the "peak of a pyramid of equations"—a fact which makes it exceedingly difficult to define the exact content of the national interest at any given time. However, these difficulties and complications do not relieve us of the necessity of drawing up and balancing the equations of ends and means. It is true that some of the factors involved do not lend themselves to precise quantitative measurement. Nevertheless, prudent men make informed guesses and estimates as to where the equations balance.[30] A true statesman will consider it his first duty to bring into balance, with a comfortable surplus in reserve, his nation's commitments and its power. His problem is to select objectives which are limited—"not the best that could be desired but the best that can be realized without committing the whole power and the whole wealth and the very existence of the nation."[31] In the world of reality there is no room for crusades, unconditional surrenders or total peace.

Lippmann maintains that acceptance of the above principle tends to promote valid and rational thinking on foreign affairs and to minimize the chances of dissension at home on foreign policy issues. Men find it easier to agree on objectives if they know that they must pay for what they want, and that, therefore, they must want only what they are willing to pay for. In the absence of this guiding principle, they lack the criterion to identify their vital interests and to choose the means of protecting and promoting them.

Lippmann thinks that since the turn of the present century the Western democracies have recklessly disregarded the vital principle of balance between ends and means. He writes:

In this epoch there is no phenomenon so alarming . . . as govern-

[30] The Public Philosophy, p. 144.
[31] Walter Lippmann, "Philosophy and U.S. Foreign Policy," Vital Speeches, February 1, 1948.

ments which are coming to depend on the votes of great masses following leaders who tell the people what they want without permitting them or compelling them to face the issues of how to provide them with what they want.[32]

Commenting on the inability of Britain and France to check the advance of aggressive totalitarianism in the 1930's, he noted that the democracies had thrown away the two essential instruments of diplomacy—readiness to fight in defense of their rights and the willingness to make concessions. They had hoped that by some miracle

they would have neither to yield anything nor to fight in order not to yield anything. In a world of rebellious great powers they have tried to combine the advantages of imperialism with the conveniences of pacifism.[33]

Again, in the postwar period, Lippmann finds that the two great European democracies—Great Britain and France—are reluctant to bring their foreign commitments and responsibilities within the limits of their present power. As a result of the two world wars the relative power of Great Britain has considerably diminished. Yet her connections and commitments abroad are so vast and complex that her policy, perforce, tends toward ambiguity and indecision. Her "friendly critics" maintain that "the British want to be in everything somewhat but not too far in it lest they be pulled out of something else that they also belong to."[34] Writing in 1950, Lippmann deplored the fact that the Atlantic powers generally had got themselves entangled in long, bloody and indecisive wars in Asia. The West, he said, had about twenty divisions engaged in Asia while only less than half that many were immediately available for the defense of Western Europe. This diversion of military power, he held, had reduced

[32] T and T, June 5, 1950.
[33] Ibid., July 11, 1935.
[34] Ibid., June 8, 1950.

the Atlantic alliance in Europe "largely to blueprints."[35] A European defense system, he argued, could become effective only if the Europeans and Americans realized that whereas their military potential was enough for the defense of their own lands and their own civilization, "it is not enough to suppress revolutions all over Asia."[36]

Speaking of the United States, Lippmann observes that the Founding Fathers were guided in the formulation of their policies by the dictum that against every desired asset there must be written down the corresponding liability in material cost and political consequences. In the twentieth century, Theodore Roosevelt acted to revive the Federalist tradition. He realized that the annexation of the Philippines called for new measures. He insisted on digging the Panama Canal, and persuaded Congress to support the construction of a large and modern navy. But from the Wilsonian era down to the present day, Americans had habitually violated this important principle of the public philosophy. President Wilson, for instance, lost his way during the war. If he had confined himself to making the world safe for the countries that were already democratic, he might have achieved his objective. He failed because he took it upon himself to make the world democratic, which was an unlimited objective.[37] After World War I the American people dissolved the alliance which had won the war. And,

knowing that Japan was the only possible enemy we had to consider in the Pacific, we nevertheless turned upon our natural partners—Britain and France—and treated them as rivals whose armaments it was a diplomatic triumph to reduce.[38]

[35] *Ibid.*, December 5, 1950.
[36] *Ibid.*, August 15, 1950.
[37] *Ibid.*, January 21, 1951.
[38] *U.S. Foreign Policy*, p. 41. Lippmann's own position during the greater part of the interwar period was not far different from the one he criticizes in *U.S. Foreign Policy*. We have noted that he advised the

In the post-World War II period also, says Lippmann, Americans have failed to measure correctly the limits of their power and influence abroad and to shape their policies and commitments accordingly. The state of imbalance between ends and means in American foreign policy became evident when in 1950 Senator Lodge proposed that, in accordance with the French and German wishes, the United States station ten divisions in Europe. But he soon discovered at the Pentagon that the United States needed as many divisions for the Korean War as she expected to have by June 1951, when the Korean War would be a year old. Exasperated, Lippmann wrote:

When we talk about the divisions that we shall station in Europe it is necessary to remember that the Korean War is a first mortgage on all our ground forces, and that it is a very big mortgage. . . . As two and two cannot be made to add up to more than four . . . so the defense of Europe cannot be improved substantially as long as the three allies have unlimited liabilities in Asia.[39]

American people, if not to turn against, at least to turn away from their "natural partners." In 1943 he denounced the Washington Conference as an "exorbitant folly," but in 1922 he had hailed it for having stopped a race of naval armaments which might have drifted into a ruinous war. He approved the underlying premise of the American position at the Conference, which he conceived as being the recognition that the United States had no overwhelming interest in the Far East. Moreover, he maintained that in making concessions to Japan this country had abandoned the dangerous illusion that she had the military power to enforce her policies in Asia. (New York *World,* January 29, 1922.)

Throughout the midtwenties, Lippmann believed that Japan's intentions toward China were peaceable. During the London Naval Conference, he noted that Japan's pre-eminence in Eastern Asia was not only compatible with the American national interest (which he had decreed to be negligible in the Far East) but was actually essential to the maintenance of peace and order in the Western Pacific. He maintained that Japan had agreed to the Washington ratios partly because the United States had promised not to fortify Guam. He suggested in 1930 that America should allay Japanese fears by neutralizing the Philippines—which, he argued, could not in any case be defended against a sudden Japanese

After his first extensive interview with Mr. Khrushchev, Lippmann reported the Russian leader's suspicion that the United States would start a hot war if she could not win the Cold War. The Russian suspicion had deepened, complained Lippmann, because of the tendency of Mr. Dulles to treat the Russian-American conflict "not as one of empires and great states but as a religious war in which the contending positions are absolute."[40] He found that on both sides of the Iron Curtain there were people who believed, erroneously, that their socio-political system must either prevail universally or perish. This desire for unlimited success obstructed the establishment between them of a tolerable *modus vivendi*, "which is the very best that is conceivable between our two societies."[41]

There may be times when the foreign commitments of a nation are too few as compared to its actual or potential power. This would mean that the country did not have an active foreign policy. Shortly before the outbreak of World War II, Lippmann began to revise his estimate of America's

---

attack, and would have to be liberated in the event of a war with Japan.

Lippmann welcomed the conclusion of the London Naval Treaty, saying that the principle of limitation adopted there was a "signal advance in international affairs." (New York *World*, June 4, 1930.)

After Japan's intentions in Eastern Asia, and Germany's designs in Europe, had become unmistakably clear, Lippmann recommended a strong navy in the Pacific, but urged a continued isolation from Europe. In May 1934 he summed up America's efforts in behalf of disarmament as follows: "Under five Presidents, from Wilson to Roosevelt, the United States has sought to protect the peace of the world by reducing and limiting armaments. . . . One result has been achieved which can be called substantial. A race of naval armaments between Great Britain and the United States has been prevented and it is as certain as anything can be in these matters that it will not be allowed to start." (T and T, May 17, 1934.)

Whereas the foregoing evidence indicates consistent adherence, on Lippmann's part, to the thesis of the balance between ends and means, it does also suggest that during the greater part of the period between the two wars he took a view of the American national interest which he found to have been erroneous only when he looked at it with the advan-

"destiny." He now maintained that in the interwar period the United States had not played a role in international affairs commensurate with her potential power. Americans had faced the world "in a mood of withdrawal, defeat, and of wishing to escape from their opportunities and responsibilities."[42] He warned that when a nation refuses to do the great things which it has to do, it fails to do the little things that it wishes to do. For "men who will not face the big things become nervous and fearful in all things."[43]

To cut one's coat according to the cloth is undeniably a sound principle in individual, national and international affairs. But the attempt to apply it strictly and rigidly at any level, and especially in foreign affairs, is likely to encounter difficulties. For one thing, situations in the arena of international politics are not exclusively controlled by any one government. It is quite possible that by the time the policy-makers of a nation have balanced the countless "pyramids of equations," they will find that time and rivals have already decided the issue against them. In other words, a government cannot always avoid taking a certain amount of risk, for it will often have to act on the basis of rough-and-ready estimates derived from inadequate data. A genuine difficulty

---

tage of hindsight. The "reckless" policies which he denounces in *U.S. Foreign Policy,* and in his subsequent writings, had his own support and blessing at the time they were initiated.

[39] T and T, September 12, 1950.

[40] Walter Lippmann, *The Communist World and Ours* (Boston: Little, Brown and Co., 1958), pp. 38–39.

[41] *Ibid.,* pp. 50–51.

[42] Walter Lippmann, "The American Destiny," *Life,* Vol. 6, No. 23 (June 5, 1939), pp. 47, 72–73. Also see "America and the World," *Life,* Vol. 8, No. 23 (June 3, 1940), pp. 103–106. Apparently this revised view of the American destiny was prompted by an awareness of the threat to America's vital interest in the safety of the Atlantic highway aroused by the imminence of war in Europe. Lippmann was returning to the thesis which he had advanced in his editorial in the *New Republic* of February 17, 1917 (*supra,* p. 50).

[43] *Life,* June 5, 1939, p. 73.

arises when one is dealing with intangible objectives. It is not easy to calculate how much the vindication of national honor and prestige or the moral necessity of fulfilling a promise is worth. Again, policy-makers cannot, at the time of making a decision, foresee accurately its long-range consequences. Nor can they assess precisely situations which unfold slowly. They must act, exercising their best judgment, and leave it to posterity to decide whether the resources deployed and the ends achieved did or did not finally balance.

The greatest national interest is national survival, which, according to Lippmann, means not only the continued physical existence of the nation but also the preservation of its values, ideals and way of life. For a fuller understanding of his position on the subject of the national interest, we should examine his views on the role of ideals in international relations.

In his *Public Opinion,* and also in *The Public Philosophy,* Lippmann observes that between man and his environment there is interposed a pseudo-environment which consists of his ideas and images of the external reality. From this pseudo-environment he receives the stimuli that move him to action.[44] The way in which the world is imagined determines at any given time what men will do, what direction their efforts will take, and where their hopes will be focussed. It follows that the student of politics cannot afford to ignore the power and influence of ideas, ideals and ideologies on the affairs of men. Insofar as people consider their ideas about the external reality as true, and their ideals as the images of the good society, their faith in them can literally move mountains. Lippmann writes:

To be sure no man's idea can remove a mountain on the moon. But if the American people took into their heads that life would

[44] Walter Lippmann, *Public Opinion* (New York: The Macmillan Company, 1922), Chapter I; *The Public Philosophy,* p. 92.

not be worth living until Pike's Peak was in the suburbs of Chicago, they could move Pike's Peak.[45]

He implies that an ideal will move a nation to pursue a given course of action for any length of time if it has at least two qualifications. It must have a wide appeal, and move not only just one man—a President or a Secretary of State—but the majority of the nation. Secondly, it should not be as difficult to realize as the task of removing a mountain on the moon.

Policy-makers should not ignore pervasive national values and ideals. In U.S. War Aims Lippmann maintained that an idealistic devotion to democracy and an opposition to imperialism had characterized American opinion on foreign affairs in the past. The Open Door, he said, was really a short name for the American way of life projected abroad. The fact that the United States supported China and sympathized with all colonial peoples in their struggle for freedom reflected that "Americans, being incapable by the nature of their own society of sustained imperialism, are the opponents of imperialism wherever they encounter it."[46] Indeed, the people of the United States were so strongly devoted to their ideals and their way of life as to have developed an intuitive feeling that they could not prosper and live securely in contact with peoples whose systems of government and whose ways of life were radically different from their own. At the same time they were convinced that their principles, founded as they were on "the laws of nature and of nature's God," must sooner or later prevail everywhere.

In U.S. War Aims Lippmann not only condones but actually defends the projection of American principles abroad and the intuitive feeling of Americans that they cannot feel happy and secure in the midst of strangers.

[45] The Public Philosophy, p. 93.
[46] U.S. War Aims, p. 38.

This persistent evangel of Americanism in the outer world . . . reflects the fact that no nation, and certainly not this nation, can endure in a politically alien and morally hostile environment; and the profound and abiding truth that a people which does not advance its faith has already begun to abandon it.[47]

The history of America's foreign relations, he says, indicates that her foreign commitments are supported and substantiated, in the final analysis, not by the instruments of diplomacy—treaties and declarations—but by the fact that they enlist American democracy as the champion of democracy.[48] It is true that when this democratic impulse is divorced from the economic, political and strategic realities of the world, it leads the nation to ill-considered and ineffective policies. Nonetheless, this same impulse constitutes that dynamic purpose which drives the American people on, "which drove it into the great commitment of the Monroe Doctrine and made it the champion of the independence and the integrity of China."[49] Lippmann goes so far as to modify his definition of the national interest. Immediately following the lines quoted above he writes that the democratic impulse which keeps the American people going expresses in its intent "the highest interest of the United States which is to live in a world environment which contains no dangerous alien powers."[50]

[47] Ibid., p. 40.
[48] Ibid., p. 154.
[49] Ibid., p. 154.
[50] Ibid. Needless to say, this is an impossibly idealistic definition of the national interest. Taken literally, it would condemn the American people to choose between a policy of complete, watertight isolation or a policy of unlimited crusades to democratize the world. In either case, they would be foredoomed to suffer failure and frustration in their foreign affairs: they could not isolate themselves, because the rest of the world would not leave them alone; and they could not democratize the world by force, because it is much too big to be subdued and made to "behave" for any length of time by any one nation or even by a group of nations. It is difficult to explain the statement except either as embodying an

Friendly relations, writes Lippmann, cannot exist between countries whose foreign policies are motivated by incompatible ideals and ideologies. In *The Political Scene,* he observed that it would be difficult to secure harmony of thought and effort among the members of the League of Nations while "half the world is socialist and the other half anti-socialist."[51] And again in *U.S. War Aims,* he argued that the United Nations could not work in cooperation and harmony unless all the governments which wielded force and influence within and without the organization were publicly accountable to their own peoples and also to the world public opinion. "The world order cannot be half democratic and half totalitarian."[52] Lippmann found it necessary to advise the Russian people that friendly relations could not develop between their country and the United State until

the basic political and human liberties are established in the Soviet Union. Only then will there be full confidence, and a free intercourse on a basis of full equality. For between states that do not have free institutions and those that do have them, international relations must necessarily be special and restricted.[53]

The reason for the relative lack of cordiality between states adhering to incompatible political and social systems is the "inequality of diplomatic intercourse" between them.

---

ultimate ideal of the civilized man, a long-range objective to create a free and peaceful good society, or as an exaggeration prompted by the hope, which Lippmann seems to have entertained during and after the war, that postwar Russia would become democratic. This latter interpretation is supported by the bulk of Lippmann's writings in which he definitely opposes the idea of crusades to alter the systems of government of other states. Even in *U.S. War Aims* (p. 151), he advised that if the Russians should refuse to democratize themselves Americans should do their very best to get along with them, employing the ordinary channels of diplomacy to prevent a third world war and at the same time, maintaining a state of preparedness to meet any eventuality.

[51] *The Political Scene,* p. 63.
[52] *U.S. War Aims,* p. 149.
[53] *Ibid.,* p. 148.

We know about a totalitarian country, and its people know about us, only that which their government permits them to know. If, for instance, Americans do not like the Russian policy of their government, they can force a change in it. But there is no appeal from the decision of the Soviet government in its American policy. The fact that it does not have to take its programs and policies to the bar of public opinion also means that it can use secrecy and surprise in its dealings with the democracies. The democratic governments cannot establish a similar quarantine without destroying their characteristic institutions. Therefore,

as long as this inequality exists there cannot be true collaboration between the Soviet Union and the Western world. There can be only a *modus vivendi,* only compromises, bargains, specific agreements, only a diplomacy of checks and counter checks.[54]

Lippmann has repeated this thesis in a number of articles in the New York *Herald Tribune.*[55] On the eve of the "summit" meeting at Geneva in 1955, he complained that both President Eisenhower and Premier Bulganin had professed to aim at a peace of understanding rather than an armistice in the cold war. Both had assumed that the conflict between the two great coalitions was due not to a fundamental cleavage of interests and ideals but to some misunderstanding.[56] Addressing himself to Premier Bulganin, Lippmann argued that the social and political structure of states was not a domestic affair alone insofar as the

great instruments of foreign policy—the military establishment,

[54] *Ibid.,* pp. 140–141.
[55] T and T, February 23, 1950; February 20, 1951; June 18, 19, 20, 21, 1951.
[56] Premier Bulganin had said: "It is sometimes said that a peaceful settlement of international disputes is prevented by the difference in the social and state structure of different countries. Yet the social and state structure is a domestic affair of the people of each country . . . Why should the difference in social and state structures prevent the peoples

propaganda, intervention—are controlled by a government which operates in the profoundest secrecy. As long as it is characteristic of the state structure of the Soviet Union that its policies for peace or for war are made without public debate, without public accountability, but privately and without notice or explanation, there cannot be that "atmosphere of confidence, mutual understanding and business-like cooperation" for which Bulganin pleaded.[57]

During his several trips to Moscow and his interviews with Mr. Khrushchev, Lippmann has found that a firm and fierce belief in the ultimate victory of communism underlies Soviet foreign policy. It imparts to the Soviet government immense self-confidence in treating with the Western powers and a relentless determination to foster communist revolutionary movements in underdeveloped areas.[58] Americans must counter the Russian ideological fervor with the vigor of their own idealism. They must develop and apply their principles, not abandon them. "I am very certain that we shall have the answer to Mr. Khrushchev if, but only if, we stop being fascinated by the cloak and dagger business and, being true to ourselves, take our own principles seriously."[59] Criticizing the advocates of a surprise invasion and speedy conquest of Cuba, Lippmann warned that a policy which deliberately violated American pledges and principles must fail. A free and open society could not successfully organize a "spectacular conspiracy." The American conscience, he emphasized, was a reality, and it would emasculate, even if it did not

---

from living in peace, respecting each other, developing mutually advantageous trade and cultural relations?" Quoted by Lippmann in T and T, July 19, 1955.

[57] T and T, July 19, 1955.

[58] This does not make Mr. Khrushchev a Woodrow Wilson. Lippmann reports that he thinks much more like Richelieu and Metternich. See Walter Lippmann, *The Coming Tests With Russia*, (Boston: Little, Brown and Co., 1961), pp. 17–18.

[59] *Ibid.*, pp. 34–35.

prevent, an un-American policy. The Bay of Pigs affair was incompetent because it was inconsistent with American character, "like a cow that tried to fly."[60]

In 1963, commenting upon the Clay Report on Foreign Aid, Lippmann criticized its major tenet that the American national interest should determine who should receive aid, and how much. In the proposed guideline he saw "an assumption of superiority which is abrasive . . . in the world we are living in—for the most part very poor and for the most part of some other color than white."[61] With their great wealth and power, Americans should have and show others humility, not pride. Lippmann noted that even after disbursing billions of dollars in aid, the people of this country were not loved or respected abroad. Yet thirty years ago, when they had no foreign aid program, they were both loved and respected. They were then struggling with their own problems of economic and political security. Then they were like the rest of mankind. Will they once again have friends abroad? Not until "this country becomes possessed . . . as it surely will when the political seasons change, in the high enterprise of making a good society."[62]

The foregoing statement of Lippmann's view of the role of ideals in foreign affairs would seem to establish the following major propositions. Ideals are a powerful factor in domestic and international relations; they can move mountains. In taking this position he inevitably implies that it would be foolish for a government to ignore their importance in its calculations of foreign policy. Secondly, in order to survive— to preserve its physical and spirtual integrity—a nation must advance its faith, its moral values and ideals, and try to develop and create a friendly international environment.

[60] *Ibid.*, p. 34.
[61] T and T, March 25, 1963.
[62] *Ibid.*

These propositions would seem to enfeeble Lippmann's assertion, noted earlier, that a government should pursue the national interest to the exclusion of idealistic considerations. It may be that this contradiction in Lippmann's thought is more apparent than real.

Even though men can honestly disagree on the relative importance of the moral and material content of the national interest, they cannot deny that physical survival is a prerequisite to the attainment of either, and is, therefore, the first and foremost constituent element of the national interest. That few nations are ever willing to stake their very existence on achieving an ideal goes almost without saying.[63] Moreover, the desire for life and the fear of death are fairly constant factors in human motivation whereas devotion to an ideal may be temporary. If ideals are mental images of the good society, they are bound to change as man marches along the road of civilization. The same is true of ideologies. "Once accepted they are held strongly, usually during the lives of one or two generations. After a lapse of time, their hold over the mind diminishes. Ultimately they are replaced by a new ideology."[64] It is rare that the adherents of an ideal are all committed to it with equal devotion. Often there are important minorities who either oppose it or merely pay lip service to it. It would then be perfectly logical for one to admit the efficacy of ideals, but insist that national survival should take precedence over any other ideal, and warn against sacrificing material interests to achieve such ideals as the nation professes only half-heartedly and superficially.

[63] As Professor Niebuhr puts it, "No nation is ever true to the cause which transcends its national life if there is not some coincidence between the defensive necessities of that cause and the defensive requirements of the national organism." See "Ideology and Pretense," *The Nation*, Vol. 149, No. 24 (December 9, 1939), p. 645.

[64] Robert Strausz-Hupé and Stefan T. Possony, *International Relations* (New York: McGraw-Hill Book Company, 1954), p. 458.

Again, one may grant that a nation's moral prestige and the persuasiveness of its ideals are vital factors in the equations of relative power, but at the same time warn that ideals, as such, do not make good objectives of foreign policy, that they have to be translated into concrete terms before they can be effectively pursued. Lippmann illustrated this point in *The Political Scene,* the most idealistic of his writings on international affairs. He complained that Wilson's ideas had never had the "precision and downrightness" of those who said, for instance, "we demand such and such territory." He recalled

the discomforting remark made to me by the diplomatic agent of one of the smaller nations shortly before the President arrived in Paris: "If he knows exactly what he wants, he can get it. Does he know? He has an ideal; but has he a program?"[65]

It would appear that the key to Lippmann's position on the issue of idealism versus realism in relation to the national interest lies in his statement that even though ideals provide that dynamic purpose which leads a nation on, they cause more evil than good when they are divorced from the realities of actual situations. A passage which he wrote on the subject in 1916 would hold good, in his view, even today.

Vision . . . will compel no one if the hope is extravagant or the fact distorted; and they see the world most effectively who see reality luminous in a cold dry light dissolving into a warm aura of probabilities. . . . Hope is dull unless its edges are sharpened on fact.[66]

And he brings out the noblest in the idealistic tradition when he reminds the "realist" interpreters of the national interest that it is not only political wisdom but a condition of survival

[65] *The Political Scene* (New York: Henry Holt and Co., 1919), Introduction, xiii.
[66] Walter Lippmann, "The White Passion," *New Republic,* Vol. 8, No. 103 (October 21, 1916), pp. 294–295.

that in determining their vital interests nations heed the vital interests of other nations. The golden rule applies to all human relations, including those between sovereign states.

The Rivalry of Nations

The great debate on the subject of the national interest is really the product of the age-old controversy over whether or not human relations are characterized by a universal harmony of interests. The Idealist contends that the real interests of all mankind are identical; that their foremost interest is to live by certain universally valid principles; and that the actual conflict between states—perpetrated by perverted politicians, greedy bankers and "merchants of death"—is by no means a permanent or inevitable condition of human existence. In emphasizing the primacy of the national interest, the Realist would be wasting his breath if he did not challenge the validity of the foregoing premise. Accordingly, he believes that the conflict of interests between nations is a fundamental and more or less unalterable characteristic of their relations.

Lippmann's position on the issue of the national interest has had similar foundations. Defending Wilsonian idealism in *The Political Scene,* he wrote: "Good democrats have always believed that the common interests of men are greater than their special interests, that ruling classes can be enemies, but that nations must be partners."[67] He urged governments to give up their "criminal rivalries," which, he warned, would destroy democracy because they led to

friction and armaments and a distortion of all the hopes of free government. They mean that nations are organized to exploit each other and to exploit themselves. This is the life of what we call autocracy. It establishes its power at home by pointing to enemies

[67] *The Political Scene,* pp. 98–99.

abroad. It fights its enemies abroad by dragooning the populations at home.[68]

Thus in 1917 Lippmann believed that the conflict of interests between nations was not a basic and permanent fact of international life, that it could be abolished, that it was about to be abolished insofar as the peoples of the world, having realized its destructiveness, were embracing the ideals of cooperation abroad and democracy at home. In *U.S. War Aims* he hoped that the great powers, which wielded the force of the world and controlled its raw materials, would respond to common ideals. Again, he implicitly upheld the doctrine of the harmony of interests when, in *The Public Philosophy*, he advocated a return to the philosophy of natural law with the concomitant principle of "right reason" as the guide to individual and state action. Moral laws and ideals had a universal validity because they were discoverable by right reasoning. Whenever and wherever disinterested men thought rationally about a problem, they must, sooner or later, all come to the same answer.[69]

Lippmann has not consistently adhered to the principle of the harmony of interests. As a matter of fact, the bulk of his writings sometimes explicitly, but far more often implicitly, point to the existence of a conflict of interests in both domestic and foreign affairs. We have noted above that before 1935 he advocated active governmental intervention and participation in the national economic life. In taking this position he implied that the harmony of interests postulated by the *laissez-faire* economists was fictitious and unreal. In *The Good Society* he denied the efficacy of state intervention, but emphasized the role of law as the composer and arbiter of conflicts. In *The Stakes of Diplomacy* he advocated international government to compose the great power con-

[68] *Ibid.*, pp. 99–100.
[69] For a detailed discussion of the subject, see Chapter VII.

flicts in the backward areas. In *U.S. Foreign Policy* and also in *U.S. War Aims* he emphasized the role of alliances and the balance of power as the regulators of international conflicts of interest. In all these works he assumed that the harmony of interests among nations, however desirable, did not exist in practice. In some comparatively recent articles he has complained that the doctrine of harmony was the underlying assumption and also the "philosophical error" of American thinking on foreign affairs. In an article entitled "The Rivalry of Nations" he wrote, "We have believed that the struggle [between nations] does not exist, or that it can be avoided, or that it can be abolished."[70] This, he maintained, was a utopian picture of the world which Americans had inherited from the "age of innocence"—the nineteenth century—when they lived in splendid isolation without the need of a positive foreign policy. They must awaken to the fact that "rivalry and strife and conflict among states, communities and factions are the normal conditions of mankind."[71] The way to deal with the struggle, he said, was to

[70] Walter Lippmann, "The Rivalry of Nations," *Atlantic Monthly,* Vol. 181, No. 2 (February 1948), p. 18.

[71] Walter Lippmann, "Philosophy and United States Foreign Policy," *Vital Speeches,* Vol. 14, No. 8 (February 1, 1948), p. 243.

Lippmann's thesis that rivalry and conflict are a normal condition of mankind has a strikingly Hobbesian flavor. However, a significant difference between the two positions should be noted. Hobbes maintains that the conflict of interests arises out of man's desire for self-preservation, which is the prime motive of human behavior. In the absence of checks and restraints, this and its subordinate urges bring about in human society a "condition which is called war; and such a war as is of every man against every man." (*Leviathan,* Chapter 13.) Conflict is a permanent condition because it arises from forces inherent in the nature of man. Lippmann, on the other hand, would argue that rivalry and conflict stem from the inability of the vast majority of men to reason and thus to establish a universal harmony of interests. In other words, he, unlike Hobbes, keeps the door open for the *ethical* validity of the doctrine of the harmony of interests.

His position should likewise be distinguished from that of writers such as Bagehot, Mahan and Beveridge, who preached the doctrine of the survival of the fittest and sang hymns in praise of conflict and war.

accept it as a fact, and then "to regulate and to moderate and to compose the conflicts and the issues, to check and to balance the contending forces."[72]

Conflicts of interest can and do arise even between nations which profess the same socio-political values. Notwithstanding the insistence of communist theoreticians that common adherence to socialism precludes conflict between nations of the Soviet bloc, the Russian-Chinese rivalry is quite real. Lippmann maintains that the conflict between them "is at bottom . . . the same conflict which existed when the Emperor of all the Russians and the Emperor of China were still on their thrones. It is a conflict of national interests . . . which has gone on for generations."[73] Between these two empires there is a 4,000-mile-long frontier which runs through the heart of Asia and along which their vital interests are engaged. Lippmann observed that common faith in the secular religion of communism was no reason why the Soviet Union and China could not fall into a great conflict. He has even suggested that a *de facto* American-Russian coalition may be in the process of developing to contain Chinese expansion toward Russia in the north and toward India in the south.[74]

For example, in *The Interest of America in Sea Power, Present and Future,* (1898), Alfred Mahan wrote: "In the rivalries of nations, in the accentuation of differences, in the conflict of ambitions, lies the preservation of the martial spirit, which alone is capable of coping finally with the destructive forces that from outside and from within threaten to submerge all the centuries have gained. . . . Not in universal harmony, nor in fond dreams of unbroken peace, rest now the best hopes of the world, as involved in the fate of European civilization." Quoted in Osgood, *op. cit.,* pp. 38–39. Lippmann does emphasize that in the world of reality the conflict of interests overwhelms the ultimate identity of interests. But in his view it is a sad and sobering, rather than a desirable state of affairs.

[72] "The Rivalry of Nations," p. 18.
[73] T and T, April 10, 1962; also July 18, 1963.
[74] T and T, May 29, 1962; also November 1 and 6, 1962.

National Power

How are international conflicts of interest composed? What is the nature of the forces which must be checked and balanced? Lippmann tells us that although domestic issues may be resolved by ballots rather than by bullets, international disputes "are decided by power, actual or potential, for the ultimate arbiter is not an election but war."[75] Power is the ability of a nation to persuade other nations to do its will. Since war or the threat of war is the final arbiter of disputes, power ultimately means the ability to decide an issue on the field of battle—the ability to raise fighting forces, to supply and to equip them.

Power is then an indispensable means by which nations protect and promote their foreign interests. Since it is a relative quality, they not only try to preserve their actual power and maintain the appearance of strength abroad, but also fear and resent increments in the power of other nations. They cannot, and should not, do otherwise, for their objectives and designs, their connections and alliances in the outside world tend to flourish or decline as their reputation for strength goes up or down. It is well known, for instance, that setbacks in Korea diminished American influence and prestige in Asia and shook up her allies in Europe. In August 1950 the West German Chancellor, Dr. Konrad Adenauer, remarked:

Until now the people in Germany maintained their spirit against the threat of communism by their faith in the United States armed forces. But the events in Korea have had a noticeable effect and there is a sense of helplessness that the Russians will take over.[76]

[75] Walter Lippmann, "A Year of Peacemaking," *Atlantic Monthly*, Vol. 178, No. 6 (December 1946), p. 38. Also see *The Stakes of Diplomacy*, p. 81.
[76] T and T, August 22, 1950.

He suggested that German morale could be bolstered by an enlargement of United States power.

As one might expect, the Soviet Union has consistently endeavored to disperse and disorganize the power of the United States and her allies. She has fomented insurrections and revolutions in Asia, and has followed the broad strategy of embroiling the West with the local nationalist and communist forces without engaging overtly in these activities or committing her own forces to these theatres of conflict. The Russians hoped, wrote Lippmann in 1950, that with American help the French could be persuaded to remain "pinned down in a cruel and indecisive little war. What could suit the Russians better than to have the only land army in Western Europe fighting guerrillas in Indo-China?"[77]

We have noted earlier Lippmann's plea to the United States to preserve her alliances and conserve her power to meet the challenge of Soviet might, if and when it should come. He has also urged that this country should employ all possible means to ensure that the forces of nationalism which prevent the formation of a world-wide Western coalition might also prevent the Soviet Union from developing such a coalition against the West.[78] But Americans should also try to reduce the existing power of Russia by a wise use of diplomacy, which in this context means the creation of situations and the offering of choices which favor and encourage the forces of disintegration already operating in the Russian orbit. In early 1953 Lippmann observed that Stalin's cruel exploitation of the satellites had aroused their national feeling and sown the seeds of revolt along the line opened up by Marshal Tito. The task of American diplomacy in this situation was not to incite rebellion, as the Truman doctrine would have it, but to open up positive alternatives to Russian domination when

[77] *Ibid.*, February 14, 1950.
[78] *Ibid.*, March 23, 1950.

the rebellion was ripe.[79] Lippmann noted that it was a wise move on the part of the United States to help Tito when he broke away from Stalin in 1948. But for this help, Stalin's empire would have reached the shores of the Mediterranean and "would now be rubbing ominously against the frontiers of Italy, Greece and Turkey."[80] Apart from diplomatic moves to diminish the power and influence of her principal foe, the United States should do everything possible to maintain her superiority of offensive power, which is the only deterrent to possible Soviet aggression against herself and her otherwise defenseless allies.

The scene of international politics is thus dominated by a struggle for power: armaments lead to counter-armaments, and issues are viewed not individually but in relation to the whole vast, complicated game of the ups and downs of power positions.[81] Writing in 1953, Lippmann predicted that Koreans would have to wait for a long time for their unification—

perhaps for years, for the day—if it ever comes—when the world powers are sufficiently secure against war to permit small but highly strategic countries like Korea to enjoy their independence. Until that time comes, the great powers will not let go of Korea. And Korea will remain a divided and however it is disguised, an occupied country.[82]

It was utopian, he wrote, of the State Department to expect

[79] *Ibid.*, January 29, 1953.

[80] *Ibid.*, February 9, 1953. Lippmann drew an analogy between Tito's secession from the Soviet orbit in 1948 and the possible desertion of Bulgaria and Albania in 1953. He seems to have overlooked a vital difference between the two situations—a difference which he himself has stressed many a time in other contexts. In 1948 the Soviet Union was unprepared to face the threat of an American atomic attack. In 1953 she was able to reply in kind. Accordingly, Bulgaria as well as the West would have thought twice before taking the risks of a showdown.

[81] *The Stakes of Diplomacy*, p. 83.

[82] T and T, April 14, 1953.

that an armistice in Korea would be followed by a treaty of peace making a permanent settlement. The administration had fallaciously assumed that it was possible to make a political settlement in a secondary theatre, the Far East, independently and ahead of a settlement in the primary theatre of conflict between the great powers—Central Europe. Lippmann emphasized that a Far Eastern settlement hinged upon a settlement in Europe, for in the absence of a European settlement "the strategic necessities of a world war would continue to dominate, and indeed frustrate, all political settlements anywhere which are related to the Soviet Union and its allies."[83] A settlement in Europe would alter the distribution of power in the world so as to encourage a feeling of security against a general war. It was precisely in such an atmosphere of growing security and relaxed nerves that political settlements in secondary theatres such as the Far East could be made.

In their quest for power, some nations lag behind while others march ahead. In the technical language of diplomacy, they are referred to as small powers and great powers. The latter are more influential in the arena of world politics, for the "effective force of the world is in their hands, and the decision of world affairs is for them."[84] The small nations follow but do not lead; they lie in the orbits of the great powers who compete with one another for the allegiance of small nations in the effort to widen their spheres of influence.[85]

[83] Ibid., April 13, 1953.
[84] The Stakes of Diplomacy, p. 82.
[85] In the preceding pages we have cited Lippmann's recent writings to indicate his opinion that small nations are, as a rule, the stakes of great-power diplomacy. We may add that he held this view as early as 1915, when in The Stakes of Diplomacy (p. 82) he wrote that the immediate cause of World War I had been the question as to whether Serbia should become a satellite of the Germanic-Magyar combination or of the Russian empire.

However, the positions occupied by the various powers on the scene of international politics are not permanent. Many a great nation has seen its star eclipsed by the rising power of other, hitherto weak or mediocre states. In the mid-twentieth century the point is well illustrated by the decline of Britain and France as first-class world powers, and the enormous rise in the power of the United States and the Soviet Union. But the current dominant position of Russia and America in the scales of relative power is, according to Lippmann, bound to be a transient phenomenon. Washington and Moscow, he says, cannot long remain the makers and masters of the world's destiny. The peoples of Europe and Asia are also going to play a part in the shaping of things to come. Germany and Japan, for instance, are bound to regain their positions as principal powers.[86] Lippmann has often emphasized that it is an illusion to think, as Americans and the British have tended to think, that Germany can be kept long in the status of a useful auxiliary. More careful observers incline to the view that at least in European affairs Germany is destined to become a greater power than Britain herself.[87]

In 1950 Lippmann noted that the decline of European nations in relative power had made them fearful and nervous. Britain and France, for instance, could not feel secure and independent so long as their very existence depended on the ability of the United States to defend them against a Russian nuclear attack. He advanced the "interesting suggestion" that the United States equip Great Britain and France with atomic bombs from her own stockpile. He argued that if these two principal allies of this country had atomic bombs, even though they had not as many as the Soviet Union had, they could well afford to talk back to the Kremlin with firmness and confidence. They would again count "as great

[86] T and T, September 6, 1955.
[87] Ibid., May 16, 1950. Also see ibid., April 23, 1953.

military Powers in the European balance of power." And, he wrote, "this action might prove to be as revolutionary an event in favor of the West as the Soviet achievement of the bomb was revolutionary to the disadvantage of the West."[88]

It is interesting to note that in the 1960's Lippmann strongly opposes the development of numerous centers of nuclear power within the Western coalition. Not only does he question the wisdom of the United States' sharing atomic secrets with France, but he sees in the emergence of an independent French nuclear striking force a threat to American security and Western unity.

The original principle of the McMahon Act is sound, that within the Western Alliance the ultimate responsibility in nuclear affairs must be in one capital, not in two or three. For the United States the predicament would be intolerable if the key to the use of our strategic nuclear forces were not in Washington. . . .

We cannot allow this power to be set in motion by others. We must keep the ultimate right to decide whether and when it shall be used. A weak and independent nuclear force within the Western Alliance, a force which could start a world war but could not finish it, would be a danger to the peace of the world and to our own national security.[89]

But of this more later.

The evidence which we have examined so far suggests that in Lippmann's view the struggle for power is a primary and inescapable fact of politics among nations. In some of his other works, he has addressed himself directly to the problems of power.

In *The Good Society* Lippmann suggests that in the heat of the struggle, the concrete objectives for the attainment of which power was originally sought may melt into insignifi-

[88] *Ibid.*, May 8, 1950.
[89] Walter Lippmann, *Western Unity and the Common Market* (Boston: Little, Brown and Co., 1962), pp. 36–37. Also see T and T, June 5, 1962.

cance, and the pursuit of power as such may become the chief concern of nations insofar as they regard it as the master key to the solution of all their international problems. By the same token a nation, insofar as it has the power to enforce its will, may not be content to settle with an opponent for this or that concession, but may want to deprive it of the future power to be an opponent at all. In *The Good Society* Lippmann wrote that this desire for absolute power had become the hallmark of international relations in the twentieth century. Wars are now fought, he said, not for tangible stakes but for complete supremacy, for the power to end any issue by superior force. The objective in total wars is "the destruction of the vanquished as an organized power in the major affairs of mankind."[90] He recalled that after World War I, the victors had imposed such terms on Germany as were designed to keep her for a long time weak, disorganized and humiliated.

In *U.S. Foreign Policy* Lippmann notes that the positions occupied by the various nations in the arena of this struggle constitute the order of power at any given time. A nation can ignore it only at the cost of her security and vital interests. He maintains that relations between the great powers as foes, as allies, and as neutrals have in the past, and will in the predictable future, regulate the issues of war and peace in the world. These relations are the major concern of a nation's policy-makers. "No great power can be indifferent to any of the other great powers. It must take a position in regard to all of them. No great power can stand against all others. For none can be great enough for that."[91] A country's foreign policy is sound and solvent only when her side is as strong as, if not stronger than, the combination of her opponents and potential enemies.

[90] *The Good Society*, p. 148.
[91] *U.S. Foreign Policy*, p. 101.

The role of power as outlined above remains unaffected by the nature of the objectives in foreign policy. Whatever its aim, whether war or peace, a nation must build up its power. "The statesman who desires peace can no more ignore the order of power than an engineer can ignore the mechanics of physical force."[92] Lippmann rejects the isolationist argument that a nation can safely ignore the order of power, that it can escape exacting requirements, risks and hazards entailed if it keeps aloof from the entangling affairs of other countries. He cites the case of the United States and argues that this country has never been able to stay out of a war in which the order of power in the oceans which surround her was at stake. Before the Revolution, Americans fought in all great wars on the side of Great Britain. After that they sought allies in Europe, and were

immediately involved in all the great wars within the order of power. During the Napoleonic Era they waged the Quasi-War against France, and the War of 1812 against England. They formed the concert with Britain to resist the Holy Alliance. They have fought in both the German wars of the twentieth century. There have been no other great wars which involved the order of power in our surrounding oceans.[93]

Thus, whether they like it or not, whether they realize it or not, the great powers are inextricably involved in, and tied to, the order of power that exists at any given time. "The principal military powers form a system in which they must all be at peace or all at war."[94] Commenting on the popular belief that wars are caused by the fact that nations play

[92] *Ibid.*, p. 101. In the mid-twentieth century, a balance of nuclear terror between the United States and the Soviet Union maintains peace between them. In the absence of such a balance, peaceful coexistence cannot be assured. See T and T, November 9, 1961, December 21, 1961, March 6, 1962.

[93] *Ibid.*, pp. 98–99.

[94] *Ibid.*, p. 98; also T and T, May 28, 1953.

"power politics," Lippmann argues that it is one thing to play politics and another to manage it. A statesman need not and, as a matter of fact, should not play power politics. But "he must with cold calculation organize and regulate the politics of power."[95]

The foregoing evidence clearly indicates that Lippmann accepts the struggle for power as the supreme and inexorable fact of international politics in a world which is organized into nation-states. It should, however, be clear that this conclusion holds only in respect of the material components of national power, which were the subject matter of the preceding discussion.

We have noted that Lippmann is not oblivious to the importance of a nation's idealistic and moral standing abroad as a constituent element of its power and influence. A relatively new factor in the present-day international situation has slightly tipped the balance in favor of the non-material components of power. The formula that war is the final arbiter of international disputes may be as true as ever in relation to, say, Bolivia and Paraguay. Its validity is somewhat questionable as regards the great nuclear powers and their allies. Both sides in the present Cold War seem to have concluded that at least for the time being war is not a practical way of settling the outstanding issues between them.[96] Their power to destroy civilization has reached a point where a slight increase in the number and effectiveness of weapons would not make an appreciable difference in their relative positions. Moreover, their power in relation to each other is the power to deter, not the power to compel. As Lippmann himself says, if either side were to mistake it

for the power to compel, it could, and it probably would, cease to be deterrent. The power to deter is effective only if the nation at

[95] *Ibid.*, p. 101.
[96] T and T, September 14, 1961; January 1, 1963.

which it is directed has been convinced that it will not be struck if it refrains from striking.[97]

Since in the present international situation military power performs an essentially negative function, and insofar as it cannot readily be used for the achievement of foreign objectives, the non-military components of power have been activated more than ever before. There is in progress an intense battle between communist Russia and the West for the minds of men. Lippmann is very much concerned with America's performance in this psychological warfare. He has urged time and again that the United States should reassure world public opinion of her desire for peace. He has maintained that the American people, having been the first to make and use the atomic bomb, and also having been the first to make the hydrogen bomb, owe it to mankind to search for a decent and honorable alternative to a war of extermination. If they were to give up the effort to find such an alternative, they "should have lost the struggle for men's souls, and the right to their trust and their faith."[98] The great powers can no longer impress the world merely by a show of force. They must also make their purposes palatable to the masses of men in different countries.[99] Americans should try to combat the Asian suspicion that the United States is an imperialist power and that her imperialism is just as arbitrary and ruthless as that of any other nation. Lippmann once suggested that as a concrete step in this direction, this country should refrain from holding Formosa by force. "It really would be better to lose the island of Formosa than to lose the confidence of all the national leaders of Asia."[100]

[97] T and T, March 8, 1951; also February 10, 1953; again, September 14, 1961.

[98] Ibid., February 9, 1950.

[99] Ibid., June 15, 1953. Also The Communist World and Ours (1958), pp. 42–45, and The Coming Tests with Russia (1961), pp. 36–37.

[100] Ibid., January 2, 1950. It should be noted that in making the above proposal Lippmann also emphasized that Formosa was not vital to American

We may conclude that in Lippmann's view it is essential for a nation to maintain a strong military posture vis-à-vis other nations, but at the same time she must make concessions to their hopes and fears and to their sense of right and wrong. What should be the relative proportion of the military and non-military elements in a nation's power? Writing more than twenty years ago, Lippmann observed that force and compromise, threat and concessions are all integral parts of effective diplomacy. Contrary to popular opinion, they go together and cannot be separated, for "the art of statesmanship is to use them both, having determined at each juncture the best proportions."[101] It pays to be known as strong and powerful, and it pays to be known as the champion of civilized, idealistic and moral purposes. The evidence thus far examined, however, suggests that the considerations of military power loom large in Lippmann's mind, and that at most junctures he himself is inclined so to mix the moral and material components of national power as to make the latter preponderant in the compounded whole.

There can be no doubt that power plays a dominant role in both domestic and international politics: whenever the issue between two governments is political, it involves their relative power. It is both futile and unwise to divorce the formulation of foreign policy from the strategy and politics of power.[102] If actions are to be judged not only by the nature

---

security. Apart from the merits of this assertion, it would then appear that he was not, after all, making a big or material concession to Asian sentiment. Secondly, it is not quite clear that in disengaging herself from the "rotten and sinking ship of Chiang," the United States would not have appeared to be "opportunist" to at least some sections of world public opinion.

[101] T and T, July 11, 1935.

[102] "And the course of things is such that as soon as a powerful foreigner enters a land, all the less powerful rulers adhere to him, moved by their envy against the one who has been in power over them. This is so true that the foreigner has to take no trouble to win the lesser rulers. . . . He has only to see to it that they do not grasp too much power and too much

of the ends pursued but also by the results actually accomplished, it would be criminal negligence for a government to ignore the politics of power, for such an omission on its part may well cause the failure of policy and bring untold misery upon the people whom it represents and governs.

How does one reconcile the prescription that nations must participate in the struggle for power with the ultimate objective of the civilized man to develop a universal harmony of interests and to work for the establishment of the good society? It would appear that the objective of victory in the struggle for power is repugnant not only to the doctrine that a universal harmony of interests actually exists but also to the ethical objective of creating such a harmony. One may argue that the participation in the struggle for power is essentially a short-term policy designed to ensure national survival, and that once survival is ensured a nation may go ahead in the pursuit of its ideals. Or one may say that the efforts to create the good society should proceed concurrently with the struggle for power.

The first argument is based on the unwarranted assumption, branded by Lippmann himself as utopian, that the struggle for power can or will one day come to an end. The fact of the matter is that there is no end to the temptation to gain a little more power and feel a little more secure. As Niebuhr

---

authority; then with his forces and their favor, he can put down those who are powerful, and remain in every way the master of that land. And he who does not attend carefully to this matter will quickly lose what he has acquired; and while he holds his territory he will have countless difficulties and troubles within it." Machiavelli, *The Prince and Other Works*, trans. Allan H. Gilbert (New York: Hendricks House, 1946), pp. 99–100.

Professor Carr has written: "The alleged 'dictatorship of the Great Powers,' which is sometimes denounced by utopian writers as if it were a wicked policy deliberately adopted by certain states, is a fact which constitutes something like a 'law of nature' in international politics." *The Twenty Years' Crisis, 1919–1939* (London: Macmillan and Company Ltd., 1954), p. 105.

says, there is "no possibility of drawing a sharp line between the will-to-live and the will-to-power."[103] Or as Hobbes has said in a celebrated passage:

I put for a general inclination of all mankind, a perpetual and restless desire for power after power, that ceaseth only in death. And the cause of this, is not always that a man hopes for a more intensive delight, than he has already attained to; or that he cannot be content with a moderate power: but because he cannot assure the power and means to live well, which he hath present, without the acquisition of more.[104]

Nor can the efforts to achieve the ideal bear fruit if they proceed alongside the struggle for power, for the ground gained will constantly be lost to the exigencies of power politics.

Power politics is unpopular, and we may submit that its notoriety is not altogether baseless. One of the philosophic foundations of the doctrine of the primacy of power is the separation of ethics and politics derived from the famous dictum, Render unto Caesar the things that are Caesar's, and unto God the things that are God's. Lippmann evidently accepts this separation in the short run. But insofar as the short run continues to stretch its tenure, the attempt to keep God and Caesar apart postpones indefinitely the establishment of a social order based upon a universal moral order.

We are faced here with a problem that defies solution. One cannot amass military might alone and be secure. One cannot rely on saintly qualities alone to enjoy the good things of life in peace, without external interference. The pursuit of military power may necessitate courses of action which are not altogether moral. And the requirements of a moral life may drastically limit the ways and means to attain physical

[103] *Moral Man and Immoral Society* (New York: Charles Scribner's Sons, 1932), p. 42.
[104] *Leviathan,* Chapter XI.

power. This is a dilemma which perhaps no one can happily resolve. As Professor Niebuhr says:

Politics will, to the end of history, be an area where conscience and power meet, where the ethical and coercive factors of human life will interpenetrate and work out their tentative and uneasy compromises.[105]

Making these "tentative and uneasy compromises," or determining, as Lippmann would say, the relative proportions of the moral and material elements of national power, is a matter of practical wisdom and statesmanship.

The following three chapters present Lippmann's views on the various ways of dealing with the problem of power which students of human affairs have suggested through the ages.

---

[105] *Moral Man and Immoral Society,* p. 4.

III

The Organization of Peace

A World State: The Ultimate Objective

WE HAVE NOTED ABOVE THAT LIPPMANN CONSIDERS THE
present organization of the world into sovereign nation-
states as a necessary evil, which imposes additional rivalries,
conflicts and wars on mankind and obstructs its progress
toward the good society. The march of civilization would be
greatly accelerated if more and more people the world over
could join together to solve their common problems and
pursue common ideals. Therefore, the ultimate objective of
thinking men who wish to see a peaceful and progressive
world is the establishment of a world state. In *The Stakes of
Diplomacy* Lippmann wrote that this might be a dream at
present, but that

It is a valiant dream which must be realized if this planet is to
fulfill man's best hopes. It is clearly the goal of human political
endeavor, and no civilized man can afford to sneer at it, or to
lay it altogether outside his mind.[1]

Lippmann predicated his enthusiasm for the ideal of a
world state with the caution that its establishment in a dem-

[1] *The Stakes of Diplomacy*, p. 143.

ocratic manner was not possible in the foreseeable future, for the simple reason that the majority of men did not want it. To force world government on unwilling men would be tyrannical and, therefore, undesirable. Moreover, the world as yet did not have the necessary administrative capacity. No Parliament of Man could muster enough time, talent and energy to deal with the enormous complexities of the earth. It would collapse, he said, under its own weight.

A democratic world government being unfeasible, Lippmann, at this time, was willing to settle instead for a benevolent despotism. He proposed that the world be led and controlled by a coalition of liberal Western powers, which would act toward it as Prussia acted toward the other German states, or as England acted toward the Empire. Lippmann acknowledged that his own plan was not without practical difficulties. The coalition of the Western powers, he feared, would be beset with internal jealousies and rivalries. He also felt that their benevolent despotism would not be universally accepted and would, therefore, have to be confined to the area of Western commercial civilization.

In short, the larger state which we are trying to create will for a long time bear slight resemblance to the Federation of Mankind. It is likely to be unequal, coercive, conservative, and unsatisfactory. In the World State those of us who dream of it today would, I fancy, find ourselves for a long time members of Its Majesty's Loyal Opposition.[2]

The creation of a world state would remain an empty dream and never become even the ultimate ideal of practical men unless someone, somewhere, made a beginning toward it. Lippmann suggested the formation of a series of miniature world governments, each charged with a specific international problem. The administration of backward areas, he main-

[2] *The Stakes of Diplomacy*, pp. 177–178.

tained, would be the best starting point. Englishmen and Germans would resent the interference of an international agency in their internal affairs but might be willing to cooperate with other nations in governing, say, Morocco. The principal merit of this approach to the problem of world government was that it called for "no more relinquishment of national sovereignty than the experience and sense of the world had already fairly well agreed to."[3] Lippmann hoped that participation in the administration of distant places would gradually lead the nations out of their habit of insisting on their "sovereign right" to pursue "independent" foreign policies. The experience of give-and-take and the lessons of cooperation learned in the government of backward areas might extend to their other interests in other spheres.[4]

International government in the backward areas should serve primarily as a continuing conference of the interested great powers, a kind of senate to hear appeals from the actions of the subordinate colonial officials. Its powers over these officials should be gradually increased until the colonial service was completely internationalized.

It will be seen that at this time (1915) Lippmann was anticipating a trusteeship system. More important, he was advocating a system of "conference diplomacy" as a means of regulating the rivalry of great powers in the backward areas which, he maintained, were the stakes of diplomacy. He emphasized that the principal virtue of all international organization, indeed its *raison d'être*, lay in its role as a perpetual conference of the representatives of national governments.[5]

Lippmann recognized in *The Stakes of Diplomacy* that the proposed international governments could not operate in

[3] *Ibid.*, p. 145.
[4] *Ibid.*, p. 186.
[5] *Ibid.*, pp. 134–135.

the face of popular opposition. However, he believed that the psychological impediments were not insurmountable. If men could love something so abstract and complicated as the British Empire, they could attach themselves not only to the limited international governments in backward areas but even to a world state. He argued:

We have seen Massachusetts patriots converted into American patriots, Bavarians into Germans, Venetians into Italians. The task of the great unifiers like Hamilton, Cavour and Bismarck looked just as difficult in their day as ours does now. They had states' rights, sovereignty, traditional jealousy and economic conflicts to overcome. They conquered them. Who dares to say that we must fail?[6]

Lippmann wrote that world government could draw on the emotions of mankind if its usefulness could be demonstrated —if it could be shown to provide more security and prosperity than the nation-state. Men fix their loyalty, argued Lippmann, on the authority that gives them security and the opportunity to make progress and advance in life. It followed that the most useful friends or the most formidable opponents of international government for backward areas were the businessmen, industrialists and other powerful pressure groups in various countries. Lippmann believed that they would never attach themselves to such a government so long as they knew that they could run to the home government for support, and could rely on it to obtain special privileges for them. Only when the interested businessman "is thrown upon the mercy of international government will he have any stimulus to loyalty."[7]

Lippmann's argument in *The Stakes of Diplomacy* is based on two assumptions. First, he assumed that the great powers would agree to maintain a so-called "open door" and the

[6] *Ibid.*, p. 180.
[7] *Ibid.*, p. 157.

"equality of commercial opportunity" in backward countries, and to share the wealth of the area in proportion to their industrial and financial ability to exploit and absorb such wealth. The fate of the open door in China, and the actual practice of the mandatory powers in the mandated territories in the interwar period, would suggest that Lippmann was being unduly optimistic about the propensity of great powers to cooperate with one another in constructive ventures.

Lippmann has ever since maintained his devotion to the ideal of a world state. However, his views on its feasibility have not remained constant through the years. We have seen that in *The Stakes of Diplomacy* (1915) he was rather pessimistic about the possibility of realizing the cherished goal. In 1917, by contrast, he seems to have thought that the establishment of world government was imminent. He was greatly impressed by the emergence of a "new internationalism" in America and a "new democracy" in Russia. The great end to the achievement of which these forces should be directed, he said, was "nothing less than the federation of the world." It should be America's foremost war aim.

We can win nothing from this war unless it culminates in a union of liberal peoples pledged to cooperate in the settlement of all outstanding questions, sworn to turn against the aggressor, determined to erect a larger and more modern system of international law upon a federation of the world.[8]

Lippmann observed that before 1914 only a few visionaries could hope for some kind of world federation. It was generally believed that each nation was appropriately concerned with its own vital interests and its own sphere of influence. This was a world, for all practical purposes, without common standards, aspirations or ideals. But times had changed. New

[8] *The Annals of the American Academy of Political and Social Science* (July 1917), p. 8.

ideas had emerged to possess men's souls, and new forces had
been released which could overcome the difficulties that beset
the internationalist in 1914. This was one of those times
"when the impossible becomes possible, when events outrun
our calculations." There were still some obstructionists, interested in their own selfish ends rather than in international
cooperation, who could be counted upon to oppose the movement for world government. But the tide, said Lippmann,
had turned against them.[9]

During the interwar period Lippmann modified his views on
the subject of international organization in general and world
government in particular. After his departure from the Peace
Conference in 1919, his enthusiasm for Wilsonian internationalism began to cool. He sharply criticized the League
as an instrument designed to enforce an unjust peace. He
opposed the ratification of the Treaty of Versailles when it
came up before the United States Senate. By the mid-thirties
Lippmann had almost become an isolationist. As was mentioned earlier, he greeted the defeat of the World Court in

[9] *Ibid.* It is difficult to understand this outburst of optimism about the
imminence of world government. It is possible that under the spell of
Wilsonianism, Lippmann believed that the hour of destiny had arrived.
Wilson himself thought so, at least for a time. At the Paris Conference he
declared: "I am confident . . . that the day is near when they [Americans]
will become as eager partisans of the sovereignty of mankind as they are
now of their national or state sovereignty." See Stephen Bonsal, *Un-
finished Business,* (New York: Doubleday, Doran and Co., 1944), p.
159. But it is also possible that Lippmann's address to the American
Academy of Political and Social Science in April 1917 was intended to
boost the general Wilsonian position on the theory that public opinion
would not support it except on appeal to high ideals. In his preface
to the second edition of *The Stakes of Diplomacy,* signed January 1, 1917,
Lippmann wrote that the realistic basis for a league of nations had been
discussed very little, "and on that basis it might never be accepted by the
American people . . . If the plan is to be popular it will not be preached
widely as practical world politics." As a maneuver in public opinion and
propaganda, the address in question might have been designed to arouse
the approving interest of the public in the ideal of world government by
impressing upon it the idea that the actual establishment of such a government was imminent.

the Senate on January 29, 1935 with the observation that the people of the United States did not favor participation in the Hague tribunal. Furthermore, he objected, the Court, like its sister institutions, was cursed with the original sin of Versailles. American adherence to the Court must be interpreted at home and abroad as a commitment to support the postwar European settlement.[10] Lippmann also denied that the Court was an independent judicial tribunal, free from power politics. The League of Nations, he said, was not a world organization but a European institution. The United States could not usefully participate in it until Europe set its house in order and resolved the question of "who is to be the master of Europe."[11]

In *U.S. War Aims* (1944), once again we find Lippmann exceedingly pessimistic, even cynical, about the feasibility of world government. It was impossible, he said, to elect and constitute such a government. The great powers, who alone had the money to foot its bills and the military power to enforce its decrees, would not accept its huge responsibilities while the power to make decisions rested with the majority in a Parliament of Man.[12] The people of the United States, for example, would not concede sovereign powers to a world legislature in which they were outvoted ten to one by Asians. And yet "on what moral principle could Americans claim that their votes should count more heavily than those of other human beings?"[13] No nation would agree to submit its vital interests to majority votes in a world legislature. If decisions

[10] T and T, February 2, 1935.
[11] *Ibid.*
[12] Lippmann's argument here is the same as that of Senators Lodge and Borah in 1919. Arguing that Wilson's advocacy of the League was based in his unlimited altruism, Borah said: "I may be willing to help my neighbor . . . but I do not want him placed in a position where he may decide when and how I shall act or to what extent I shall make sacrifices." Quoted in Osgood, *op. cit.*, p. 286.
[13] *U.S. War Aims*, p. 183.

were taken by a unanimous vote, nothing at all would ever be decided in such a parliament.

If we could not have a world government elected by the adult suffrage of mankind, we were obliged to come back to an organization of the existing nation-states as the only alternative. But this organization would exercise only such powers as were given to it by the participating national governments. Even if it had an assembly, a secretariat and a police force, it would still not be a world government. It would meet its expenses out of what the member governments gave it, and their contributions would depend not on its power to tax but on their willingness to pay. Now, if the national governments were to pay the world officials, specify their powers, and mark out their jurisdictions, then "no matter what the covenants and charters may say, the world organization is a voluntary association of diplomats who confer."[14] Let us then not mislead ourselves and the world by dressing it up in different words.

In 1946 Lippmann expressed the view that world government could not be created by decree or even by treaty, but must evolve through the slow process of trial and error. Its construction should proceed from bottom to top rather than vice versa: the process of uniting the world should begin at points where civilizations meet and overlap, not at the centers and the interior. Nations with diverse ways of life could not be fused into one socio-political entity. At present, they could only be joined in a loose federation or an association. Any further progress toward world government must hinge upon the maintenance of peace among nations, and the responsibility to maintain peace, wrote Lippmann, must rest with those nations who knew how to use power, and to keep all power, including their own, in equilibrium. While the nations of the world were at peace,

[14] *Ibid.*, p. 185.

if the conviction begins to take hold that they may look forward to a longish period of peace, then, gradually, constructive and creative individuals in all countries will begin to communicate. They will push out threads of common effort and of a world-wide humanism across the dividing lines. And so they will begin to weave the pattern of a higher union of mankind.[15]

It will be noticed that Lippmann is advancing the familiar argument that the emergence of government presupposes the existence of a community, that world government cannot be created so long as a world community does not exist. This school of thought asserts that a government can perfect the order and justice of the community but cannot create the community. Professor Niebuhr, an exponent of this school, observes, "The community cannot be coerced into basic order; the basic order must come from its innate cohesion."[16] It is further contended that communities or unions cannot be created by the fiat of government or law or constitutional conventions. They grow. The world community lacks the essential element of togetherness, and neither law nor police power can supply this defect.[17]

The foregoing argument must be confronted with the opposing argument that the community and government have a relation of interaction. They grow together and reinforce each other. This is, says Robert M. Hutchins,

what the Greeks had in mind when they said that law was an educational force and that the city educates the man. . . . We are so used to thinking of law as repressive and constitution as the embodiment of pre-existing agreement that we neglect the tre-

[15] Walter Lippmann, "One World of Diversity," *Vital Speeches*, Vol. 13, No. 5 (December 15, 1946), p. 140.
[16] Reinhold Niebuhr, "The Myth of World Government," *The Nation*, Vol. 162, No. 11 (March 16, 1946), p. 312.
[17] Among the earlier writers on the subject, Kant was the forerunner of Lippmann and Niebuhr in emphasizing a gradualist approach to the problem of world government. He advocated a federation of free states which

mendous force which any constitution and any system of law exerts in behalf of its own acceptance and perpetuation.[18]

In 1948 Lippmann revived his plea for a world state as the ultimate objective of civilized men, and advocated that the United States make its establishment a principal objective of her foreign policy. Americans, he said, had a traditional distrust of power politics and believed that "security and serenity require a universal order of equal laws, and can never be had in a mere equilibrium of sovereign states."[19] Nations of the world, to be sure, would have to struggle and strive for a long time before they could achieve the ideal of a world state. In the meantime, economic, territorial and political problems would continue to arise and challenge the statesmanship of their leaders. The battle of the civilized and the enlightened against the ignorant and the malicious would not come to an end. But

how different would be the assumptions and the expectations of diplomacy if, as a great power in the company of other nations who would surely be with us, we were committed to the formation of a world order of universal law. Merely to have begun on this enterprise, though the first steps be small and difficult, would be to introduce into all the calculations and judgments of international affairs a new orientation, and into men's lives a compelling purpose.[20]

Once again, Lippmann advanced a practical proposal to

should develop and expand its jurisdiction slowly. But, at the same time, he urged governments not to try to move too rapidly toward this goal lest they jeopardize its realization. L. Larry Leonard, *International Organization* (New York: McGraw-Hill Book Company, 1951), p. 27.

[18] Robert M. Hutchins, "The Constitutional Foundation for World Order," *Foundations for World Order* (University of Denver: Social Science Foundation, 1947), pp. 105–106. Also see Schuman, *op. cit.*, p. 471.

[19] Walter Lippmann, "How to Enforce International Agreements," *Readers Digest*, Vol. 48, No. 4 (April 1946), p. 142.

[20] *Ibid.*

expedite the formation of a world order under law. He observed that if there was anything in the field of political science that could be called a proved discovery, it was that a system of law could produce peace, justice and order only if it operated on individuals. It would be a contradiction in terms to speak of law enforcement in reference to sovereign entities, for by definition they would be outside the jurisdiction of law or law-enforcing agencies external to them. International law, he said, was ineffective because it was inoperative, because its subjects were not individuals but sovereign nation-states. Hamilton was applying this principle when he argued that if a government rather than a league were wanted, "we must extend the authority of the Union to the persons of the citizens."[21]

World government could not operate without a body of world law. Therefore, Lippmann argued, in order to make international law effective and to broaden the popular base of a future world government, that law must be made to operate on individuals. This could be accomplished by international agreement that a treaty should be deemed ratified only after its content had been made into national law by domestic legislation. Then international law would truly become universal law. The offender against this law would nowhere find quarter, for no one would harbor him. He would be an outlaw who could be arrested and punished in any of the United Nations. Lippmann went on to suggest that if a national government coerced its citizens to violate the world law, they could appeal to the United Nations. In fact, "no one would owe allegiance to his state when that meant that he had to violate the world law." A patriotic man would feel free to expose the officials of his national government conspiring to violate the law of the world and, also, the law of their own country. He could do so with good conscience "just

[21] *Ibid.*, p. 137.

as he would expose them if, in the United States, they were conspiring against the Bill of Rights, or for that matter to rob the treasury. They, not he, would be the traitors, the criminals and the lawbreakers."[22]

Lippmann maintained that the United Nations had already accepted his principle in that they had participated in the indictment, trial and punishment of war criminals. They had "embraced the principle that crimes are always committed by persons and that only those sanctions which reach individuals can peacefully and effectively be enforced."[23]

While Lippmann proposed these blueprints of world government and law, he acknowledged that in the predictable future "the affairs of the world will be determined by rivalries, combinations and an uneasy equilibrium among the sovereign and powerful states."[24] However, a long step toward the final goal would be taken if these proposals were adopted.

It will be seen that the above proposal is illogical. Lippmann offers a plan to hasten the establishment of a world state, but in drawing it up he assumes that such a state is already in existence. For otherwise how could the United Nations punish an individual violating the world law, or save its adherents from the punitive action of a national government bent upon breaking the world law? We cannot expect world patriotism to rise against national governments hostile to the world law, unless we assume that men and women the world over have already developed a system of dual allegiance, as in a federation, in which their loyalty to the world authority transcends their national loyalties. Lippmann's proposal is all the more surprising because it came at a time when the Cold War had already begun to split the world into two rival coalitions. It was somewhat utopian in 1946 to expect that

[22] *Ibid.*, p. 139.
[23] *Ibid.*, p. 141.
[24] *Ibid.*, p. 142.

the Soviet government, or for that matter any government, would allow its citizens to serve any but the national interest, or permit international law to operate directly on its workers engaged, say, in making nuclear weapons.

From an over-all view of the positions which Lippmann has taken over the years on the issue of world government, the following striking *facts* emerge. He has always maintained that the elimination of the present struggle for power between nation-states, and its replacement by a "pool of power" managed and controlled by a world state, is a worthy end of human political endeavor. With one exception—his address to the American Academy of Political and Social Science in April 1917—he has always insisted, albeit with varying degrees of emphasis, that this goal cannot be realized in the predictable future. The principal reason for its infeasibility is the lack of will on the part of mankind to work for it. "Unregenerate and immature" men, who constitute the vast majority of mankind, desire the impossible: they wish to avoid the hazards of national rivalries, and would seek the fruit of international cooperation and world government without having to give up the freedom to follow "independent" policies for independently chosen ends.

Is the establishment of a world order under law an ever-receding goal? There is no conclusive answer to this question. It is possible that mankind is in the grip of forces beyond the scope of its comprehension and outside the span of its control, which are leading it to self-destruction, and that one day, as Henry Adams put it in 1901, "the world will break its damned neck." Again, it is possible that men will be united, and that they will be liberated from the tyranny of fear engendered by the ever-present danger of infinitely destructive wars—not through the courage of their convictions but by the might of a great power which, by the sword, subversion, or economic aid, may subdue the rest of the world.[25] And, of course, it is possible that mankind will continue indefinitely to live in an unsafe world kept from destruction or disintegration by a series of uneasy compromises. Finally, we may submit that there is nothing sacrosanct about world government. It is only a way to fulfill man's desire to live in a peaceful and orderly world. There may be other ways to satisfy this vital human need.

Collective Security

We have noted Lippmann's view that the evolution of the world state must hinge upon the maintenance of peace for an extended period of time. Many students of international affairs have believed that man's desire for peace and security could be fulfilled by organizing an international agency to maintain world peace. We have seen that in April 1917 Lippmann pleaded for an association of nations "pledged" to cooperate in the settlement of international disputes and "sworn to turn against the aggressor." A great many of his contemporaries who shared this view meant to pledge

[25] On the premises that force is the greatest unifier and that the authority of government is the principal promoter of social cohesion, some writers have argued that the only way to establish world government is by force. Bertrand Russell, for instance, maintains that "a federal [world] government formed by mutual agreement, as the League of Nations and the United Nations were formed, is sure to be weak, because the constituent nations will feel, as the barons felt in the Middle Ages, that anarchy is better than loss of independence. And just as the substitution of orderly government for anarchy in the Middle Ages depended upon the victory of the royal power, so the substitution of order for anarchy in international relations, if it comes about, will come about through the superior power of some one nation or group of nations. . . . I agree, of course, that it would be far better to have an international government constituted by agreement, but I am quite convinced that the love of national independence is too strong for such a government to have effective power." The fact that such a government will be undemocratic is a necessary evil and must be faced. However, after it "has been in power for a century or so, it will begin to command that degree of respect that will make it possible to base

the proposed organization to the principle of collective security. The association of nations should act to restrain the violators of world law and order, if necessary with the force of arms. Lippmann, however, stood apart from them.[26] He did not pin his hopes for world peace on the exercise of police power and functions by the world organization. As a matter of fact, he has consistently argued against the theory of collective peace enforcement.

The principle of collective security, which means "the enforcement of international agreements by sovereign states against [other] sovereign states"[27] is oppressive in its operation. Even if we assume that the principle is workable, the peace that it might maintain must be a very bad peace. For one thing, it would draw the small and middle-sized nations into great power conflicts, and burden them with heavy costs in men and materials.[28] Secondly, the principle of collective security works in practice as the custodian of the status quo. Criticizing the League Covenant in 1919, Lippmann argued that Article 10, which bound the members to preserve the

---

its power upon law and sentiment rather than upon force; and when that happens, the international government can become democratic." *New Hopes for a Changing World* (London: George Allen and Unwin Ltd., 1951), pp. 77-78.

[26] In his preface to *The Stakes of Diplomacy* (pp. xiii-xx) Lippmann observed that the "real value" of the idea of the League to enforce peace lay in the development of a postwar defensive alliance between the United States, Great Britain and France to guarantee pacific settlement of international disputes but more especially to offset a possible future alliance between Russia, Germany and Japan. A number of Lippmann's contemporaries also advanced the same idea. See Ruhl F. Bartlett, *The League to Enforce Peace* (Chapel Hill: The University of North Carolina Press, 1944), p. 65.

[27] "How to Enforce International Agreements," *Readers Digest*, April 1946.

[28] It may be recalled that under Article xvi of the Covenant, the members of the League were pledged to "support one another in the financial and economic measures which are taken under this Article, in order to minimize the loss and inconvenience resulting from the above measures." But for all practical purposes the provision was disregarded when sanctions

territorial integrity and political independence of one another, was an attempt to seal the status quo, "an effort to be wiser than the next generation, and to curb the action of the future by a magic set of words."[29] The League would become the sanctuary of illiberal states which would invoke Article 10 to perpetuate their oppressive policies, and would denounce any proposal to modify them as aggression against their sovereignty and political independence.

Again, assuming that it is workable, Lippmann maintains that the way to achieve peace through collective security is crude and barbaric. It calls upon

great masses of innocent people to stand ready to exterminate great masses of innocent people. No world order can be founded upon such a principle; it cannot command the respect of civilized men, least of all of democratic men who . . . consider it the very essence of justice to distinguish between the guilty and the innocent.[30]

Lippmann rejects the argument that the wars of collective security would not be necessary since the mere threat of collective punitive action would be sufficient to deter ag-

---

were imposed against Italy during the Italo-Ethiopian War. Of all the countries applying sanctions, Yugoslavia was the hardest hit, for something like a quarter of her total exports normally went to Italy. Great Britain did make certain concessions in respect to Yugoslav farm products, but "the fruits of the attempt to organize 'mutual support' were exceedingly meagre . . ." The Royal Institute of International Affairs, *International Sanctions* (London: Oxford University Press, 1938), p. 210.

[29] *The Political Scene*, p. 56. Most writers support Lippmann's view that in the absence of an adequate machinery to facilitate peaceful change, the institution of collective security must operate as the guardian of the status quo. See Stefan T. Possony, "Peace Enforcement," and Edwin Borchard, "The Impracticability of 'Enforcing' Peace," in *Yale Law Journal: Symposium on World Organization* (August 1946); also Werner Levi, *Fundamentals of World Organization* (Minneapolis: The University of Minnesota Press, 1950), pp. 50–60; Hans J. Morgenthau, *Politics among Nations* (New York: Alfred A. Knopf, 1948), p. 332.

[30] "How to Enforce International Agreements," *Readers Digest*, April 1946, p. 137. We may submit that this is an argument not against col-

gression. He argues that this theory would work only if everyone knew that the threat was not an empty bluff. Moreover, it is in the early stages of aggression that collective security would have to be effective if a major conflagration were to be avoided. But it is precisely here that collective security is likely to be the least effective. The peace-loving states cannot be expected to plunge themselves into war "over what appear to be in themselves minor disputes." The aggressor can be counted upon to know this and treat the threats of collective action as bluffs. And when the conflict does assume serious proportions, stopping it would mean not a minor police action but a major war.[31]

In 1944 Lippmann pleaded that the proposed international organization should not contain pledges to use military force for the maintenance of peace. The principle of collective security, he contended, is unworkable in a world of nation-states. For one thing, it is much too vague and nebulous to be accepted as a norm of conduct. It tries to do the impossible in that it seeks to commit a nation to wage a hypothetical war in the indefinite future against an unknown enemy under unforeseeable circumstances. This hypothetical and generalized nature of the commitment makes it both valueless and dangerous: everyone accepts it because it demands nothing concrete at the time of acceptance, and nobody honors it because the hazards involved were not foreseen by the signatories.[32]

Since everyone knows that the commitment to wage wars

---

lective security but against war as such. For in every war masses of innocent men exterminate masses of innocent men. Yet Lippmann does not condemn all war.

[31] *Ibid.* Even some advocates of collective security concede this point. See, for instance, Senator Joseph H. Ball, *Collective Security* (Boston: World Peace Foundation, 1943), p. 44.

[32] Walter Lippmann, "Big Four and World Peace," *Newsweek*, Vol. 24, No. 8 (August 21, 1944), p. 104.

of collective security is nebulous, no nation, if it can help it, will rely on it for the defense of its vital interests. Lippmann maintained that Americans were certain to rely on their own armed strength and on their alliances to safeguard their security. They would use the world organization only as a reinforcing agent, not as a substitute for the aforementioned arrangements. The other great powers were sure to do the same.

The greatest danger to the peace and tranquility of the world arises not so much from the isolated conflict of two small nations as from the clash of great powers, which tends to spread like wildfire and engulf the whole community of nations. Small nations cannot restrain the great powers, which hold the force of the world in their hands, from breaking the peace of the world. Thus, the principle of collective security is meaningful only in a context in which the great powers act as policemen and enforce peace when it is broken by small powers. In other words, the principle is applicable to relatively harmless conflicts; for when the policemen fight each other, no one can restrain them.[33] When a combination of the great powers tries to police one or more other great powers, it is no more a police function but a world war.

In December 1944 Lippmann wrote that the peace-enforcing function of the United Nations was predicated on the assumption that the great powers would remain at peace. Their special position in the Council was designed to prevent an alignment on issues that could disrupt the enforcing and pacifying powers. The question then was: "Shall the Charter assume that bad faith among the guardians of peace is possible, and prepare for it, or shall it assume that their good faith is indispensable if the peace is to be maintained by force?"[34] The Russians answered this question at Dumbarton Oaks by arguing that they could not subscribe to a Charter which gave

[33] U.S. War Aims, pp. 160–162.
[34] Walter Lippmann, "Pacification for Peace," Atlantic Monthly, Vol. 174, No. 6 (December 1944), pp. 50–51.

other nations the right to wage war against them.[35] It became quite clear that the universal society could not prevent war between the great powers, and that, on the contrary, war between them must be prevented so that the organization might have a chance to live and prosper. It should be remembered, said Lippmann, that

when a great power, itself one of the policemen, has to be coerced the police force is split in two and arrayed against itself. It is only when the policemen act together that the enforcement is not the equivalent of a great world war, but is a police function requiring only the show, and in rare areas the use, of limited military forces.[36]

In 1946 Lippmann observed that the United Nations had actually rejected the principle of collective security. The Charter, he wrote, nullifies the provisions for collective security by requiring the unanimous support of the permanent members of the Security Council for collective action against aggression. The method cannot lawfully be used against any great power without its consent, which means that it can never be used. For "the rule of unanimity protects all other states against collective coercion unless, perchance, there is some state so small, so isolated, and so unimportant that it is not the ally or the client of any one of the great powers."[37]

The theory of collective security, as regards the small states,

[35] President Roosevelt and Secretary Hull in vain sought Russian agreement to their proposal that a permanent member of the Security Council should not exercise her right of vote if she were involved in a dispute being considered by the Council. Cordell Hull, *Memoirs* (New York: The Macmillan Co., 1948), Vol. II, p. 1700.

Generally speaking, Americans also favored the right of veto and the principle of the unanimity of the great powers. Hull himself maintained that "without an enduring understanding between these four nations upon their fundamental purposes, interests and obligations to one another, all organizations to preserve peace are creations on paper and the path is wide open again for the rise of a new aggressor." Hull, *op. cit.*, p. 1651.

[36] "Pacification for Peace," *Atlantic Monthly*, December 1944, p. 51.
[37] "How to Enforce International Agreements," *Readers Digest*, April 1946, p. 140.

is that if they join in a war against the aggressor they will not be very much hurt, for their big allies will keep the enemy too busy to pay much attention to them. Lippmann argues that this theory has become obsolete in the nuclear age. When there are bombs so powerful that one of them can knock out a small country, and two or three of them can subdue a middle-sized state, the main assumptions of collective security are wiped out. Small countries within the reach of a nuclear power are not likely to join hands in war against it. Addressing himself to the advocates of collective security in 1954, Lippmann wrote:

Here we are, having public tantrums about how we may be demolished by atomic weapons, flown in across the Atlantic Ocean, lobbed in at us from submarines, carried in among us in suitcases. And yet we cannot seem to appreciate why small countries that are much nearer, that have no defenses, do not want to go half-way around the world to take part in wars of collective security.[38]

The foregoing does not mean that there is nothing the small nations can do to promote international peace and order. They can promote order among themselves; they can help colonial and dependent areas in developing the institutions of self-government. They can play a fully equal part in the development and adoption of the civilized principles of international law. In short, says Lippmann, "they can do . . . what they are capable of doing. They cannot do more, and if they tried to do more they would end by doing less."[39]

[38] T and T, April 1, 1954.
[39] Walter Lippmann, "The Four Policemen," *Vital Speeches*, Vol. 10, No. 5 (December 15, 1943), p. 139. It should be emphasized that Lippmann wrote these lines in 1943. At that time, and in fact until recently, the opinion seemed perfectly justified that the small state could best remain a passive participant in the politics of world power within or without a world organization, and "specialize" only in "cultural" affairs. It is an ironical, but perhaps a revolutionary, phenomenon in international affairs that at the highest point of development in military science its most effective

Lippmann contends that the principle of collective security is not only unworkable but also dangerous. Naively entrusting their security to the non-existent protective power of the universal society, nations fail to take necessary measures to safeguard themselves against aggression and even proceed to dismantle their existing buildup. He recalls Wilson's injunction that nations should reduce their armaments to the lowest point consistent with national safety—which in the official commentary on the Fourteen Points was interpreted to mean internal order and protection from external invasion. In saying this Wilson was exhorting the nations of the world to commit themselves to a course of passive defense and to give up the right to organize regional defense.[40] Lippmann goes on to suggest that Wilson's devotion to the principle of collective security was a rebound from the traditional American distrust of alliances. According to the President's Five Particulars of September 27, 1918, there could be "no leagues or alliances, or special covenants or understandings within the general and common family of the League of Nations."[41] In urging the nation-states to outlaw alliances, the President was asking them to lay down one of the most effective weapons of national defense. Wilson looked upon collective security as both remedy and substitute for alliances, which, he maintained, were a principal cause of wars. In spite of the Wilsonian propaganda, an influential minority of the American people maintained that a nucleus of great powers, allied for the defense of their vital interests, was needed to enforce

weapons have been neutralized, with the result that the balance of influence and prestige has tilted somewhat in favor of the small state. The small nation is still the stake of great-power diplomacy, but it does not seem to be an altogether helpless pawn. We are passing through an age when the words—if not the moods, expressions and gestures—of the statesmen of many a small or middle-sized nation are studied and analyzed with care in the foreign offices of the greatest military powers on earth.

[40] *U.S. War Aims*, pp. 171–172.
[41] *Ibid.*, p. 172.

peace by a system of collective security. Thus Wilson's refusal to see the need for alliances split the nation on the issue
of international organization. The opponents of the League
saw clearly that if the organization was going to enforce
peace, then it must amount to an Anglo-American alliance.
And if it was not intended to be such an alliance, then its
generalized commitments were too vague and "unpredictable
to be intelligible." Here was the Wilsonian dilemma: If the
League was to be effective, it had to be an alliance, and all
"good" men, including Wilson, equated alliances with un-
holy intrigues. Thus the League was criticized "both as a
concealed alliance in the realm of power politics and as a
utopian pipe dream. The dilemma was presented because
Wilson wanted the omelet, but rejected the idea of cooking
the eggs."[42]

It may be worth while to take note here of Lippmann's
comments on the attempt of nations to organize collective
measures against aggression on three momentous occasions
in the history of collective security, namely the Manchurian crisis, the Italo-Ethiopian conflict and the Korean
war.

About two weeks after the Japanese army seized Mukden,
Lippmann wrote that the question in Manchuria was who
should control the large and potentially rich province. For a
generation, Japan had been building there a network of vested
interests. The Chinese were colonizing the area at the rate of
one million men a year. This was a real conflict of vital interests which no peace machinery could resolve. Lippmann
predicted that even though the Japanese army had violated
both the spirit and the letter of the League Covenant, the
Kellogg Pact and the Nine Power Treaty, the machinery of

[42] U.S. Foreign Policy, p. 76. The belief that collective security serves
to outlaw rather than necessitate a working alliance between the great
powers, persisted in official American thinking long after Wilson. See Hull,
op. cit., pp. 1542–1543, 1638 and Ball, op. cit., pp. 33–35.

the League would not be set in motion to call a halt to the Japanese advance in Manchuria. The powers at Geneva, being too weak to challenge Japan, would continue to evade the issue in the hope that the civilian and commercial classes in Japan would be able to restrain the army. He wrote:

It is disheartening to have to confess that the Powers are not in a position to do more, to vindicate law and order majestically and set justice upon her throne. They are not. The Manchurian issues lie beyond the present resources of our civilization.[43]

When, some weeks later, the Council of the League ruled that Japan had violated the Kellogg Pact, Lippmann greeted the move with mixed feelings. It was a gamble, he said, with the prestige of the postwar peace machinery. If successful, "it should bring untold benefits in the way of increased human faith and confidence"; but if it failed, it would be a "disastrous disillusionment to all the peoples."[44] The decision to gamble having been taken, there was no other course but to see it through. However, this did not mean that the powers should even consider the coercion of Japan. Lippmann advised that they should confine themselves to applying moral pressure upon Japan, and that in doing so they should stand united. Furthermore, they must continue unremittingly to seek a settlement by negotiation that would give Japan her full rights, but no new advantages as a result of the adventure.[45]

After Japan occupied South Manchuria, Lippmann noted that the peace machinery had completely failed to halt aggression. It had failed because the principal League powers, the Western democracies, were unprepared and—rightly—unwilling to use force against Japan. Moral force had been shown to be no force at all to achieve immediate results.

[43] T and T, September 29, 1931.
[44] Ibid., December 10, 1931.
[45] Ibid.

Lippmann interpreted Secretary Stimson's note of January 7, 1932 as a recognition of this failure. The note was meant "to stop humiliating ourselves by making further protests, and to leave the whole business in such a way that perhaps in time Japan will find it wise to square her position with the treaties she has violated."[46] He observed that even though much could be said in favor of a league to enforce peace, the fact had to be faced that for all practical purposes such an organization did not exist. Therefore the United States should oppose all further denunciation of Japan, and reject the proposal to withdraw ambassadors from Tokyo on the ground that it implied a threat of war. Lippmann recognized that such a course of action would be severely criticized by the friends of the League. But he insisted that under the circumstances this was the only logical and coherent step to take, especially since this country had deliberately rejected the theory of collective security.[47]

Lippmann's attitude toward the organization of collective effort to check Italy's aggression on Ethiopia was quite similar. He maintained that the Hoare-Laval Pact had merely registered the realities of the situation, to wit, that Britain and France had not found it worth while to defend the integrity of the Ethiopian empire at the risk of a war with Italy. Such a war, they had calculated, not only would be expensive, but would also drive Mussolini into the arms of Hitler. The vital interests of Britain and France were not at stake in the conflict. In fact, their interests called for non-intervention.[48]

Writing on the question of oil sanctions against Italy, Lippmann observed that the British government had been brought face to face with the harsh reality that effective sanctions

[46] *Ibid.*, February 2, 1932.
[47] *Ibid.*, February 26, 1932.
[48] *Ibid.*, December 17, 1935.

against a great power constituted an act of war. The League powers, he said, were not ready for such a war, and had therefore been confined to issuing a series of bluffs. The moral of the experience was that

the world has to rid itself of the dangerous illusion that peace can be preserved by condemning the aggressors and then annoying them. It has to learn that collective security is a snare and a delusion unless the collective force is overwhelmingly greater than the force of the aggressor—unless the collective force is not only greater in theory but can, in fact, be mobilized, unless it will, if challenged, be employed.[49]

Significantly enough, Lippmann predicted that even though the machinery of collective security had not been used against Japan and Italy, it would be used in the case of a European upheaval in which the vital interests of the great powers were unmistakably involved.

As in the Manchurian case, Lippmann maintained that the United States should remain aloof from the collective effort of the League powers to stop the Italo-Ethiopian dispute. The attempt of the State Department to put pressure on Italy was a "serious mistake." Lippmann condemned that section of American opinion which held that the United States should use its moral influence against aggression as if it were a member of the League. "For a power which is not a part of the same system of public law, in this case the Covenant, to

[49] T and T, December 24, 1935. Stanley Baldwin and his colleagues in the Cabinet indeed feared that effective interference with Mussolini's plans to conquer Ethiopia might provoke him into making war with Britain and France. Supporting the motion to lift the sanctions in May 1936, the Tories shouted at the Labor Opposition, "Do you want war?" However, the postwar publication of documents, diaries and memoirs seems to suggest that the Tory fears were largely unfounded. See Duff Cooper, *Old Men Forget* (New York: E. P. Dutton and Co., 1954), pp. 191–192. Also see Winston S. Churchill, *The Gathering Storm* (Boston: Houghton Mifflin Company, 1948), Chapter 10, esp. pp. 176–177.

arrogate to itself the right to apply that law, though it is not itself bound by it, is both dangerous and . . . immoral."[50]

Lippmann's views on the attempt of the United Nations to halt aggression in Korea have been less clear-cut than on the two other occasions noted above. He endorsed the administration's decision to dispatch military aid to South Korea, and to refer the question of the North Korean invasion to the United Nations. It was a sound decision especially because Americans could not become unilaterally committed to a military enterprise on the Asian mainland. They would need the support and advice of the Asian powers, which could most readily be had only within the framework of the United Nations. He felt that one could not expect the Asian governments to have any enthusiasm for the South Korean government as such. "But for their obligations in the Charter and their interest in avoiding a general conflagration, it would be hard to interest most of Asia in the fate of that Korean government."[51]

Two days later, Lippmann hailed Truman's decision to commit American forces to Korea. The President, he said, had met the obligation "without flinching and without fumbling." Significantly enough, he also remarked that President Truman alone had all the necessary information to come to a decision. The North Korean attack was a naked act of aggression and clearly a defiance of the United Nations. To accept the aggression passively would have been fatal to its authority and influence. "If a wretched little satellite government in North Korea can thumb its nose at the U.N. then all hope would be lost that through that universal society the nations of Asia and the nations of Europe and the Americans can find a way to work together."[52]

[50] T and T, December 31, 1935 and February 1, 1936.
[51] *Ibid.*, June 27, 1950.
[52] *Ibid.*, June 29, 1950.

It would appear that at the time of writing these two articles, Lippmann was not aware that the North Korean invasion had come as a surprise to the administration, and that President Truman had decided to commit American forces to the theatre of conflict without previous planning and detailed examination of facts. For within four days of the above-noted article he was stressing the fact that "it would be an incalculably great Soviet success if the United States were to become involved and pinned down in a long, bloody, expensive, indecisive struggle on the Asiatic mainland with the Chinese-Korean forces."[53] A week later, Lippmann was already condemning the Korean venture as an evidence of the bankruptcy of the Truman Doctrine, which had once again been invoked to contain communism in Asia without making the necessary preparations.[54]

Lippmann vacillated on whether or not the other members of the United Nations would and should dispatch troops to Korea. In July 1950 he wrote that it was their moral support which counted, for without it Americans would be fighting a "dirty little war."[55] However, by September 1950 he was fed up with the idea of American forces being wasted in Korea. With evident bitterness, he commented that the Korean war had become the first mortgage on the ground forces of the United States. Theoretically, he said, American forces could be replaced by the troops of other nations. But the assemblage of such a heterogeneous force would take time, and little was likely to come of it unless the leadership of the whole undertaking were promptly handed over to India. Even this, he admitted, was not easy to bring about. For

all the normal hesitations and delays, all the natural reluctance of any government to become entangled in the nasty business of

[53] *Ibid.*, July 3, 1950.
[54] *Ibid.*, July 11, 1950.
[55] *Ibid.*, July 20, 1950.

policing guerrillas, will be reinforced and rationalized by the fact
that on the deeper questions of Asian politics there has been no
meeting of minds.[56]

In January 1951 Lippmann noted that the United States was
fighting a lone struggle in the Far East. He returned to his
usual firm denunciation of the principle of collective security.
Summing up the lesson of the Korean experience, he wrote:

It has long seemed to me that . . . no universal society can survive
if it is expected to execute the principle of collective security. . . .
Both the League and the U.N. have shown that you cannot rally
all the nations to a collective war to enforce peace.

The trouble with collective security is that when the issue is
less than the survival of the great nations, the method of collective security will not be used because it is just as terrifying to the
policeman as it is to the lawbreakers. . . . There would be little
enforcement of law in our cities if in order to arrest burglars . . .
the police had to start a fight in which the courthouse, the jail
and their own homes were likely to be demolished. Men will not
burn down the barn to roast a pig.[57]

We may conclude that Lippmann categorically rejects that
concept of collective security which envisages the entire
membership of a universal society united, in righteous indignation and with a missionary zeal, to fight any violator of
world law at any time and at any place. He rejects the
fundamental assumption of collective security, that the maintenance of world peace is the supreme concern of all national
governments but one—the aggressor. Even the so-called
peace-loving states are infinitely more interested in the peace
and security of their immediate neighborhood than in "world
peace." Furthermore, Lippmann maintains that no nation
is inherently or permanently peace-loving. His contention
that international politics are characterized by a conflict of

[56] *Ibid.*, October 3, 1950.
[57] *Ibid.*, January 15, 1951.

interests and a struggle for power is only another way of saying that there is always a group of nations which actively strives to alter the status quo. The paramount interest of this group is not the maintenance of world peace but the modification of the status quo by peaceful means if possible, by war if expedient.

Finally, we may submit that Lippmann's rejection of the theory of collective peace enforcement naturally follows from his rejection of world government as a practical policy for the present. The maintenance of peace and of law and order is typically a governmental function. The difficulties which confound the actual operation of collective security arise principally from the absence of a universally accepted authority with a unified police force at its command. There can be no universal peace enforcement outside of a world state.

The Scope of the Universal Society

What is the true nature and scope of the universal society if it is not to be treated as a peace-enforcing agency? Lippmann maintains that an organization such as the United Nations should be viewed as a meeting place for the plenipotentiaries of national governments, as "a voluntary association of diplomats who confer."[58]

In 1917 Lippmann looked upon the proposed League of Nations as "a constitution of common action adopted by the stable powers in a period of unpredictable change."[59] This great enterprise was to be managed by the Western powers under the leadership of Great Britain and the United States, whose liberal tradition, power and influence fitted them well for this role. In *The Political Scene* he wrote:

[58] *U.S. War Aims*, p. 184.
[59] *The Political Scene*, p. 32.

An Anglo-American entente means the substitution of a pool for a balance, and in that pool will be found the ultimate force upon which rests the League of Nations. For if the united power of Britain and America—potential and actual—is wielded for the ends they now both officially profess, they are assured of the active assistance of the smaller nations everywhere.[60]

John Bull and Uncle Sam had a great deal of very important work on their hands. But their individual foreign offices, acting through the traditional channels of diplomacy, could not salvage the future of Europe and of the world.

If there is one method of insuring the irritation of ignorance and suspicion, it is long distance telegraphic communication between the heads of government. The mere fact of committing ideas to paper for the scrutiny of biographers stiffens the mind and arouses the disastrous desire to pose nobly. There is little good humor in official dispatches; like most newspaper editorials they are sick with infallibility, and there is nothing worse for the peace of the world than two infallible diplomats uttering strong sentiment at each other from opposite ends of a cable.[61]

A new kind of diplomacy was needed to meet the requirements of the postwar era. Lippmann pleaded that the League should act as a conference in continuous session to take up problems as they arose. The great managing powers should meet in secret sessions for heart-to-heart talks conducted not in the inflexible postures of righteousness but in the relaxed and conciliatory spirit of give and take. After they had worked out common policies on the points at issue, they would admit other members of the League into their discussions. There would thus be some open debate of the issues before the League. But such debate would take place at the instance and under the direction of the great powers, who in their secret conversations had already agreed on the disposition of those issues.

---

[60] *Ibid.*, pp. 41–42.
[61] *Ibid.*, pp. 36–37.

Writing in a mood of optimism in 1944, Lippmann envisaged a wide scope for the deliberations of diplomats at the meeting place which the projected international organization was to provide. He repeated his thesis that the promotion of "deep and continuing consultation" was the true function of the universal society.

It is the duty of every state to explain what it wishes to do and that it is the right of other states to be heard. I cannot imagine a more pregnant principle than that. For instead of holding the nations to a code of ambiguous rules like the Atlantic Charter, it holds them accountable for all their international acts. The right of all nations to be consulted and the duty of all to consult on such actions, is as searching and comprehensive a principle of international conduct as can be found.[62]

If at this time Lippmann was suggesting that the foreign policy of every nation was to be examined and debated by every other nation in the universal society, he soon rectified that position. In U.S. War Aims he wrote:

We shall not, I believe, further the comity of nations by establishing an international assembly of which the avowed purpose is that every nation is there to inspect and police every other nation.[63]

The critical issues, he said, must be discussed and decided quietly and confidentially by the nations directly involved, and by those which by virtue of their power and influence were generally responsible for the maintenance of international peace and security. Lippmann warned that if the proposed international organization met in the mood and manner of an international parliament and presumed to examine and pronounce upon the conduct of individual nations, its sessions would cause the tension in world affairs to

[62] "The Big Four and World Peace," Newsweek (August 21, 1944), p. 105.
[63] U.S. War Aims, p. 167.

rise. Every time it sat to discuss an important international issue, there would be limitless intrigue and gossip in its lobbies and corridors—which would promote suspicion, distrust and friction among the peoples of the world rather than bring about the triumph of reason and justice. The propagandists everywhere would agitate the issues, acclaiming the protagonists and denouncing the opponents of their points of view. The meetings of the universal society would become enveloped in an atmosphere of climax and crisis. A world that needed peace, compromise and accommodation would get fiery speeches and dramatic debates ending in the aggravation rather than the reconciliation of differences.

It will be recalled that when, in *The Political Scene*, Lippmann charted out a course of action for the League of Nations, he made provision for both secret and public consultations between the member states. By contrast, the advocacy of open diplomacy is conspicuously absent from the discussion of international organization in *U.S. War Aims*. The reason may be that in this latter work Lippman is on the whole pessimistic about the cooperation of great powers in the postwar world organization. But if the great powers, because of their own differences, could not contribute to the resolution of international disputes, the nations concerned would then be forced to go to the international assembly and present their case openly before the bar of world opinion. The temptation to do so would be irresistible, and yet the outcome could be nothing but the heightening of international tension.

It was probably this dilemma that induced Lippman in *U.S. War Aims* to limit rather severely the scope of the universal society. He seems to have recognized that since open diplomacy was likely to accentuate differences unless it was steered and guided by the great powers acting in concert, and since there was little chance that in the postwar period the

Western nations and Russia would see eye to eye on substantive issues, the only alternative was that the international organization should be concerned with relatively
harmless and unexciting matters. The true function of the
universal society, said Lippmann, was to facilitate intercourse among nations that were already at peace. It should
eschew the issues of war and peace between the great powers,
and should concentrate on those dispuites between small
nations in which the great powers were not interested or involved. This was a sound political principle for the proposed
organization to follow, especially in its initial, formative
years. He explained: "Hard cases do not make good law; it
is in the treatment of the easier cases that the principles of
international comity will develop, and decisions will be
rendered that become precedents, expanding the common
law of the nations."[64]

The universal society could also do a great deal to alleviate
the social and economic problems facing the world and especially the underdeveloped countries. Lippmann proposed
that it should develop the principles and standards of trusteeship for those parts of the world where the people were not
yet ready for self-government. Again, the new international
organization should facilitate and promote the exchange of

[64] U.S. War Aims, p. 165. Lippmann's thesis that the international
organization should devote itself to "facilitating" the settlement of international disputes, rather than sit in judgment on them, is shared by other
writers. It was the starting premise of some of the architects of the United
Nations. See Leo Pasvolsky, The United Nations in Action (University of
Illinois Press, 1951), p. 79.

Professor Goodrich maintains that "to a considerable extent, the task of
the United Nations will be educational: to help peoples and their representatives know each other better and to understand each other's purposes
and interests . . . and to assist them to develop attitudes and procedures for
facilitating the resolution of differences. It should not be claimed that the
U.N. as it stands offers an adequate means for dealing with matters of
international concern." Leland M. Goodrich, "The Amount of World
Organization Necessary and Possible," Yale Law Journal (August 1946),
p. 963.

information in the fields of science, technology and culture. It could bring together men and women belonging to the arts and sciences among whom intercourse was most likely to be fruitful. These men, said Lippmann, had passed through professional discipline and were therefore more able than others to disengage themselves from the issues of profit and power in their contacts and conversations with one another. Thus there were many things with which the universal society could usefully concern itself. Broadly speaking, it should focus its attention on the problems of individual rather than national security.

The principles of these constructive works . . . will have to be put together by precedents, developed out of practical experience in combating disease, destitution and ignorance; in working out projects for the conservation and development of the natural resources of the earth, the improvement of transportation and communication; in arranging for an orderly extension of international commerce. . . . There must then be many concrete things to collaborate about. These concrete things cannot be the things men ordinarily fight about: their frontiers, their sovereignty, their security. They must be the things they do not ordinarily fight about. These are the arts of peace.[65]

In saying that the universal society should devote itself to promoting the "arts of peace"—to promoting individual rather than national security—Lippmann obviously means that it should concentrate on economic, social and cultural rather than political affairs. He believes that the international organization can be more successful in these fields than it can in its conventional role as the guardian of world peace. It will be seen that in advocating this non-political role for, let us say, the United Nations, Lippmann makes the following basic assumptions: first, that the economic, social and educational problems facing the world are so im-

[65] U.S. War Aims, pp. 165-168.

portant and urgent in their own right that even if the universal society addressed itself exclusively or primarily to their solution, it would still be rendering an invaluable service to mankind and merit a high place in their estimation; second, that these non-political problems can be isolated from the political domain and thus rendered "unexciting" and more amenable to cooperative enterprise; third, that the habits of international cooperation thus formed will gradually be carried over into the political sphere, and enable the universal society ultimately to become the guardian of international peace, law and order.

If the universal society brings about international cooperation for enriching the economic, social and cultural lives of the masses of men everywhere, it will more than justify its existence. But can it perform the role which Lippmann has assigned to it?

Non-political questions are generally undramatic and unexciting; men do not fight over the merits of a new vaccine to check and prevent tuberculosis. The average citizen does not understand the intricacies of, let us say, modern international economic relations. To him these issues are technical matters to be taken up by the "experts." The experts, in turn, have no incentive to take stiff and rigid positions, since there is no audience to pose for. But the indifference of the common man to non-political questions is not an unmixed blessing. The indifference of men is as fatal to the stability and prosperity of human institutions as their hostility.

There are some other difficulties also. It so happens that the nations of the world are committed to different, and in some cases incompatible, economic systems and social ideologies. Moreover, the world is divided into "haves" and "have-nots" so far as the distribution of natural resources is concerned, and into advanced and underdeveloped countries so far as technological progress is concerned. The resulting differences in systems and structures, aims and objectives obstruct international economic cooperation. The record of both the League and the United Nations shows that international economic cooperation means different things to different nations. To the United States it may mean lower tariffs, abolition of discriminatory practices, the open door, and the equality of commercial opportunity. Other nations may see in this program a threat to their economic interests, even a design for American economic imperialism.

Even though international economic organizations, past and present, have done valuable work, their achievements have not been great enough to warrant the thesis that the future of the universal society now lies in the economic domain. The thesis is erroneous also because it is based on the untenable assumption that economic issues can be insulated from political considerations and influences. In the mid-twentieth century economic resources of all kinds constitute a weapon of war. Power politics and power economics march in step in the battle for supremacy among nations. So long as the struggle for power continues, "no amount of manipulation can make international economic trends move counter to the trends of other international relations."[66] The Cold War which has dominated postwar international relations has not spared the specialized agencies of the United Nations. Several member states, especially the nations of the Soviet bloc, have used them exclusively as forums of hostile propaganda against the West.

International cooperation is equally difficult in the social and cultural spheres. Power politics as well as genuine ideological differences make such cooperation well-nigh impossible. This becomes evident when we consider that one of the two great partners in the proposed non-political reconstruction of the world, the Soviet system, is committed not only as a matter of policy, but also as a matter of creed, to promot-

[66] Levi, *op. cit.*, pp. 94-95.

ing social unrest in the non-communist world. In the cultural field, it stands for unity and does not tolerate diversity.

The fact of the matter is that the distinction between the political and the non-political, though perhaps valid in a framework of deductive reasoning, is in practice so hazy that it has little bearing on the organization of human affairs in the context of modern international relations. One must then conclude that to tie the future of the universal society to the "arts of peace"—the non-existent sphere of the non-political —is to impose upon it a life of inaction which must eventually mean its death.

The record of Lippmann's postwar writings suggests that he himself has not rigidly or uniformly adhered to the formula that commits the universal society exclusively, or at least primarily, to the "arts of peace." In fact, he has often proceeded on the assumption that the United Nations is deeply concerned with the questions of international peace and security, including the issues of war and peace between the great powers.

Now it cannot be gainsaid that American aid to Greece and Turkey in the spring of 1947 was a link in a chain of political issues between the United States and the Soviet Union; it inaugurated the policy of containment which has since been the cornerstone of American strategy in the Cold War. Lippmann himself acknowledged at the time that the purpose of intervention in Greece was "to exert American military power upon the Soviet power." The administration, he said, should make it clear to the Russians and to the rest of the world that American aid to Greece and Turkey was

a strategic operation designed not only to check the expansion of the Soviet power but to bring about its contraction. . . . We have selected Turkey and Greece . . . because they are the strategic gateway to the Black Sea and the heart of the Soviet Union.[67]

[67] T and T, April 1, 1947.

Yet Lippmann pleaded that the United States should take
the issue of intervention in Greece to the United Nations. He
conceded that the U.N. lacked the power to dispose of the
matter. But he insisted that its inability to deal effectively
with the issue did not confer upon this country the right to
act unilaterally. And even if the United States had the right
to act independently in Greece, it was "inexpedient" to exercise this right. He declared that

the heart of the U.N. Charter and the soul of the whole undertaking is the covenant to consult with the other members, particularly the permanent members of the Security Council, when
an issue of international security and peace is raised.[68]

There were several ways to consult the U.N. The American ambassador to the organization could go to the Security
Council and explain the intended policies of his government,
and promise to submit periodic reports to the United Nations
on the progress of action in Greece. He could also invite the
interested nations to send observers to the scene of action.
The advantage of all this, Lippmann explained, was that "it
would at once rehabilitate the moral authority of the United
Nations and would reaffirm our loyalty as a member of the
organization."[69] A few days later, Lippmann upheld as both
right and expedient Senator Vandenberg's amendment to the
Greek-Turkish Bill, seeking to direct the President to withdraw American aid from the area if requested by a "proce-
dural" vote in the Security Council or by a majority vote in
the General Assembly. There was no danger, he reassured his
readers, that this country would fail to obtain the support of
at least a majority of the United Nations.

Here, then, was a case in which the two greatest military
powers of the world were arrayed against each other. Lipp-

mann could not have doubted that the Soviet bloc would oppose with all the force, skill and eloquence at its disposal a move which was professedly designed to capture the "gateway to the heart of the Soviet Union." He must have foreseen that in the ensuing open debate the participants would not address each other in conciliatory tones and gentle manner but would roar at their opponents in anger and indignation. It seems that Lippmann's desire "to rehabilitate the moral authority" of the U.N. was mixed with the desire to arouse world public opinion against the Soviet Union.

It is interesting to note that within six months of the date of the articles referred to above, Lippmann was protesting at the unintended consequences which flowed from his recommendation. In *The Cold War* he observed that the "true friends" of the United Nations must oppose the entanglement of the world organization in the Soviet-American conflict. It was folly to use the Security Council and the General Assembly as an arena of the Cold War. He wrote:

Judging by the speeches in the Greek affair of the British and the American delegates, Sir Alexander Cadogan and Mr. Herschel Johnson appear to be acting on instructions which treat the U.N. as expendable in our conflict with Russia. Nothing is being accomplished to win the conflict, to assuage it, or to settle it. But the U.N., which should be preserved as the last best hope of mankind that the conflict can be settled and a peace achieved, is being chewed up. The seed corn is being devoured.[70]

The mood of *The Cold War* continued for some time. When in June 1948 Count Folke Bernadotte, acting with the diplomatic support of the great powers, succeeded in mediating a truce in Palestine, Lippmann greeted his initial success as vindicating the "basic conception" of the United Nations, namely that *"when* the great powers are able to

[70] *The Cold War* (New York: Harper and Bros., 1947), p. 59. Also see T and T, September 30, 1947.

agree that they prefer peace to war, *then* small wars can be localized, the fighting regulated and reduced, and the opportunity to mediate the issues created."[71] This conception did not satisfy the advocates of a strong U.N., but no careful student of the Charter and of the realities of world politics could expect any more.

But in April 1949 one finds Lippmann once again taking an activist view of the United Nations. This time he proposed that the United States should go to the United Nations and "explain" the Atlantic Pact—a military alliance directed against a permanent member of the Security Council, the Soviet Union. He maintained that not only Russia and her allies but all the United Nations were entitled to an "accounting, and it is our duty to them and to ourselves to make that accounting."[72] The attempt to evade this "obligation to explain" would undermine popular confidence both in the Pact and in the Charter. Again, writing in April 1950, Lippmann recalled that Great Britain had disengaged herself from a difficult situation in Palestine by passing it on to the United Nations. The French, he said, were in a similarly difficult position in Indo-China. They could continue the fighting there only if this country gave them an infinite amount of moral and material aid. If the United States did support French colonialism it would shatter her prestige in Asia. A practical way for Americans to resolve the dilemma might be to "turn now to the United Nations to take the problem there deliberately rather than to let it be dumped into the U.N. later on."[73] We have already noted in a previous section that in the earlier stages of the Korean War, Lippmann was satisfied that the United Nations had taken charge of that "dirty little war."[74]

[71] T and T, June 15, 1948.
[72] *Ibid.*, April 11, 1949.
[73] *Ibid.*, April 4, 1950.
[74] See pp. 114–115 above.

The foregoing evidence indicates that until about the end of 1950 Lippmann was generally inclined to take a rather inflated view of the political jurisdiction of the United Nations. It is difficult to understand his insistence during this period on the "obligation" of a member state to consult and the "right" of other nations to be consulted. After one has urged the nation-states to keep the United Nations out of their cold and shooting wars, it is surely illogical to invite them, nay to require them, to come and defend before the international organization their plans and policies vis-à-vis their friends and foes. It appears that, in spite of his protestations to the contrary, Lippmann has, at least in the instances cited above, tended to look upon the United Nations either as a Parliament of Man to which every nation was in duty bound to explain its international conduct, or as a forum of propaganda which every nation was free to use to vilify its enemies.

The disappointments of the Korean experience turned Lippmann definitely against the idea of an extensive and active political role for the United Nations. Commenting on the reports in 1951 that Hungary, Rumania and Bulgaria were planning to attack Yugoslavia, Lippmann urged the administration to consult immediately with Britain and France. At the same time, he emphasized that the clarification of American policy on the issue should not be "entangled now with the confused machinery of the U.N."[75] Instead, the three Western great powers should formulate policy and take a stand on the question not as members of the United Nations but as signatories to the treaties of peace with these East European states. In March 1951, Lippmann pleaded that the Korean issues should be taken out of public diplomacy at the United Nations. Responsible people in this country and abroad agreed that the solution of the Korean

[75] T and T, February 6, 1951.

stalemate lay in a "quiet and secret" effort to work out a
formula that reflected the actual balance of military power in
the Far East. But such a realistic and unglamorous objective
could not be achieved before the television cameras at Lake
Success. In a scathing denunciation of the *modus operandi*
of the collective diplomacy at the United Nations, he wrote:

When statesmen become actors they not only stick to their parts
in the show but they are stuck with their parts. They can be
more and more of what they have been. But on pain of un-
popularity—even if it might be of denunciation and Congressional investigation—they cannot appear to be a little bit less.

Thus by the hoop-la system of diplomacy—which some say is
wonderfully enlightening—every difficult issue, not infrequently
a comparatively easy issue, is likely to become insoluble as each
actor-statesman rises to such peaks of public righteousness that in
public he cannot possibly descend again into common sense.

Then there is no hope except to turn off the lights, to shut down
the microphones, to take away the stage props, to wash off the
make-up, to disperse the crowds, and to let a few men absent
themselves from publicity a while.[76]

In 1952, Lippmann observed that the United Nations was
in grave trouble. It was being torn apart by "the pressure
groups, the machine politicians and the demagogues of the
universal society" who felt that they owed no obligation to
the United Nations except to go there and try to obtain
whatever benefits they could for their governments and
popularity for themselves as the procurers of those benefits.
They felt free to put all kinds of insoluble issues on the
agenda and then force the member states to take positions
pro and con. This unfortunate practice could only destroy
the United Nations, for it undermined that popular confidence in the organization which alone could sustain it in our
divided and embittered world.

[76] *Ibid.*, March 27, 1951.

The worst thing that can be done to the United Nations is to force it to deal with questions it cannot answer, with problems it cannot settle, with undertakings that it cannot complete, with conflicts in which it is unable to intervene. The result of that is not only failure, not only heightened intolerance and intransigence, but also the diversion of the energies of the U.N. from its own constructive, useful and necessary work.[77]

That necessary and constructive work was to function as a congress of diplomats from all quarters of the globe and provide facilities for contact and negotiations between them. The acid test of the success of the General Assembly lay in whether the volume of serious, private conversation between the diplomats was greater than the volume of their public oratory. In 1953, Lippmann observed that as a result of unlimited and reckless debating, the United Nations, instead of facilitating diplomatic intercourse between nations, had become a positive obstacle to the use of diplomacy. He recommended the constitution of a committee that would screen and examine the proposed agenda before it was finally approved, and would make sure that all the normal procedures of diplomacy had been exhausted before an issue was permitted to come before the United Nations.[78]

In the 1960's we find Lippmann favorably disposed toward the United Nations' involvement in the Congo. He finds the world organization performing a function which he had envisaged for it a half century ago, in *The Stakes of Diplomacy,* and later in *U.S. War Aims.* The U.N. is trying to put an underdeveloped country on its feet. There is no possibility of the Congo becoming truly independent, self-governing and stable in the foreseeable future. The country is abysmally lacking in educated and trained personnel to run its government and to manage its economy. It will take

[77] *Ibid.,* October 14, 1952.
[78] *Ibid.,* January 12 and 13, 1953.

a long time to create a native governing class. In the meanwhile, says Lippmann, the only solution to the Congolese
problem lies in instituting some sort of tutelage over it. The
great powers and the former colonial powers are precluded
from providing the needed tutelage because of the rivalry
among them and also because of their unacceptability to
most of the other parties concerned. That leaves the United
Nations, which can provide an "unostentatious tutelage
carried on by that new breed of officials, the international
civil sevants," who would work under its aegis and over-all
control.[79]

Even the limited success which the U.N. has had in maintaining a semblance of order in the Congo encourages Lippmann to think that one of its important functions is "to
preside over the troubles which arise from the death agony
of the old empires and birth pangs of the successor states."[80]
Lippmann is pleased about the U.N. operation in the Congo
also because it has prevented a confrontation of the great
powers in that area.[81] Together with the U.N. Emergency
Force along the Arab-Israeli border, the Congo operation is
playing a "mighty part in keeping the peace in the Middle
East and in the heart of Africa."[82]

The U.N. operation in the Congo may have the appearance of a venture in international government. This should
not lead us into thinking that the United Nations is a world
government. "It is and always has been an association of
national governments in which the most powerful ones have
a veto on action."[83] The U.N. remains a "grand piece of
conference machinery," which can debate and mediate for
peace but which cannot enforce peace except on those rare

[79] T and T, December 26, 1961; also January 3, 1963.
[80] T and T, December 28, 1961; April 5, 1962.
[81] T and T, March 27, 1962.
[82] T and T, February 20, 1962.
[83] T and T, December 17, 1961.

occasions when the great powers can unite in doing so. Addressing himself to some American critics of the U.N. who "like spoiled children wish to stop playing if they cannot always win the game," Lippmann wrote that the U.N. was indispensable because it facilitated contact between the old powers and the emerging nations of Asia and Africa.

What really matters is that so many nations have representatives in one city at the same time, and that they have their recognized place to meet and that they can talk with one another frequently and casually in the lounges and the corridors, and in private apartments and houses. No one can ever measure the amount of good that this does.[84]

Lippmann opposed the Soviet proposal for a "troika" executive to head the U.N. secretariat on the ground that it would destroy the greatest of the Secretary General's functions, which was "to be a father confessor to the member governments." The Secretary General knows, from the confidences he receives, the real positions of the parties to an international dispute. This knowledge enables him to mediate.[85]

Lippmann recently wrote that one should not expect the world to move in one leap from a condition of "virtual anarchy" to that of political order and stability. Not being a world government, the United Nations cannot maintain "perpetual peace" in the world. But even the limited contribution which it makes towards the "pacification of the world" is significant and also fabulously cheap, considering the amount of money which member nations contribute for its maintenance. Each success which the U.N. is able to attain in fulfilling its various missions is a step "onto new, firm and higher ground."[86]

Is it possible to keep difficult political problems out of the

[84] T and T, December 21, 1961.
[85] T and T, November 7, 1961.
[86] T and T, January 18, 1962.

United Nations? Apparently, Lippmann hopes to accomplish this objective by moral suasion, through the development of a new tradition, a new way of looking at the United Nations. One suspects that he wants this change of attitude to take place not among the masses of men but only among their rulers. For if both the peoples of the world and their governments begin to look upon the universal society as a congress of diplomats who confer, then it will indeed become just that. And if it does become merely a meeting place for diplomats, then there would be no reason to treat it with that care and tenderness which Lippmann insists it needs and deserves. After all, every country has its plenipotentiaries in every other country. There are as many congresses of diplomats as there are national capitals in the world. The U.N. needs to be handled with care precisely because it is not a mere "association of diplomats who confer." It is also the nucleus, the "seed corn" of something bigger and better—a world state which, as Lippmann once said, is the dream of civilized men all over the world.[87] Being a believer in the ultimate desirability of world government, Lippmann would want to preserve the popular belief that the U.N. is a peace-enforcing agency. His insistence that it should not be used as such in practice probably emanates from the desire to perpetuate the myth so that it can one day become the foundation on which the structure of a world state can be built.

Creating a dual personality for the United Nations—one for the masses to see and revere, and the other for the diplomats to recognize and to work with—is not altogether utopian. It is not much more difficult today than it was in the past to make and maintain political myths. Surely the average Cockney speaker in London and Her Majesty's Prime Minister do not have the same concept of constitutional monarchy: to one the Queen is an object of reverence, to the other she

[87] See pp. 89, 98.

is perhaps nothing more than a useful political "symbol" or "institution." If we can create the conditions which Lippmann hoped would attend the working of the League and the United Nations, and which both the Covenant and the Charter assumed to be available—cooperation between great powers—the scheme of a dual personality for the universal society is perfectly practicable. If, for instance, an Anglo-American alliance had managed the League, and if a Western alliance with a reformed Russia had guided the U.N., the universal society would surely have settled a far greater number of international disputes than it has. Then it could also have remained aloof from any number of political issues, and men would have continued to hold it in esteem and affection and to reckon it as a peace-enforcing agency.

Assuming that Russia and the West were not partners, but were nonetheless peaceably settled in their respective spheres of influence—the alternative to active cooperation which Lippmann advanced in *U.S. War Aims*—they could still cooperate in an *ad hoc* manner to compose a large number of international disputes within or outside the universal society. Accordingly, it would still be possible to create and perpetuate the proposed myth about the U.N. But the question is that now that the two greatest powers on earth—the United States and the Soviet Union—are engaged not in a joint venture to create a more beautiful world but in a struggle which often assumes the bitterness and the ferocity of a battle for life and death; now that their power and influence are not available for the reconciliation of international disputes outside the United Nations; can the member states be prevailed upon to keep their political troubles out of the universal society? It seems quite clear that they cannot.

When two nations go to war, it is safe to assume that they have pretty much exhausted their reserves of patience and self-restraint. It may still be possible to restrain them if third powers intervene and promise to settle their dispute to their mutual satisfaction. But it is idle to expect that while the weaker side fights for its very existence and sees no way of escape except that which it may forge by its own effort, it will stay away from the U.N. lest it should disturb the repose and tranquillity of the universal society. It is true that if the dispute were allowed to come before the United Nations and had to stay there unsettled, the prestige of the organization would be undermined. But if a victim of aggression was not allowed even to present her case to the U.N. its prestige would still be undermined. In fact, it is probable that if the member states were not allowed to bring their political disputes, even though insoluble, to the United Nations, they would leave the organization.

Lippmann complains that the great powers are using the universal society as an expendable instrument of propaganda in their cold war. He urges them not to fight their battles in the United Nations, which should be treated as a holy city, respect for which is made part of the international law of war—in this case the Cold War. Unfortunately, the Cold War in which the great powers are engaged is largely a war of nerves in which propaganda is an important weapon. If then the U.N. is a good place to propagandize one's position, it is unlikely that the great powers will forego the advantage of using it.

It is possible that Lippmann exaggerates the evil effect of open debate and public quarrels in the United Nations on the general tone of international relations. It is likely that the battles which are fought in the U.N. merely register the general international situation. One tends to agree with the Brookings Institution in the following assertion:

The operations of the United Nations Organization could do no more than reflect the actual state of international relations. . . . The close relation between the operations of the United Nations and the state of the world was further illustrated when member

states began to use its forum and its councils to appeal their conflicting positions to the judgment of world opinion.[88]

To summarize, Lippmann maintains that in the political
sphere the universal society should generally confine itself
to providing facilities for negotiation between the representatives of nations. As a rule, it should eschew those international disputes which touch upon the vital interests of the
member states, with the possible exception of those on which
the great powers are willing to cooperate and act in concert.
It should not act as if it were a judicial tribunal or a sovereign
parliament unless the members who compose it, including
the great powers, are willing to see it act as such. On these
rare occasions it may even let the spotlight of publicity fall
on its activities, for since success is assured, publicity will
help raise its prestige. In the absence of cooperation among
nations, especially the great powers, the universal society
should concentrate on economic, social, cultural and educational affairs.

[88] *Major Problems of United States Foreign Policy 1952–1953* (Washington, D.C.: The Brookings Institution, 1952), pp. 33–34.

IV

The Organization of Power

Alliances

THE CONFLICT OF INTERESTS AMONG NATIONS, UNLESS IT IS
more than counterbalanced by the identity of interests,
makes them all potential rivals of one another.[1] The true
statesman will therefore locate the identity of interests between his nation and other nations, and will try to develop
friendship and, if necessary, alliances with them. He must
do this; for, as we have noted above, no state is strong enough
to afford the rivalry of all others. If a country does not
act promptly, her potential allies may become actual rivals.
In international relations, says Lippmann, the rule that "if
you cannot fight him, you must join him," also means that
if you do not join him, you may have to fight him.[2]

Alliances are an important factor of national power; the
power of a trustworthy ally is your own power. Power attracts
more power. A strong combination will command the respect
and possibly the allegiance of states which have not yet made
up their minds as between the opposing coalitions. Failure to

[1] *U.S. Foreign Policy*, p. 55.
[2] *Ibid.*, p. 119.

organize a position of strength may push such states into the opponent's camp. Thus purely by default a nation may lose friends, and strengthen the hands of its enemies. This is what happened in the period between the two world wars. The victorious powers dissolved their alliances, and the new combination of aggressor states was formed without opposition.[3] The Western democracies courted the disaster of Hitlerian aggression in that they allowed themselves to be isolated from one another. They ignored the rule that to be isolated in the arena of power politics is the worst of all predicaments, and that to be the member of a combination "which can be depended upon to act together, and, when challenged, to fight together, is to have achieved the highest degree of security which is attainable in a world where there are many sovereign national states."[4]

Lippmann has often emphasized that alliances are an indispensable instrument of foreign policy. We have noted above that in 1917 he strongly advocated the creation of an Anglo-American alliance to act as the moving force behind the League of Nations.[5] During World War II he pleaded that the United States, Britain and the Soviet Union should carry their wartime alliance over into the postwar period. He advanced reasons in support of this proposal which are interesting and which should be noted here in some detail. The three great powers, he said, were natural and permanent allies, for they all had a vital interest "in preventing the rise of . . . a conquering power in Europe."[6] Their solidarity was

[3] *U.S. Foreign Policy*, p. 104.
[4] *U.S. Foreign Policy*, p. 105.
[5] See p. 117.
[6] *U.S. Foreign Policy*, p. 164. It should be noted that in time Lippmann discarded the thesis that the United States, Britain and Russia were "natural and permanent" allies. In *U.S. War Aims* he was skeptical about the future of the "nuclear alliance." And in *Isolation and Alliances* (Boston: Little, Brown and Co., 1952; p. 38) we read that the Soviet Union was not really an "ally" of Britain and the United States in World

the "irreducible minimum condition" of their own security and of world peace and order.[7] Just as in *The Political Scene* he had emphasized that the coalition to run the League and manage the affairs of mankind must have a liberal character, in *U.S. Foreign Policy* he insisted that the "nuclear alliance" of the United States, Britain and the Soviet Union must wield its power for liberal ends.[8]

Lippmann conceded that the defeat of the Axis powers would reduce the compulsion for the three great powers to remain united. The conflicts of interests which lay dormant or remained secondary during the war would tend to come to the surface. However, if the great powers acted rationally, these forces of discord would be more than counterbalanced by the identity of their foremost interest, which was to prevent the re-emergence of their wartime enemies as great powers. The Allies would realize that only by remaining united could they remain secure, for only by concerted action could they prevent the rise of Germany and Japan to a position from which they might once again set out to dominate the world. After the great powers had clearly understood that their unity was indispensable to their security, they would be obliged to manage the affairs of mankind in a liberal fashion. For they would know that self-aggrandizement at

---

War II; she was merely an "associated" power. It seems that the fact that both the United States and Britain had in the past sided with Russia in fighting a great aggressive power on the Continent led Lippmann to believe in 1943 that a permanent identity of interests existed among these powers. The logic of the political geography of Europe studied in the light of history suggested that cooperation between the wartime allies was vital to their future security. However, Lippmann did not foresee that the war would not only effect a radical change in the distribution of power in the world, but would, for practical purposes, alter the political geography of Europe itself. Nor did he realize that for a long time after the war the threat to world peace would come not from the defeated and mutilated nations of Europe but from one of the non-European victors.

[7] *U.S. Foreign Policy*, p. 166.
[8] *Ibid.*, p. 168.

the expense of one another or the rest of the world would break up the alliance, even make them competitors for the friendship of their wartime enemies, whose rise to power such a course of action would then make certain. Thus the realities of their situation dictated that they must remain united to be secure, and that they must pursue liberal domestic and foreign policies to remain united.

The inexorable logic of their alliance demands that they [the Allies] recognize the liberties of the peoples outside the alliance. For in no other way can they avoid becoming rivals and then enemies for the domination of these other peoples. In no other way but by supporting a world-wide system of liberty under law can they win the consent, earn the confidence, and insure the support of the rest of the world in the continuation of their alliance.[9]

In *U.S. War Aims* Lippmann advised that if the Soviet Union refused to abandon her despotism at home and imperialistic aggrandizement abroad, and thus made it impossible for the West to continue its wartime alliance with her, the nations of the Atlantic Community must nevertheless maintain their unity.[10] Later, in *Isolation and Alliances*, he observed that the Western states should have preserved their partnership and entered the postwar negotiations to make the treaties of peace and to establish the United Nations not as separate states but as a community. There were men, he recalled, who urged during the war that the United States and her Western allies should consolidate the Atlantic Community before they negotiated a settlement with the Soviet Union. However, the administration, under the influence of Secretary of State Cordell Hull, deemed these suggestions a vicious heresy—a violation of the Wilsonian injunction against alliances. The postwar developments, said Lippmann,

[9] *U.S. Foreign Policy*, p. 173; also see Chapter X.
[10] *U.S. War Aims*, p. 194; also see Chapter XI.

had forced the Atlantic states to renew their alliance and had made them realize that the failure to maintain and strengthen it during and immediately after the war was an expensive detour.

But, of course, we are finding it harder to repair the error now. For now we are having to re-create our Western partnership in defiance of, in the very teeth of, the Soviet Union. Had we never dissolved the Atlantic system, Stalin would have found himself dealing with us after the war as he had had to deal with us during the war.[11]

In the postwar period generally, Lippmann has continued to stress the importance of alliances. In 1954 he wrote that American foreign policy inevitably rested upon alliances. Americans were only six per cent of the world's population, and therefore they could neither safeguard their security nor play a leading role in international affairs without reliable allies.[12]

Where should a nation seek allies? Lippmann holds that an alliance is good and useful in direct proportion to the identity of interests which exists among the participants. A nation which shares our strategic, political, economic and cultural interests is our "natural" ally. This is true, for instance, of the alliance between the United States and Canada. The same is more or less true of the bigger area which Lippmann calls the Atlantic Community. Among the members of this community there exists a

vital connection founded upon their military and political geography, the common tradition of Western Christendom, and their economic, political, legal and moral institutions which, with all their variations and differences, have a common origin and have been shaped by much the same historic experience.[13]

[11] Isolation and Alliances, p. 41.
[12] T and T, May 4, 1954; also June 1, 1953.
[13] The Cold War, pp. 24–25.

In Lippmann's view, an important factor making for a "natural" alliance is the identity of strategic interests among the allies. It follows that global alliances formed between powers which have vital interests all over the world should not include states whose interests are confined to a particular region. Otherwise the alliance becomes burdensome for its small and middle-sized member states, which are local or regional powers. "As between a global power and a regional power," writes Lippmann, "a complete two-way alliance is impossible—that is to say if the regional power is not a dependency or a satellite."[14] In 1951 he noted that the admission of Turkey into the NATO alliance would extend the area of the Pact beyond the strategic interests of at least some of its members, such as Norway and Denmark. These nations would find themselves among the guarantors of peace in the Middle East, a region which to them had always been a remote part of the world. "This, for small, highly vulnerable countries is an enormous commitment, not to be undertaken lightly or expected of them imperiously."[15] Lippmann observed that the Atlantic Pact should have been confined to the North Atlantic area, leaving the way open for local alliances such as, for instance, a Scandinavian alliance consisting of Norway, Denmark and Sweden, and a Mediterranean alliance including Italy, Greece, Turkey and Spain. The United States should have offered these alliances such support and guarantees as she might have deemed necessary.[16]

Lippmann also maintains that a great power should not enter the strategic orbit of another great power to seek alliances with its member states. Such alliances are entangling and interventionist in that they bring an alien power in a neighborhood and disrupt its solidarity. No one would ques-

[14] T and T, May 17, 1951.
[15] Ibid., May 17, 1951.
[16] Ibid.

tion America's alliance with Canada or Mexico. But if Mexico made an alliance with the Soviet Union, everyone would know at once that the peace of the world was threatened. "If we made an alliance with . . . Rumania, all the world would have every right to think the worst of our intentions."[17]

There is an additional difficulty in reaching out for alliances in other neighborhoods. They are expensive and difficult to maintain. Writing in 1946, Lippmann criticized British Foreign Secretary Ernest Bevin and the United States Secretary of State, James F. Byrnes, for subjecting the small states of Eastern Europe to the ordeal of having to stand up publicly to say whether they were with Russia or the West. "As a result," he noted, "we have compromised the political leaders and parties in Poland and elsewhere who wished to be independent of Moscow. We have sponsored them without in fact being able to support them."[18]

Lippmann is especially hostile to the idea of a great power seeking alliances with far-flung, small and backward nations in order to use them as a "bulwark" against the opposing combination of another great power. In *The Cold War* he wrote that it was an impossibly difficult task to organize a coalition of feeble and immature states, and to hold it together for any length of time. It required constant intervention by the great power in the affairs of these "allies" to make sure that they did not pursue "undesirable" policies.[19] In the very nature of things, such allies were no allies, they were satellites. And for our own sake, he wrote in 1952,

---

[17] *U.S. War Aims*, pp. 136–137. Russia's recent humiliation in Cuba, and the threat to world peace which arose from her alliance with that country, provide a good case in point. The Soviet government found it inexpedient to aid her distant ally against the United States and, under the threat of American retaliatory action, withdrew her offensive weapons from Cuba. See T and T, November 6, 1962.

[18] "A Year of Peacemaking," *Atlantic Monthly*, Vol. 178, No. 6 (December 1946), p. 37.

[19] *The Cold War*, pp. 21–22.

we must wish to live among equals, among peoples who trust us but do not fear us, who work with us but do not fawn upon us. Only equals can really be trusted, only governments that speak candidly and do not say what they think we want to hear, what they think will keep the dollars flowing. There is no health in satellitism, and even the most ruthless imperialism can never trust the satellite.[20]

When a country sponsors a coalition of puppets and satellites to assist her in her battles with a formidable foe, she stakes her own security and the peace of the world on partners whom she may know little. In spite of watchful intervention, these mercenaries will often act independently and confront their sponsor with accomplished facts, thereby creating crises for which the latter may not be ready. In the end, the promoter of the alliance "will have either to disown [her] puppets . . . or support them at an incalculable cost over unintended and perhaps undesirable issues."[21] A front composed of agents and clients is useless also because the great power against whom it is organized can easily disorganize it.[22] Above all, the effort to develop these unnatural and expensive alliances alienates one's natural allies, who are deprived of the assistance and support that might otherwise have gone to them.

Since the firmness and vigor of an alliance depend upon the solidarity of its members, they should not pursue objec-

[20] T and T, January 7, 1952.
[21] The Cold War, p. 23. Also see "Waging World Peace," Vital Speeches, Vol. 13, No. 7 (June 15, 1947), p. 528. We may submit that in almost every alliance some members are bound to be weaker than others. The tendency to present one's allies with a *fait accompli* or to force a given course of action upon them is not confined to puppets and satellites, far-flung and backward states. In some measure it is characteristic of most alliances. Again, nations may take independent action and force the hands of their allies, not by way of exploiting them but by the sheer compulsion of a habitual desire to exercise their "sovereign will." This pull toward independent action is especially characteristic of alliances which require long-term cooperation for encountering a threat the specific details of which are not clearly known or foreseen.
[22] The Cold War, p. 26.

tives which injure the vital interests of their allies. Lippmann
holds that this fundamental condition is not fulfilled by the alliances of the two great powers—the United States and the
Soviet Union.[23] He criticizes that section of opinion in the
United States which disregards the national interests of her
allies. "There is no one so crazily ignorant of the reality of
things as the American isolationist who wants to have all of
Asia and Europe say, yes sir, when we speak, and feels deeply
hurt when they don't."[24] Lippmann wrote these lines in
1954. Eight years later, we find him advising his countrymen that while President Kennedy is in some ways the leader
of the Western world, he is in no way its master. He must
consult with his allies before he can negotiate a settlement of
outstanding issues with Mr. Khrushchev.[25] Americans should
realize that they now must deal with an adversary of equal
military power and with allies who have economic strength
comparable to their own. They must learn to live in a world
where their "own will is not the only law."[26]

Likewise, American alliances to contain communism in
Asia could not operate successfully without the popular support of the Asian people. Lippmann observed that it was
futile, indeed harmful, to rely on the corrupt and discredited
rulers in Asia, for when they were thrown out by popular
movements "we are thrown out with them."[27] Asians would
support the West only if the total picture of its objectives
and purposes appealed to them. The United States could
enlist their support for her policies if she convinced them that
"we understand, and respect and support their vital interests
—not merely our own."[28] Indeed, this country should en-

[23] See pp. 52–54.
[24] T and T, May 4, 1954.
[25] Ibid., March 1, 1962.
[26] Ibid., January 9, 1962.
[27] Ibid., August 5, 1952.
[28] Ibid., May 11, 1954.

courage them to follow the neutral course which their instinct urged upon them, and she should help them with their plans for social progress and economic development in spite of their non-alignment in the cold war.[29]

An alliance cannot work if the leading power in it begins to dictate policies to its associates. The area of an alliance is not like the territory of an empire ruled from one capital. The gradual breaking up of the two-power system, the appearance of cracks and fissures in the coalitions of both Washington and Moscow, suggests that the world is too big and also too unwilling to be organized into two tight alliances governed from two capitals.[30]

In an article in 1952, which might be said to sum up Lippmann's position on the postwar alliances of the United States, he observed that the formation of an alliance was like the covenant to create a business partnership, which should be undertaken with extreme care and forethought. Americans, he said, had tended to think that since alliances were necessary they should have as many of them as possible. They had ignored the cardinal fact that the chain of alliances was not made stronger by adding weak links to it.

A great power like the United States gains no advantage and it loses prestige by offering, indeed peddling, its alliances to all and sundry. An alliance should be hard diplomatic currency, valuable and hard to get . . . One of the consequences of making unnecessary alliances is to depreciate the necessary and valuable alliances. For the inclusion of weak and unwilling states in an alliance merely increases the liabilities of the stronger state.[31]

Three salient facts about Lippmann's thinking on the sub-

[29] *The Communist World and Ours* (1958), p. 42, and *The Coming Tests With Russia*, (1961), pp. 36–37.
[30] Walter Lippmann, "Break-up of the Two-Power World," *Atlantic Monthly*, Vol. CLXXXV, No. 4 (April 1950), pp. 25–30.
[31] T and T, August 5, 1952.

ject of alliances emerge from the foregoing. Alliances are a necessary instrument of foreign policy. This proposition logically follows from his view of the nature, significance and role of power in international affairs, which we have considered earlier. He implicitly rejects as irrelevant the charge that alliances lead to war; the supreme end of foreign policy, he would say, is not the maintenance of peace but the preservation of national security in war and peace.

One may argue that while any two states have a perfect right to make common cause against a common enemy, the rest of the international society cannot but view the formation of alliances and counter-alliances with apprehension. The emergence of opposing coalitions serves notice on the world that war is intended or threatened. Consequently, tension in international relations rises. States which lie in the neighborhood of the major contestants or their seconds fear, not without reason, that they may be embroiled in an "unnecessary" war. This is not to argue that alliances should not be formed. They are certainly beneficial to those who need them. The point is that nations are bound to frown upon the alliances of *other* nations, especially the great powers, as being potentially dangerous to their own security and well-being.

Second, Lippmann holds that a great power should not form alliances with small, backward and remotely situated states. We have seen that he has no objection to an alliance between the United States and Mexico, even though the latter is both small and backward. Nor would he condemn the NATO ties between, say, the United States and Luxembourg, which is a tiny state. The idea of remoteness calls for some explanation. Ceylon and Chile are indeed remote from each other, and a military alliance between them would surely leave the world puzzled. But for Great Britain, which is a global power with vital interests scattered all over the world, Ceylon is not at all remote. Korea is situated at a great distance from the United States. Yet many Americans have died on Korean battlefields defending their vital interests. It follows that physical distance between two nations is, in itself, no reason against an alliance between them.

It would then appear that it is the combination of these characteristics—smallness, backwardness and remoteness—in a state which in Lippmann's view disqualifies it for an alliance with a great power. He opposes American alliances with those Asian countries which are at once small, feeble and distant. These alliances may be useful for a lesser objective than the one for which they were organized, namely the containment of Soviet power. They are evil, not absolutely, but relatively to the large cost of maintaining them. Not all alliances or spheres of influence add to one's power or security. As Machiavelli advised his friend Francesco Vettori,

You must remember that rulers often gain territory without gaining power; and if you consider carefully, you will see that the King of France when he gains land in Italy will . . . get position but not power. . . . And as to any difference that the possession of Milan would make, the King of France would need to fear the more, for he would have a state that he could not trust.[32]

Lippmann has often condemned the alliance between the United States and Formosa, which, according to him, is a "classic case of an entangling alliance." The vital interests of the United States, he says, are not involved in Formosa. Formosa is useless as an American strategic base: being too close to the Chinese mainland, it can be devastated by missiles and blockaded by submarines.[33] The United States should liquidate its commitment to defend Formosa as soon as a "satisfactory solution" of the Formosan problem is found. This country should propose to the "international community" a settlement

[32] The Prince and Other Works, p. 245 (Letter to Francesco Vettori, December 20, 1514).
[33] T and T, October 2, 1958.

which aims at preserving Formosa for the Formosans and at preventing the Red Chinese from making it a base against the Philippines. By international agreement and under international supervision, Formosa should become autonomous, neutralized and demilitarized. The mainland Chinese on Formosa should be repatriated to the mainland. Chiang Kai-Shek and his deputies should be given asylum at a safe place.[34] Lippmann did not insist on the expulsion of Chiang and his compatriots from Formosa. A few days after publishing the article referred to above, he observed that the United States should seek to "preserve Formosa's independence from the mainland —to preserve it as an independent center of non-communist Chinese culture and to keep it militarily neutral.."[35] Lippmann conceded that neither Mao nor Chiang would welcome a settlement which recognized two Chinas. Nevertheless, two Chinas would continue to exist because neither could subdue and absorb the other. The world would learn to live with both of them and they with each other. Lippmann assumed that the United States would continue to protect Formosa until an international agreement about its future was made. He advised Chiang to renounce his "illusions" about returning to the mainland, concentrate on the economic development of Formosa, and reduce his army to the level necessary for maintaining internal order.[36]

Needless to say, Lippmann strongly opposed the proposition that the United States should assume responsibility for defending Quemoy and Matsu and thus enable Chiang to maintain his forces there. He observed that by placing a substantial part of his forces on these islands Chiang had laid a trap to entangle the United States into a full-scale war with

[34] T and T, October 2, 1958 and September 11, 1958.
[35] October 14, 1958.
[36] Ibid.

Red China.[37] President Eisenhower and Secretary Dulles
must not fall into this trap. Instead, they must negotiate a
cease fire with the Red Chinese on the basis of the withdrawal
of Chiang's forces from the off-shore islands. Quemoy and
Matsu were not worth defending, for they had no bearing
upon the defense of Formosa. They were merely the symbol
of Chiang's unrealistic desire to return one day to the mainland and of the "fiction" that real China was in Formosa.[38]
Those who opposed withdrawal from the off-shore islands as
an act of appeasement which would demoralize small nations
of Asia should remember, said Lippmann, that these nations
regarded the American connection with Chiang as "sinister."[39]
Moreover, withdrawal would be infinitely better than a war
with Red China which might become a general nuclear war.

Lippmann abhors the prospect of the United States fighting
a war with Red China. But it appears also that he is averse to
any Western power, and especially the United States, becoming engaged in a war anywhere in Eastern and Southeastern
Asia. Not only are these places far from home, they are muddy
and marshy and full of jungles. Their governments are no
better; being inefficient, reactionary, corrupt and cruel. Western military efforts in these parts of the world are unpopular.
They please only the communists, for they pin down Western
military power in dirty, indecisive battles with the guerrillas.
Lippmann's attitude in this respect is well illustrated by his
opposition to American involvement in Southeast Asia.

During 1959, 1960 and 1961, Lippmann wrote a number
of articles opposing American military effort to defeat the
communist rebels in Laos, and urging a "political solution" of
the Laotian civil war. Military intervention "would be a
miserable way to engage American forces in a most inacces-

[37] T and T, September 4, 1958.
[38] T and T, September 11, 1958. Also see *Ibid.*, October 11, 1960.
[39] T and T, September 25, 1958.

sible place" and would mean a "prolonged and indecisive jungle war."[40] Moreover, it would lead to a violent Red Chinese reaction. Laos was as close to Red China as Cuba was to the United States. We must not forget the Red Chinese reaction when, during the Korean war, American forces crossed the thirty-eighth parallel and approached the Yalu River.[41] A political solution meant the restoration of Laotian neutrality, which was upset when the United States unwisely urged the Laotian government to act vigorously against the communist party and army in that country.[42] Lippmann conceded the possibility that a neutralist Laotian government might quickly turn communist, but this did not trouble him. He wrote: "Laos is not a primary interest of the United States. For we are not the arbiters of human destiny in every corner of the globe."[43] Lippmann also suggested that the United States should pass on to Great Britain, France, and India—whose knowledge of an interest in Southeast Asia was much greater than her own—the main responsibility for solving of the problems of Laos.[44]

Lippmann maintained that the United States could no longer defend Indo-China by threatening massive retaliation, for the Soviet Union could now make a similar threat against the United States.[45] A Korean-type war must also be ruled out. The United States should therefore permit, indeed encourage, the countries of Southeast Asia to become neutral in the cold war. She should propose a "regional system of independence and security and neutrality for the old colonial lands of South(east) Asia."[46] The system of American "protectorates,"

[40] T and T, September 10, 1959.
[41] Ibid., September 10, 1959 and December 29, 1960.
[42] Ibid., September 10, 1959.
[43] Ibid., December 29, 1960.
[44] Ibid., December 29, 1960.
[45] Ibid., June 23 and July 7, 1960.
[46] Ibid., May 16, 1961.

which Mr. Dulles had created during the days of American nuclear supremacy, was now crumbling partly because the United States could no longer defend them and partly because the "American-client governments" there—in Korea, South Vietnam, Laos—were not only corrupt but "intolerably reactionary." Americans should not become unduly perturbed at the break-up of their empire. The British and French empires had also been liquidated. This was the age of revolutions! At any rate, "there is no conceivable way in which Laos, which has two communist states on its frontiers, which is a country of trackless jungles, can be made finally secure against infiltration and guerrilla fighting. We cannot seal off Laos from the communist states which it touches."[47] The situation of South Vietnam was equally hopeless. Ngo Dinh Diem, the "friend and client" of the United States, had lost much of the country to the communists. His regime was both reactionary and corrupt and lacked popular support.[48] Here too the United States should settle for a neutral government. South Vietnam could not become a bastion against the communist powers. Ever since the Soviet Union had become a great nuclear power, the "wiser men of the West" had believed that military outposts could not be maintained on the frontiers of the communist world. "Just as Cuba is not now, and will never be allowed to become, a Soviet military outpost, so in reverse for peripheral positions like Laos, South Vietnam, Quemoy and Matsu, and some others."[49]

Cuba has indeed become a Soviet military outpost. Lippmann's reactions to this development should be noted. During 1959 Lippmann maintained that Castro's rise to power in Cuba represented a genuine popular revolution, "the real thing," and not merely "a change of guard at the top." The

[47] T and T, January 10, 1961.
[48] Ibid., May 4, 1961.
[49] Ibid., May 4, 1961.

United States government should offer to help Castro and try to advise him. There was no alternative to such a policy, for this country could not install a "puppet" government in Cuba to replace Castro. In this age of popular revolutions, the old gestures of imperialism and overlordship were neither morally correct nor feasible. Moreover, the Charter of the Organization of American States absolutely precluded this country from intervening in Latin America. Nor would it help to denounce Castro as a communist, for such action would make him regard the United States as his enemy. "The thing we should never do in dealing with the revolutionary countries . . . is to push them behind an iron curtain raised by ourselves. On the contrary, even when they have been seduced and subverted and drawn across the line, the right thing to do is to keep the way open for their return."[50]

In 1960 Lippmann saw in Castro's seizure of United States property without compensation and in his anti-United States propaganda the suggestion of a "vast international action," a "sinister design" to provoke the United States into armed intervention in Cuba. He warned that such intervention would seriously damage this country's standing in Latin America, Africa and Asia. Latin Americans feared United States intervention, which was a historical fact, much more than they feared Russian intrusion, which was still "only talk."[51] He also advised against the economic coercion of Castro on the ground that it would persuade the Soviet Union to aid him just as the United States aided certain countries on the periphery of the Soviet Union.[52] Lippmann urged the United States government to seek the cooperation of a few "liberal" Latin American states—Brazil, Mexico, Colombia, and Venezuela—for controlling the traffic of arms from and to Cuba

[50] T and T, July 23, 1959.
[51] Ibid., July 19, 1960; also see Ibid., July 5, 1960.
[52] Ibid., July 5, 1960.

and for containing the Cuban revolution within the island. But the United States should not try to overthrow Castro and his revolution. She would have to learn to live with it. "The more we allow ourselves to be jockeyed into the position of being a great counterrevolutionary power, the more will sympathy with Castro grow in this hemisphere."[53] With the overthrow of the old order and its privileges, there was "no future in the support of counter-revolution."

In August 1960, Lippmann urged a policy of "magnanimity" towards Cuba. The United States should tell the Latin American governments that it did not desire a "license to intervene in Cuba." Instead, it should seek their good offices in composing Cuba's quarrel with this country and in convincing Castro and the Cuban people that it did not wish to make war upon them. This would indeed be "a policy of turning the other cheek. But is that an ignoble policy for a great state?"[54]

Lippmann's reader will find one constant theme in his observations concerning Cuba during the last three years: the United States must not use its military power in order to overthrow Castro.[55] "There is no conceivable way," he wrote in 1961, "in which we can deal with Castro except to contain him gradually with the growing collaboration of the other

[53] *Ibid.*, July 19, 1960.
[54] *Ibid.*, August 18, 1960. About this time Lippmann made another rather interesting proposal for dealing with Castro's subversive influence in Latin America. The United States, he said, should make friends with the intellectual leaders of Latin America and through them with their peoples. However, Americans could not buy this friendship by offering aid to the Latins. They must cultivate a sense of humility, stop treating Latin Americans as "under-developed" and stop regarding themselves as "a virtually perfected model of a free society." "If this country becomes again the scene of a movement to improve and reform and develop itself, we shall again win friends abroad and influence them. It is no accident but the very nature of human affairs that in the times when we have been most liked and respected abroad . . . we were the least smug about our own affairs and the least satisfied with ourselves." T and T, July 19, 1960.
[55] T and T, September 6, 1960, October 25, 1960.

American states. We cannot exorcise the revolutionary spirit of idealism."[56] After the Bay of Pigs fiasco, he suggested that those government officials who had advised President Kennedy to authorize the affair should resign their offices.[57]

Lippmann's comments during the Cuban crisis of 1962 provide a good illustration of his view of the nature of international politics. It should be noted that while he regards the installation of Soviet military power on Cuba as an unfortunate development from the standpoint of American interests, he does not consider it an act of villainy on the part of the Soviet Union. Writing a few weeks before the crisis, he had the occasion to observe: "We have in fact achieved the same kind of penetration of the communist world as Moscow has done in our world in Cuba."[58] When the President's "quarantine" of Cuba went into effect on October 24, 1962, Lippmann urged him to keep open the channels of diplomatic communication with the Soviet Union. He should avoid the "tragic mistake" which Wilson and Roosevelt had made, the mistake of suspending diplomacy "when the guns began to shoot." Lippmann observed that when the President met Mr. Gromyko on October 18, he should have confronted the latter with the evidence of Soviet missile build-up in Cuba and should have "told him privately about the policy which in a few days he intended to announce publicly." Having done that, the President "would have given Mr. Khrushchev what all wise statesmen give their adversaries—the chance to save face."[59] Mr. Khrushchev might then have taken steps to avoid a confrontation of Soviet and American power, which on October 24 seemed to be imminent.

Lippmann maintained that the need for diplomacy was

[56] *Ibid.*, January 10, 1961.
[57] *Ibid.*, May 2, 1961.
[58] *Ibid.*, October 2, 1962.
[59] T and T, October 25, 1962.

especially urgent with reference to the President's demand that the Soviet missile installations already in Cuba be dismantled and removed. While he would not recommend a "Cuba-Berlin horse trade," some "face-saving agreement" might be in order:

The only place that is truly comparable with Cuba is Turkey. This is the only place where there are strategic weapons right on the frontier of the Soviet Union. . . . There is another important similarity between Cuba and Turkey. The Soviet missile base in Cuba, like the U.S.—NATO base in Turkey, is of little military value. The Soviet military base in Cuba is defenseless, and the base in Turkey is all but obsolete. The two bases could be dismantled without altering the world balance of power.[60]

Lippmann was pleased with the outcome of the crisis. The President, he wrote, had "used military force boldly and successfully to achieve a limited and specific objective." He did not demand the unconditional surrender of the Soviet Union and he did not seek the unlimited objective of dismantling Castro's communist regime. The United States had promised not to invade or blockade Cuba and the Soviet Union, in turn, had agreed to remove its strategic weapons from Cuba. Lippmann congratulated the President for doing what Wilson, Roosevelt and Truman had failed to do: "He did not fall in with those who in this war crisis, as in all other war crises of this century, wanted not a settlement but a crusade."[61]

Alliance with small, remote and relatively backward Cuba has not been an unmixed blessing for the Soviet Union. At the time of crisis, she was unable and unwilling to defend Cuba against the military power of the United States. She was forced to dismantle and remove her missiles from Cuban soil in apparent humiliation which the whole world saw. However, Soviet military power is still present on the Island of Cuba. It

[60] *Ibid.*, October 25, 1962.
[61] *Ibid.*, October 30, 1962.

is interesting to note that Lippmann's reaction to this situation
has been one of moderation and even philosophical detach-
ment. He is not as harshly critical of the Soviet alliance with
Cuba as he has been of American alliances in Eastern and
Southeastern Asia. A tentative explanation of his attitude may
be offered. While Lippmann probably feels that he is in duty
bound to criticize, in the hope of correcting, the mistakes of
the government of his own country, there is no reason to think
that he feels a similar sense of obligation to the government of
the Soviet Union. A few other considerations, which appear to
figure in Lippmann's thinking, may be noted. In establishing
a military outpost in the orbit of the United States, the Soviet
Union has done that which is common occurrence in international politics. For the last fifteen years or so, the military
power of the United States has been stationed at many points
along the frontiers of the communist world. Furthermore,
there are limits to the ability of the United States to compel,
under the threat of military action, a complete Soviet withdrawal from Cuba. Mere denunciation of the Soviet Union
or a diplomacy of threats, which cannot be carried out, would
therefore be futile. Lippmann seems to feel also that Castro,
the "client" of the Soviet Union in the Western Hemisphere,
is a popular hero, representing a revolution of the masses,
while Chiang Kai-Shek, Ngo Dinh Diem and other "clients"
of the United States in Asia are reactionary and corrupt tyrants, hated by their peoples. American alliances in Asia are
thus even more "sinister" than the Soviet alliance with Cuba.
There is some indication that according to Lippmann the immense power of the United States is not entirely an asset in
the cold war. It is somehow not quite right, he seems to think,
for this country to be so rich and powerful in a world where
the vast majority of men are unspeakably poor and miserable.
In this age of popular revolutions, shows of wealth and power,
gestures of imperialism and overlordship are especially dis-

advantageous. Writing in the New York *Herald Tribune* as recently as May 7, 1963, Lippmann observed that the people of this country were too rich and too powerful to win the confidence and friendship of Latin Americans. He proposed that Europe and the European Economic Community should be involved in Latin America to make it once again the "three-legged stool" that it was during the nineteenth century when British sea power backed up the Monroe Doctrine.

Are equals necessarily better allies? Lippmann says that they alone are trustworthy. He cannot mean it literally, for history is replete with instances where equals have stabbed one another in the back. He must mean that they are more trustworthy than others. That may be so. But it is clear that at least in one respect they are less desirable as allies than smaller states: equals remain rivals even when they are allied. And the greater the two states which are allies the larger must be the area in which their interests will come into conflict.[62] The conflict of interests may overshadow the identity of interests among the allies if their alliance becomes a long-drawn-out affair. This leads us to the third interesting point which emerges from the preceding discussion.

We have seen that after World War I, and during World War II, Lippmann advocated the formation of a "permanent" alliance between the great victorious powers to promote and

[62] The Soviet government fired the first shot in its cold war with the United States in 1944, while the war against Germany was still in progress. *Izvestia* termed the presence of American troops in Iran illegal and unauthorized on the ground that, unlike Great Britain and the Soviet Union, the United States had no treaty arrangement with the Iranian government to station troops on Iranian territory. Lewis V. Thomas and Richard N. Frye, *The United States and Turkey and Iran* (Cambridge: Harvard University Press, 1952), p. 235. For an account of Anglo-American rivalry for Middle Eastern oil during the war, see *The Memoirs of Cordell Hull*, Vol. II, pp. 1511–1527. For an expression of Lippmann's own indignation at President De Gaulle's current policy of limiting American and increasing French influence in European affairs see T and T, May 17 and 24, 1962.

superintend, so to speak, the progress of man toward the good society. He insisted that the nations of the Atlantic Community should go ahead and organize a permanent alliance even if the Soviet Union refused to join them. In all these cases, the idea of an enduring concert among the great powers for the general good of mankind seems to have persisted in Lippmann's thinking.

One may ask whether it is at all possible to organize in times of peace a permanent alliance to wage war on evil or to promote, as Lippmann has put it, the rule of "liberty under law" among the peoples of the world. If we assume, as Lippmann does, that nations in their dealings with one another are motivated by their interests, and that as a general rule these interests clash, then it is difficult to see how great powers, with great conflicting interests, could cooperate for any length of time for peaceful purposes. We have already noted in a previous discussion that hopes of international cooperation in promoting the social, economic and cultural objectives of the League and the United Nations have remained largely unfulfilled.

It is not without reason that alliances are typically associated with war. As Professor Schwarzenberger writes,

Any statesman, who has ever concluded an alliance, is unlikely to dissent in the heart of his heart from the statement in Hitler's *Mein Kampf* that "an alliance which is not for the purpose of waging war has no meaning and no value." Even though at the moment when an alliance is concluded the prospect of war is a distant one, still the idea of the situation developing towards war is the profound reason for entering into an alliance.[63]

The stresses and strains to which the Atlantic Alliance is currently subjected by the desire of the French to assume the leadership of Western Europe and to exclude Anglo-Ameri-

[63] *Power Politics* (New York: Frederick A. Praeger, 1951), p. 176.

can influence from there is also a case in point. According to
Lippmann himself, the French policy is predicated upon the
belief that the United States in any event will maintain a
balance of nuclear power against the Soviet Union, thus pre-
cluding Soviet aggression upon Western Europe. In the
French view, the Atlantic Alliance is then superfluous or at
least of diminishing importance to the defense of Western
Europe. "Once again," comments Lippmann, "as is usual in
human affairs, a wartime coalition begins to break up as peace
begins to break out."[64]

We may then conclude that whereas it is possible to talk
about permanent unions between states in which their separate sovereignties are merged to create a larger unit, it is
self-contradictory to talk about permanent alliances between
them. And one suspects that when Lippmann advocates
a permanent alliance between the great Western democracies, it is some sort of political union—*de facto* if not *de
jure*—rather than an old-fashioned alliance, that he has in
mind. His emphasis on the liberal character of its membership
and mission reminds one less of Machiavelli's thesis on alliances than of Aristotle's distinction between an alliance and
the polis:

It is true that . . . peoples have . . . written terms of alliance for
mutual defense. On the other hand, they have no common offices
of state to deal with these matters; each, on the contrary, has its
own offices, confined to itself. Neither of the parties concerns itself to ensure a proper quality of character among the members of
the other. . . . But it is the cardinal issue of goodness or badness
in the life of the polis which always engages the attention of any
state that concerns itself to secure a system of good laws well
obeyed. The conclusion which clearly follows is that any polis
which is truly so called . . . must devote itself to the end of en-

[64] T and T, February 14, 1963.

couraging goodness. Otherwise a political association sinks into a mere alliance.[65]

It follows from Aristotle's argument that if nations want to have "common offices of state," as Lippmann urges the Atlantic Community to do, in order to secure a "system of good laws," or as Lippmann says, the "rule of liberty under law," then they must organize a "polis" and not a "mere alliance."

The Balance of Power

In the preceding pages we have examined two suggested ways of dealing with the rivalry for power among nations: the institution of world government and the device of collective security, both of which seek to end the struggle through the agency of an all-embracing, universal pool of power. We have seen that Lippmann rejects these proposed remedies as impracticable and utopian. But he is quite favorably disposed to a classic, though unpopular, technique of dealing with the phenomenon of power. This is to confront power with power, to manage and organize the order of power so as to balance it.

Lippmann has consistently adhered to the principle and advocated the policy of the balance of power.[66] Addressing himself to the critics of the balance of power, he writes:

There is the idealistic tradition, which Wilson formulated, that this country cannot with a good conscience recognize any settlement which rests on a balance of power and the existence of spheres of special influence. The tradition holds that only one

[65] *Politics*, Book III, Chapter IX, Barker's translation (Oxford University Press, 1950), pp. 137–138.

[66] The one time he went on record against the policy of the balance of power was in 1917, when he wrote in *The Political Scene*, (pp. 40–41) that the world could not return to a system of the balance of power "unless supreme madness descends upon the English-speaking peoples."

world of like-minded states is tolerable, and all the arrangements which the diplomatists have made in the past, to accommodate the perpetual rivalry of nations, are intolerable. This tradition, noble though it is in purpose, is not compatible with peace in a world where great powers are not like-minded, and do not mean to be.[67]

The problem of peace, he says, cannot be solved merely by devising and negotiating a formula of agreement. It can be met only by making a series of moves over a long period of time in order to establish and perpetuate a balance of power between the great rival states.[68] In the absence of such a balance, it is possible to talk about the surrender of one side to the other but not about a satisfactory negotiated settlement.[69] Political settlements can be had only when nations know that their power to get what they want is limited, checked and balanced.[70] For when the balance of power turns decisively against one side or the other the stronger coalition can force its opponent to choose between surrender and a destructive war.[71] In order, therefore, that war may be prevented while both sides make preparations to sit down at the conference table and negotiate a settlement, a balance of power between them must be maintained. The underlying idea, as Lippmann put it succinctly in 1955, is that "when the ponderable forces are in balance, neither being able or willing to exert decisive force, the imponderable means of reason become efficacious."[72]

[67] T and T, March 29, 1948.
[68] Ibid., January 9, 1947.
[69] Ibid., March 11, 1947.
[70] Ibid., December 22, 1947.
[71] Ibid., March 15, 1948.
[72] The Public Philosophy, p. 158. Also see T and T, March 15, 1948. Several writers on international law and politics have emphasized the point that law and reason in international conduct become efficacious only when the contending forces are in balance. Oppenheim writes: "A law of nations can exist only if there be an equilibrium, a balance of power,

It is precisely the maintenance of a balance of power between the West and the Soviets which, according to Lippmann, has so far prevented them from plunging the world
into another war. On this balance of forces between them
"rests, not the peace we would like to have but the avoidance
of that total war which would mean the end of our epoch
and almost certainly of our civilization."[73] The United States
must continue to maintain a nuclear balance of power with
the Soviet Union. Only then will coexistence be practiced and
a world war prevented.[74] Lippmann suggests that the Soviet
Union has refrained from going to war over Berlin because
of the existence of such a balance.[75]

Lippmann's thesis that the establishment of a secure and
stable equilibrium in the world is the irreducible minimum
condition for the maintenance of peace, should not be taken
to mean that war can never break out among states which
belong to a system of the balance of power. Many wars have
been fought in the past, and some may be fought in the
future, to forestall or redress a disturbance in the balance of
power.[76] Indeed, just as the principle of collective security

---

between the members of the family of nations. If the powers can not keep
one another in check, no rules of law will have any force, since an over-
powerful state will naturally try to act according to discretion and disobey
the law." Quoted in Quincy Wright, *A Study of War* (Chicago: University of Chicago Press, 1942), Vol. II, p. 745.

According to Prince Metternich, ". . . the balance of power offers us the
drama of the unified efforts of several states in restraining the hegemony of
a single state and limiting the expansion of its influence, and *thus forcing
it to return to public law*" (italics mine). Quoted in Ernest B. Haas, "The
Balance of Power: Prescription, Concept or Propaganda?", *World Politics*,
Vol. 5, No. 4 (July 1953), pp. 469–470.

[73] T and T, September 21, 1950. Also see *ibid.*, January 1, 1952,
September 22, 1953.

[74] *The Communist World and Ours* (1958), p. 39, and T and T,
November 9, 1961.

[75] *Ibid.*, February 13, 1962.

[76] According to Cobden, the maintenance of "what is denominated the
true balance of European power has been the fruitful source of wars from

calls upon "peace-loving" states to make war on the breakers of peace, the doctrine of the balance of power requires its devotees to move against the actual or the probable disturbers of the balance.[77] It is interesting to note here that when war broke out in Korea, Lippmann greeted President Truman's decision to dispatch American troops to the theatre of conflict by saying, "Now that force is being used to upset the existing balance of power in the Far East, force must be used to right it again."[78]

Lippmann does not look upon the balance of power as the absolute guarantor of international peace. Like some other writers, he considers it the best available means by which a nation can safeguard its independence, and by which a group of nations can hope to prevent a great, dynamic and aggressive power from establishing its hegemony over them.[79] During the post-World War II period, he has often said that the existence of a balance of power between the two great coalitions has prevented the Soviet Union from extending its empire to Western Europe, and that it has likewise kept the

---

the earliest time. . . . And yet we have able writers and statesmen of the present day, who would advocate a war to prevent a derangement of what we now choose to pronounce the just equipoise of the power of Europe." *The Political Writings of Richard Cobden* (London: T. Fisher Unwin, 1903), Vol. 1, p. 5. For a similar view see Sidney B. Fay, "The Balance of Power," *Encyclopedia of Social Sciences*, Vol. II, p. 398.

[77] In his essay, "Of Empire," Bacon states this position in unequivocal terms. "First for their Neighbours; there can no general rule be given (the occasions are so variable), save one, which ever holdeth; which is, that princes do keep due sentinel, that none of their neighbours do overgrow so . . . as they become more able to annoy them than they were. . . . *Neither is the opinion of some of the schoolmen to be received, that a war cannot justly be made but upon a precedent injury or provocation. For there is no question but a just fear of an imminent danger, though there be no blow given, is a lawful cause of war*" (italics mine). *The Essays of Francis Bacon* (London: Macmillan and Co., 1906), pp. 46–47.

[78] T and T, June 25, 1950.

[79] Machiavelli states clearly what might be called the very core of the idea of the balance of power, to wit, that states must throw their weight on the weaker side in a contest in order to prevent a strong neighbor from

forces of the Atlantic Community from "liberating" the states of Eastern Europe. In 1949 he wrote that the Red Army, encamped deep in Europe, had not advanced against the practically unarmed states west of the Elbe because of the knowledge in the Kremlin that a war upon Western Europe would mean a war with the United States.[80] In 1953 Lippmann noted that the British felt secure in their independence because they realized that a balance of military power between the Atlantic Community and the Soviet orbit had been achieved.[81] In 1958 he observed that the fear of American retaliation restrained Mr. Khrushchev from moving against Turkey and West Germany.[82] Indeed, the bonds of unity between the Western allies tend sometimes to loosen because of the security which the existing balance of terror provides them. For instance, President De Gaulle is currently trying to exclude American influence from Western Europe as far as possible. He also wants to exercise a veto on the right of the United States to negotiate the issues of war and peace with the Soviet Union.[83] De Gaulle is convinced that the Soviet Union will not start a nuclear war. But this conviction is based, says Lippmann, on the existence of American, not French, nuclear deterrent power. The "lofty disdain" in Paris

---

becoming stronger and thus destroying the independence of the whole neighborhood. "A prince," he says, "should be careful not to join company with one more powerful than himself, in order to attack someone. . . . If your powerful ally conquers, you remain his prisoner. . . . The Venetians joined the King of France against the Duke of Milan, when they were able to avoid making that alliance, and it resulted in their ruin." *The Prince*, Chapter 21, para. 7.

Hume cites several instances to illustrate the same point. Referring to the frustration of the French expansionist ambitions in the eighteenth century, he wrote: "And such is the influence of the maxim here treated of [the balance of power], that tho' that ambitious nation [France], in the five last general wars, have been victorious in four, and unsuccessful only in one, they have not much enlarged their dominions, nor acquired a total ascendant over Europe. . . . Britain has stood foremost in the glorious struggle; and she still maintains her station, as guardian of the liberties of Europe, and patron of mankind." David Hume, "On the Balance of

is thus no more than "hitch-hiking diplomacy."[84] Lippmann complains that the allies of the United States take the present balance of power for granted, forgetting that its maintenance costs this country a great deal of money.[85]

Is the balance of power an absolutely reliable instrument for preserving national independence, if not international peace? Lippmann is right in saying that the imponderable means of reason become efficacious when the ponderable forces are in balance, being neither willing nor able to strike. But the ponderable forces never are exactly in balance, for it is impossible for statesmen to make accurate guesses about their own power and about that of their friends and foes.[86] It is probably the consideration of this element of uncertainty, that leads Lippmann to reject the policy of an even balance of power as a bulwark against aggression. In his *U.S. Foreign Policy* he wrote:

no state is secure. It cannot know whether it would win or would

When the alliance is inadequate because there is an opposing alliance of approximately equal strength, the stage is set for a world war. For then the balance of power is so nearly even that

---

Power," in *Essays Moral, Political and Literary*, edited by T. H. Green and T. H. Grose (London: Longmans, Green and Co., 1882), Vol. I, pp. 350, 353.

[80] T and T, April 14, 1949.

[81] *Ibid.*, October 22, 1953; also August 18, 1955.

[82] *The Communist World and Ours*, p. 17.

[83] T and T, December 21, 1961 and May 15, 1962.

[84] *Ibid.*, March 8, 1962.

[85] *Ibid.*, May 15, 1962.

[86] Professor Fay maintains that since the factors of power are numerous, diverse and elusive in character, the policy of the balance of power "has never achieved a satisfactory equilibrium for any long period of years and has signally failed in its purpose of preserving peace and the status quo or even of preventing states or groups of states from imposing their will upon others. Any international system to be successful in the long run must take cognizance of the inevitable factor of growth and change." Fay, *op. cit.*, p. 398.

Some writers, however, have suggested that the precise measurement of relative power is not vital to the success of the policy of the balance of

lose the war which it knows is probable. . . . The combination must be so strong that war against it is not a calculated risk, in which much might be won at a great price, but is instead an obvious impossibility because there would be no chance whatever of winning it.[87]

We are not living in the good society where nations practice self-restraint and tolerance in their relations with one another. People acquire these qualities as civilization progresses. But the wheels of civilization move slowly, and in the meantime the impossibility of success is the only deterrent to aggression.[88] It follows that a statesman should aim at establishing a balance of power which is distinctly favorable to his nation.

Writing in 1948, Lippmann maintained that the existing balance of power, which prevented the Red Army from marching westward and which kept the Atlantic Community from reducing the Soviet sphere of influence, was "inherently unstable and unsatisfactory." It had to be "redressed." The Western states, he observed, should seek to secure a withdrawal of the Red Army from Europe and, at the same time, should develop the power to strike at the vital centers of the Soviet Union.[89] The United States would not withdraw her

---

power. For it is unnecessary, they say, to have an exactly even balance. What really matters, according to Gentz, is "eternal vigilance" to ensure that no state acquires enough power to overawe the rest. Cited in Ernest B. Haas, "The Balance of Power: Prescription, Concept or Propaganda?", *World Politics*, Vol. 5 (July 1953), p. 471. "The scales of the balance of power," writes Lord Bolingbroke, "will never be exactly poised, nor is the precise point of equality either desirable or necessary to be discerned. It is sufficient in this as in other human affairs, that the deviation be not too great. Some there will always be. A constant attention to these deviations is therefore necessary." *The Works of Lord Bolingbroke* (Philadelphia: Carey and Hart, 1841), Vol. II, p. 291.

[87] *U.S. Foreign Policy*, pp. 106–107.
[88] Walter Lippmann, "One World of Diversity," *Vital Speeches*, Vol. XIII, No. 5 (December 15, 1946), p. 140.
[89] T and T, February 2, 1948.

forces across the Atlantic Ocean. "The true equivalent of the Russian withdrawal would be an American withdrawal into Western Europe."[90] In other words, a "satisfactory" balance of power between the two coalitions meant a balance which enabled the Atlantic Community to cripple the Soviet power without fear of retaliation.

Lippmann interpreted the Russian moves to incorporate Finland and Czechoslovakia into her strategic system to mean that the Russians were trying to extend their military frontiers so deep into Europe that while their homeland remained invulnerable, the whole continent would be at their mercy. Their second and no less important objective was to dominate by means of their troops the area which the West would need in order to use its superior military weapons. They could thus intimidate and divide Western Europe. Lippmann maintained that this trend in Soviet policy was designed to turn the balance of power decisively against the West. He considered the Russian moves so gravely imperiling Western security as to warrant immediate American mobilization—the restoration of selective service, the re-establishment of war power over industry, the restoration of lend-lease, and the declaration of a state of national emergency.[91] In 1950 Lippmann noted that the Soviets were trying to develop their air defenses to the point where these would neutralize American deterrent power. The logic of the situation, he wrote, demanded that the United States must constantly keep the development of her striking power superior to the Soviet defenses, and the development of her own defensive techniques ahead of the Russian offensive power.[92]

In 1958 Lippmann noted his impression, gained from con-

[90] Ibid., October 28, 1948.
[91] Ibid., March 15 and 16, 1948.
[92] Ibid., September 21, 1950.

versation with Mr. Khrushchev, that the Soviet Union was unwilling to make any concession that would give the United States even a slight tactical advantage, not to speak of a strategic advantage, in case of war.[93] Again in 1962 and 1963, commenting on the repeated failure of negotiations for a nuclear test ban treaty, he observed that neither the United States nor the Soviet Union was ready to trust the other with nuclear superiority. Each believed that it must have supremacy in order to have security.[94]

It follows that when Lippmann advocates a policy of the balance of power for the United States, he means the establishment of a balance that would be decisively favorable to this country.[95]

But it follows also that a state will do everything within its means to prevent the balance of power from becoming or remaining favorable to its enemy. The contestants will then live under the constant shadow of war. They will arm furiously, each trying to outdo the other, to "redress" the balance of power. Theoretically, the race could go on *ad infinitum*. But actually either one side will attack the other when it thinks, rightly or wrongly, that it has "righted" the balance, in which case one of the contenders will lose its independence, or one of them will collapse during the race by sheer exhaustion. It may disintegrate internally or it may

[93] *The Communist World and Ours*, p. 37.

[94] T and T, March 6, 1962, March 12, 1963.

[95] Lippmann's position here confirms the opinion of writers on the subject that nations, as a rule, seek to establish a favorable, and not an even, balance of power. "The word balance itself has two meanings: it can mean equilibrium, and it can also mean preponderance, as when we say we have a balance in the bank. This is the distinction between the objective and subjective view of the balance of power. The historian will say that there is a balance when the opposing groups seem to him equally strong. The statesman will say that there is a balance when he thinks that his side is stronger than the other." Martin Wight, *Power Politics* (London: Royal Institute of International Affairs, 1946), p. 45.

Professor Spykman maintains that "states are always engaged in curbing the force of some other state. The truth of the matter is that states are

come to the end of its resources, in which case, again, it will lose its independence. We may then say that in the absence of third parties who may act as balancers, the balance of power has a natural tendency to move to the point of equality of power and finally to break down.

Lippmann has often submitted that third states which might act as balancers between American and Russian power are bound to appear on the scene of world politics. Occasionally he has even urged the two super powers to encourage the emergence of powerful states which are independent of both Washington and Moscow. In 1950 he emphasized that the hazards inherent in the existing bipolarization of power could be overcome only by "the reappearance of independent powers, who have the energy and the will to take their own course."[96] Again, supporting Winston Churchill's plea for a "supreme effort to bridge the gulf between the two worlds," Lippmann observed that the world needed more than two "spheres of influence." Not every state, he pleaded, should be asked to join the Atlantic Community or the Soviet orbit. A settlement between these two systems could endure only if both sides acknowledged "the right and the need of many smaller powers to exist and act as buffers and mediators, and indeed as guardians of the balance of power."[97] In June 1953, Lippmann noted that the East Germans had rioted against the Soviet regime, and that Sygman Rhee had rebelled against United States policy in Korea. He hailed these events as indicating that the two-power system was breaking

---

interested only in a balance which is in their favor. Not an equilibrium, but a generous margin is their objective. There is no real security in being just as strong as a potential enemy; there is security only in being a little stronger. . . . The balance desired is the one which neutralizes other states, leaving the home state free to be the deciding force and the deciding voice." Nicholas John Spykman, *America's Strategy in World Politics* (New York: Harcourt, Brace and Co., 1942), pp. 21–22.

[96] T and T, March 23, 1950.

[97] *Ibid.*, February 16, 1950. Also see *ibid.*, June 21, 1951.

up. This breakup, he said, was "predestined and appointed," because Russia and America had become super-powers in the extraordinary postwar situation which found all other great powers prostrate with the exhaustion of war. But these powers were now beginning to recover, and as they recovered, they were bound to challenge the right of Moscow and Washington to determine exclusively the destiny of mankind.[98]

Lippmann thinks that an increase in the number of effective competitors for the prizes of power would diminish the present tension in world affairs to the extent that it stems from the heavy concentration of international rivalry at two points—Washington and Moscow. Moreover, some of the new entrants in the arena of world politics would, by virtue of their independence and power, occupy the position of the "balancer" which, to the detriment of security and stability in international relations, has remained vacant so long.[99]

It is generally assumed that the role of the balancer is a difficult one and that not every nation can play it. It is an assignment for those states whose own standing is unchallenged and who are not rivals among rivals. Lippmann observes that Great Britain was able to function as the balancer of Europe only so long as her position of preponderance remained unquestioned and her commercial and territorial interests lay not on the Continent but in regions beyond the seas. As soon as Germany made her appearance as a great power and challenged the position of Britain, the latter lost her ability to hold the balance of power in Europe. She had to call a Wilson or a Roosevelt from the new world to

[98] *Ibid.*, June 30, 1953. Also see *ibid.*, July 12, 1955.

[99] For an excellent presentation of the view that security and independence are attainable only in a system of complex balance of power, see DeWitt Clinton Poole, "Balance of Power," *Life*, Vol. 23, No. 12 (September 22, 1947), pp. 77–92.

redress the balance of the old.[100] Similarly, it is out of question today for the United States to act as the balancer because she is a principal, and not a disinterested bystander, in the current struggle for power.

There is no possibility that small nations, acting individually or collectively, may exert decisive influence on the policies of the great coalitions and become the guardians of the balance of power between them. Lippmann has often asserted that among the stakes of the great power diplomacy the small state is a mere pawn on the chessboard of international politics. In U.S. War Aims he noted that before World War I the small states of Europe had depended on the balance of power for their security. They staked their independence on "a delicately poised balance of power among the great states."[101] The foreign policy of Poland for example, and likewise of Finland, was not one of strict neutrality. Both hoped to survive by leaning on Germany against Russia, and upon Russia against Germany. "Disliking and fearing both their great neighbors, they sought to stand between them, aligning themselves definitely and finally with neither."[102] Lippmann signficantly added that this policy did not work in the twentieth century because the unchallenged balancer, Great Britain, had disappeared from the scene. The small states of Europe were then not the manipulators but the beneficiaries of the pre-World War I balance of power on the Continent. In the mid-twentieth century, technological revolutions have rendered the small states altogether too small to manipulate the balance of power or even to pursue an independent policy.[103]

The theory of the complex balance of power assumes

[100] U.S. Foreign Policy, pp. 115–116, and Isolation and Alliances, pp. 36–37.
[101] U.S. War Aims, p. 81.
[102] Ibid., p. 81.
[103] U.S. War Aims, p. 83.

that a number of great states of more or less equal power, constituting the system, not only desire to maintain a balance among themselves but also are willing to move collectively against the state which seeks aggrandizement and overlordship. They may all desire increments in their relative power, but they will not all act to satisfy this desire at the same time. Nor will they all seek such increments in the same quarter. It is therefore probable that one could always find some among the great powers who were disinterested in any given dispute between two or more members of the system, and who, by virtue of their power, disinterestedness and the jealousy of the balance, would be willing and able to act as balancers.

It should be clear that none of the powers would be permanently disinterested, or satisfied or dissatisfied with the status quo. The disinterested balancers of today would be the interested contenders of tomorrow, and the membership of the various combinations would therefore vary from time to time. In other words, the whole system would have to rest on unceasing watchfulness by each great power over the actions of every other great power, and on the shifting sands of temporary alliances. One might say that even if a complex balance-of-power system could, during its lifetime, preserve the independence of great states, it would not lend stability to the international order or give a sense of security to mankind. It could do both—protect the independence of its members and at the same time stabilize their relations—only if it operated under the patronage of a supremely disinterested super-power, greater than all others, which was ever willing and able to wield its force to restrain the upstart.

We have assumed in the foregoing discussion that the membership of a complex balance-of-power system will consist only of great powers that are securely settled in their strategic neighborhoods. They are all overlords in their own spheres of influence, where their supremacy is unchallenged and unencumbered by local balances of power. This is an unavoidable assumption, for it is clear that a great power which must always reckon with hostile leagues and combinations in its region cannot exert appreciable influence on the global balance. Indeed, if all states followed the principle of balance, none among them would ever rise to greatness, and their energies would be so devoted to preventing increments in the relative strength of their neighbors that life on this planet would become extremely impoverished. It is therefore no accident that Lippmann advocates the establishment of regions and spheres of influence, and that several other writers prescribe political federation of existing sovereign states into larger political units as a prerequisite to the successful functioning of a complex balance of power.[104]

A complex balance of power can operate smoothly if the constituent members of the system possess more or less equal power. In the event that they do not, the more powerful states will dominate the system. If the latter unite, they may conquer the world. If they are arrayed against each other, most of the lesser states will join one or the other coalition. The remaining disinterested powers, if any, will be too weak to hold the balance between the great coalitions. But even if the members of the system all start out as equals, some of them will bungle their affairs and thus weaken themselves as compared to those who have managed their business prudently and efficiently. The system will then once again split into two rival coalitions. One may say that it is a tendency inherent in a balance-of-power system that its smaller members are cumulatively eliminated as independent agents in its politics, and that the resulting disparity of power among the remaining states sets in motion forces that make for the bipolarization of power, eventually turning the complex into a simple balance of power.

[104] See, for instance, Poole, *op. cit.*, pp. 77–78.

Another difficulty afflicting a balance-of-power system may be noted in passing. Nations are interested not only in preserving but also in augmenting their power. To preserve it, they tend to join forces and to curb the strongest. But to enhance their power, they are likely to exploit the quarrels between others to their own advantage.[105] Thus the two rules of power politics—"curb the strongest" and "divide and rule"—though they are mutually incompatible in the long run, simultaneously enter into the calculations of statesmen and make it impossible for the latter to cooperate wholeheartedly in preserving the balance of power.

The critics of the principle of the balance of power charge that it is immoral in its application.[106] Its advocates deny the charge, pleading either that it is amoral or that it is morally beneficial in its operation.[107] It should be interesting to examine Lippmann's view on the moral position of the principle of the balance of power in the testament of the good society.

We have noted earlier that Lippmann's cherished alliance between American and British sea power after World War I, and likewise the "nuclear alliance" at the end of World

[105] Arguing that the advocates of the balance of power used the phrase merely to cloak their designs of aggrandizement, Cobden wrote that "the balance of Europe has merely meant . . . a desire, on the part of the great powers, to 'hold the balance of Europe.' England has, for nearly a century, held the European scales—not with the blindness of the goddess of justice herself, or with a view to the equilibrium of opposite interests, but with a Cyclopean eye to her own aggrandizement. The same lust of conquest has actuated . . . the other great powers." Cobden, op. cit., p. 201.

[106] Cobden wrote that the principle of the balance of power "would interdict the growth of morality and freedom." Op. cit., p. 205. Professor Fay maintains that it is "a principle based not upon justice but upon expediency and force." Fay, op. cit., p. 398. Professor Haas notes that it runs counter to the moral law. Haas, op. cit., p. 443. For similar opinions see also Edward V. Gulick, The Balance of Power (Philadelphia: The Pacifist Research Bureau, 1943), pp. 14–15; and Frank Tannenbaum, "The Balance of Power Versus the Coordinate State," Political Science Quarterly, Vol. 67, No. 2 (June 1952).

[107] Professor Morgenthau maintains that rules of morality are irrelevant

War II, were to promote the rule of liberty under law and
to work generally for the good of mankind. There can be no
doubt that at least in the former instance he looked upon
the proposed pool of Anglo-American power as the guardian
of a global balance. In the concluding chapter of *The Stakes
of Diplomacy* he wrote:

If any of our finer hopes are to be realized, it will be because the
more enlightened democracies assume a decisive position in world
politics. Unless the people who are humane and sympathetic, the
people who wish to live and let live, are masters of the situation,
the world faces an indefinite vista of conquest and terrorism. . . . I
realize that this sounds suspiciously like the old doctrine of
balance of power. This is just what it is, and there is no need to
be afraid of a bad name.[108]

The Anglo-American combination was to maintain a preponderant position in order to "balance off" the power of
those who opposed its liberal mission.[109] Thus the balance of
power was to function as an instrument of liberalism.

Lippmann addresses himself directly to the issue in *The
Public Philosophy*. He concedes that as a technical device the
balance of power may be used for moral, immoral or amoral
purposes. A warring lord who wants to dominate others, or
secure himself against the rest, may do so by applying the

to international politics. See *In Defense of the National Interest*, pp.
33–39. Also see Spykman, *op. cit.*, p. 18.

    The point is stated more positively by most eighteenth-century writers,
who viewed the principle of the balance of power as related to the "law of
nature" and "the harmony of spheres." The state of equilibrium was
something inherently beautiful, and also morally elevated in that it served
the cause of peace. Fénelon, the great philosopher of the reign of Louis
XIV, noted: "To hinder one's neighbor from becoming too strong is not to
do harm; in a word it is to work for liberty, tranquillity and public
safety. . . . This attention to the maintenance of a kind of equality and
equilibrium between neighboring states is what assures peace for all."
Quoted by Sidney B. Fay, *op. cit.*, p. 396.
    [108] *The Stakes of Diplomacy*, pp. 220–222.
    [109] *Ibid.*

principle of balance, as indeed many have done in the past. But it does not follow, says Lippmann, that the holder of the balance must always become a tyrant who seeks to subdue and rule his neighbors. Taking note of Professor Spykman's assertion that "the truth of the matter is that states are interested only in a balance which is in their favor," he asks, "Of what 'matter' is this the 'truth?'"[110] It may be that states, particular parties, factions and individual politicians are interested in a balance which is to be in their favor. "They have Hobbes's desire for power after power." However, this is the truth about "the first or the fallen nature of man," not about the balance of power. "It is the truth about the condition which the balance of power can be used to correct."[111] One may concede that each contender for power will seek to rule and dominate the rest. But the most vital question is: What does he want to do after he has achieved a position of predominance? Does he mean to use his position to aggrandize his own power, or is he primarily interested in the preservation, harmony and development of the system itself? There is a radical difference, says Lippmann,

between being a contender for power, a rival among rivals, and being the guardian of the order which intends to regulate all the rivalries. In the one, the technique of the balance is used as an instrument of aggression and defense. In the other, it is used as the structural principle of public order in the good society.[112]

The fact that the balance of power has been used in the past for immoral ends does not stop us from urging that it should henceforth be used as "the structural principle of public order in the good society."

In other words, Lippmann maintains that the balance of power is one of those basic and fundamental principles on

[110] The Public Philosophy, p. 159; Spykman, op. cit., p. 21.
[111] The Public Philosophy, p. 159.
[112] Ibid.

which rests the edifice of good government. In saying this, he would seem to refer not so much to the mechanism of checks and balances, characteristic of some democracies, as to the principle underlying that mechanism, the tenet that persons and groups other than the governors have a right to preserve their individual entities and personalities. In the context of the good society, the idea of the balance of power is a representation of "the awareness," as Alfred Vagts has put it, "of the need for opposition in politics, as well as in the sciences and arts, a willingness to admit a modicum at least of reason to the adversary. The image for this readiness . . . is the political balance."[113]

It is clear that when we talk of the political balance we imply that there is a superior power which is to be restrained by the opposition. It must be a superior power, for if the power to be checked is that of a minority in opposition, the mechanism of the balance does not work to civilize the "desire for power after power," prompted by the "fallen nature of man." Instead, it becomes the keystone of a system of tyranny, in which government becomes the "warring lord." In the domestic sphere, then, the power to be checked is the power of organized government, which is the largest single holder of the means of coercion in the state.

How do we relate this concept to the international sphere, which has no institution analogous to the national government? One suspects that in Lippmann's view the "public order" in international politics, of which the balance of power is the "structural principle," is the aforementioned permanent alliance of the Western democracies to manage the world. Some additional evidence which lends support to

[113] Alfred Vagts, "The Balance of Power: Growth of an Idea," *World Politics,* Vol. I, No. 1 (October 1948), p. 83. Vagts adds that this awareness prevails only in the world west of the Iron Curtain, "west of the Byzantine, the monolithic order of things."

this interpretation may be noted. When World War I broke out, Lippmann exhorted the two great English-speaking democracies to lead mankind in creating a better and happier world. Addressing the American Academy of Political and Social Science in July 1916, he declared:

The kind of world we desire, a world of stable, autonomous, interdependent democracies *acting as the guardians of less developed peoples* [italics mine]—that vision depends upon the cooperation of the United States and Great Britain. . . . No one need pretend that within it complete justice will prevail. The American Negro, the Hindu, the Irish, the Egyptian would still suffer oppression. But if there were enough freedom from external danger, the mind of the West would be freed for the solution of these questions.[114]

And to those who feared that having once tasted the heady wine of power they would get drunk with it and would eventually lose touch with their democratic heritage, he impatiently said: "If that is the kind of people we are, how impudent of us to say one word in criticism of the military empires."[115] On the eve of World War II he told the American people that history had decreed greatness for them. They had to open their eyes and see the "splendor of their destiny." They had to awaken to the fact that they had "the opportunity, the power and the responsibilities of a very great nation at the center of the civilized world."[116] And in *The Public Philosophy*, as we have seen, Lippmann clearly implies that a contender for power who seeks to rule mankind should not be censured if he intends to use his preponderant

[114] Walter Lippmann, "What Program Shall the United States Stand for in International Relations," *Annals of the American Academy of Political and Social Science*, Vol. 66, No. 155 (July 1916), pp. 64–65.

[115] *The Stakes of Diplomacy*, p. 223.

[116] Walter Lippmann, "The American Destiny," *Life*, Vol. 6, No. 23 (June 5, 1939), p. 73. Also see "America and the World," *Life*, Vol. 7, No. 23 (June 3, 1940), p. 103.

position to develop, improve and make more beautiful the world which he governs.

Behind Lippmann's desire to see the democracies take charge of the world is the conviction that having gained power they would use it to serve the cause of peace, freedom and justice. They would promote the rule of law, for that is their way of life. They would serve the cause of peace because the common man, who has nothing to gain by wars of conquest, and who in the democracies has the right and the opportunity to examine the policies of his government, would not sanction such wars.[117] Moreover, the freedom of debate and expression in democratic societies makes it virtually impossible for them to wage aggressive war or to catch their victim by surprise.[118]

It is interesting to note here that until about the beginning of the nuclear age, Lippmann had also another argument. The democracies could be trusted to promote peace and freedom for mankind because they wielded a form of force— sea power—which was irresistible in conflict, and yet could not be used "to conscript and enslave" alien people. There were exceptions, to be sure. Nevertheless, "the record of history proves that under the aegis of sea power alone is there progress toward freedom."[119] The British Empire, he wrote in 1940, lay in all the seas, and it was a growing community of increasingly independent states. It was significant that Ireland had been able to remain neutral while the Empire fought for its existence. But how different was the fate of the "land-locked Czechs and Poles who live in the midst of the German and Russian land power."[120] He concluded:

[117] *The Political Scene,* p. 43.
[118] T and T, July 19, 1955.
[119] "The Weapon of Freedom," *Life,* Vol. 9, No. 18 (October 28, 1940), p. 112.
[120] *Ibid.*

The realm of sea power is the realm of human freedom: in the realm of sea power there is law and there is order which regulate the affairs of men without regimenting their lives or occupying their homes or breaking their spirits.[121]

It is quite clear that Lippmann would like to see an enlightened, humane and liberal aristocracy take the world—or the greater part of it—under its wing and rule it in the manner of "liberal" rather than popular democracy.[122] The principle of the balance of power fits well into this pattern. While the managing powers, backed by irresistible force, rule the world in the interest of mankind, a less powerful minority, within or beyond their jurisdiction, would perform the function of an opposition party. The rulers would balance the power of groups and factions within the empire so as to regulate their rivalries and to prevent any one of them from devouring the rest. They would fill the indispensable position of an unchallenged, disinterested balancer who uses his power to preserve and improve the system. The existence of an opposition, ready to exploit discontent in the empire in order to unseat the ruling aristocracy, would serve to keep the latter on the path of disinterestedness.

We may submit that this is the only framework in which the balance of power can promote the ends of the good society. We have seen that as between independent entities it guarantees neither peace, nor freedom, nor justice. What is more, it tends to turn back the wheels of civilization and to retard human progress.[123] Thus it is not without significance that most eighteenth-century writers on the subject conceived of Europe as a "system," a "commonwealth," a "union" or a

---

[121] *Ibid.*

[122] For a discussion of liberal democracy see Chapter VII.

[123] In a world of sovereign nation-states, says Professor Toynbee, "the Balance of Power operates in a general way to keep the average calibre of States low in terms of every criterion for the measurement of power: in territory, population and wealth. For any state which threatens to increase

"family" of nations bound together by the ties of a common code of religion and ethics. In such a Europe, they argued, the balance of power would operate to safeguard the rights and possessions of the European princes. One may infer that they did not look upon the balance of power as a secular, amoral principle that could protect the independence of states which bowed to no common spiritual or temporal authority but were all independent and sovereign, bearing no relation to one another except rivalry. Security in the enjoyment of rights and possessions can be attained only in some kind of ordered society, not in the "state of nature." One would therefore think that the balance of power should, in order to operate as a reliable means of obtaining such security, call for the establishment of a system in which the member units submitted to a common higher authority— religious, moral or political. Even in this world of sovereign nation-states, when a government consciously accepts the principle of balance as a guide to policy, it comes

on the threshold of conceding that the stability of the community of states is an interest superior to its domestic interests. Doubtless it concedes this only because it believes that stability is a *sine qua non* of its own survival. The concession is, however, an enlightenment of self-interest which approaches altruism or the submergence of the self in a larger whole.[124]

It follows that before the balance of power can operate as the structural principle of good government, either there must evolve a system of liberal democracy all over the world or, failing that, the existing powerful democracies must establish something akin to a world state. In this age of fierce conflict

---

its calibre above the prevailing average becomes subject, almost automatically, to pressure from all the other states within reach." Arnold J. Toynbee, *A Study of History* (one-volume abridgment), (New York: Oxford University Press, 1947), p. 233.

[124] Quincy Wright, *A Study of War*, Vol. II, p. 749.

between democracy and totalitarianism, it takes an extraordinary amount of optimism to expect that the peoples of the world will, in the foreseeable future, voluntarily embrace the ideals of liberalism and thus give themselves a set of common political values. Nor is it any more certain that the Western democracies will soon overwhelm the tremendous forces that are arrayed against them, and become the governors and guardians of mankind. But assuming for the sake of argument that they will do so, we can still not count on them to rule the world altruistically, or to employ the mechanism of the balance of power as the structural principle of public order in the good society. In the first place, it is not a proved fact that democratic states are inherently generous, selfless or even peace-loving. In fact, the proposition is seriously challenged in certain quarters. Hamilton criticized it in his advocacy of the Union versus the Confederation, saying:

There are still to be found visionary or designing men who stand ready to advocate the paradox of perpetual peace between the states. The genius of republics, say they, is pacific; the spirit of commerce has a tendency to soften the manners of men, and to extinguish those inflammable humors which have so often kindled into war. . . . Have republics in practice been less addicted to war than monarchies? Are not the former administered by men as well as the latter? . . . Are not popular assemblies frequently subject to the impulses of rage, resentment, jealousy, avarice, and of other irregular and violent propensities?[125]

It is true that freedom of debate makes it well-nigh impossible for a democracy to launch a surprise attack on its enemy. It is also true that a democratic people will not be pushed into an aggressive war by their government if they do not want it. But freedom of debate cannot ensure that people will not want war. Sea power, unaided by land power,

[125] *The Federalist Papers* (The Federalist No. 6), p. 29.

may not be a good instrument for subjugating alien peoples. However, this is only one of its limitations, not a proof that its holder is necessarily virtuous and contented, free from greed and ambition. It would be difficult to establish that sea power exercised a moderating effect on the aggressive imperialism of Germany and Japan between the two world wars. Furthermore, the democracies cannot convert mankind to the gospel of liberalism unless they first set things right in their own house, which according to Lippmann is in a state of grave disorder. As we shall see in a subsequent chapter, he maintains that they have lost touch with the traditions of civility and fallen prey to Jacobinism. Their governments are paralyzed, unable to give leadership and direction, and unfit to meet the crises of our times.

When all is said, it seems that in the present context of world affairs and organization, Lippman's concept of the balance of power as the structural principle of public order in the good society is relevant to international politics only as an ideal which men may cherish and strive to realize. It is not a tool of analysis for understanding the behavior of sovereign states.

What is then the meaning or the significance of the principle of the balance of power in a world torn asunder by the rivalries of sovereign independent states? It means that in a city where robbers abound, citizens must keep watch and fortify themselves as best as they can. It is a dictate of plain common sense that where there is no law, and no one to enforce the law if there had been any, men must take adequate precautions to safeguard their lives and protect their possessions. Individually, or in concert with others, they must acquire the kind and the amount of power needed to subdue the robber and restrain the tyrant.

It may be that the mechanism of the balance of power is unreliable as a means of protecting national independence and security because sooner or later it is likely to break down. But we must remember that mortal men cannot seal a given arrangement of affairs once for all in a world where everything moves and changes. The cyclical process of construction, decay, collapse and reconstruction is an integral part of life on this planet. Balances of power will be made, broken and remade, and thus the cycle will go on. And if the process of change in international relations is sometimes violent and painful, the fault lies not with the mechanism of the balance but with the organizational structure of the international society.

Lippmann views the balance of power in a number of ways. In the short run, while the political organization of the world remains unchanged, the mechanism of the balance is the best available instrument which nation-states can employ to defend their vital interests. It is complicated and difficult to operate. Yet it is more reliable as an instrument of defense than such institutional arrangements as collective security, which is almost completely unworkable. In the long-range view, Lippmann visualizes a state of affairs in which the world, or the greater part of it, will become one political unit living under a liberal form of government. In this context, the balance of power serves to ensure that rulers do not become tyrants, and that they rule according to law. It guarantees freedom, not sovereign independence. It is no longer an instrument of aggression and defense; it has become a principle of government. There is an intermediary stage between the immediate reality and the distant ideal, between the present system of sovereign nation-states and the universal state. This is the world of regionalism and of a complex balance of power in which the nation-state gives way to great associations of states as the participating unit in international relations.

V

Regionalism

THE WORLD OF NATION-STATES IS THE THEATRE OF CONFLICT
and of wars of destruction between organized groups of
mankind. Institutional arrangements intended to bring international rivalry under the civilizing influence of law have
had only limited success. The politics of power, designed to
mitigate or compose the conflict, affords only a precariously
uncertain protection against the onslaught of ambitious and
aggressive force.

At one time the Western peoples turned to the nation-
state as the guardian and promoter of their spiritual and
material cultures. Today, millions in Asia are eagerly tread-
ing the same path. Yet certain quarters advance the view
that the nation-state, as a unit of human political organization, has already become obsolete.[1] It cannot assure its mem-

[1] Professor Carr observes that the nation-state which "was created by a
cumulative process of combination between individuals to protect themselves against the devastating consequences of unfettered economic individ-
ualism has become in its turn a threat to the security and well-being of the
individual . . ." *Nationalism and After*, pp. 47–48.

Raymond Aron sees in the continued division of Europe into separate
sovereign states a grave obstacle to its development and progress in not
only the political and economic but also the cultral sphere: "[Nation-
states] no longer exist at the advanced level of our epoch; their fate is
similar to that of the feudal principalities in the age of national states.

187

bers that freedom from fear, want and ignorance which is indispensable to the enrichment of their lives and the development of their personalities.

What is the alternative to the nation-state as the operative unit in international affairs? Lippmann, together with several other writers,[2] offers regionalism as the only escape from the dilemma posed by the inability of the nation-state to answer the various aspirations of its people and the unwillingness of men to merge their separate sovereignties in order to create a world-wide political union. The national frontier symbolizes, and thus accentuates, the separateness of nations and their interests. However, among certain groups of nations the community of interests outdoes the conflict of interests, enabling them to cooperate in the pursuit of common objectives. Lippmann suggests that it is here, among these nations, that one should begin to build institutions which may eventually replace the modern nation-state. The test of whether the ground is fertile for regional cooperation and organization is not whether a complete harmony of interests prevails among the member nations. The test is whether, when their common

They become mere stakes in the game of power between the empires—just as the cities of Italy and Germany became pawns of the rivalry between the Kings of France and Spain in the sixteenth century. . . . For how many years will intellectuals be crushed by material difficulties—so unfavorable to leisure and creative activities? When will that minimum of security and comfort—without which culture appears as something superfluous—be reestablished? . . . Wars of nationalities in the epoch of empires: Europe condemns itself to death . . . because it remains a prisoner of the principle of yesterday." Raymond Aron, "Can Europe Achieve Political Unity?," *Modern Review*, Vol. 1, No. 7 (September 1947), pp. 492–493.

[2] For instance, K. M. Panikkar, a prominent Indian geo-politician and diplomatist, maintains that "the work of economic, social and cultural advancement can be undertaken only on a regional basis. The conditions of the different regions in the world differ so much that the promotion of higher standards of living, for example, has a different meaning in relation to the people of South East Asia to what it has in European countries." *Regionalism and Security* (New Delhi: Indian Council of World Affairs, 1948), p. 5.

interests are threatened, they find themselves acting together.
For example, the vital interests of the British nations, the
American nations, and the Latin nations are so interwoven "by
geography, by strategic necessity, and by historic formation
that their permanent interests are, when tested in the fires
of total war, inseparable."[3]

In *U.S. Foreign Policy*, and again in *U.S. War Aims*,
Lippmann observed that regional groupings of states should
not be too difficult to bring about since one of them, the
Altantic Community, already existed and others, especially
the Russian orbit, were emerging.[4] It would be futile, even
dangerous, to ignore them or to try to dissolve them. For only
by perfecting them could we make any progress toward
stabilizing international relations. In the postwar period
Lippmann continued to emphasize that regional groupings,
such as the Atlantic Community, had become a living reality which no universalist formula could undo. In 1949 he
observed that the United States government should not attempt to justify the Atlantic Pact on the legalistic ground
that it derived from Articles 51 and 52 of the United Nations
Charter. Rather, it should tell the critics of the Pact that
"the formation of these blocs is an historic development
unforeseen and undesired in 1945, to which the U.N. is
now compelled to adjust itself."[5] The blocs and groupings,
he pointed out, already existed in the United Nations, and
it was therefore vain to deplore and denounce them.

It would appear that the harmony of interests which forms
the core of Lippmann's ideas on regionalism is strategic in
character. The "communities" or the "associations of states,"
as he calls them, constitute separate strategic systems. A
strategic system exists when the defense of its members is

[3] *U.S. Foreign Policy*, p. 132.
[4] *Ibid.*, Chapter VII and *U.S. War Aims*, Chapters VII and VIII.
[5] T and T, April 11, 1949.

so interdependent and interrelated that when one is in peril, the others are in peril too. Britain, France, Canada and the United States may think in time of peace that they can go their separate ways, but in war they must stand together.[6] In *U.S. War Aims* Lippmann noted that Russia was the nucleus of another regional community. The strategic interests of the East European states were linked not with the Atlantic Community but with the land power of the Soviet Union. The two world wars, he said, had proved that the Western nations could not safeguard peace east of the Rhine or prevent a German invasion of Eastern Europe and Russia. The aid which Great Britain and the United States had given the Soviet Union did not alter the fact that German armies could not be expelled from East European and Russian territory without the exertions of the Red Army and the sacrifices of the Russian people. One might then conclude that Russia lived in and made part of a strategic system separate from the Atlantic powers.[7] China was the nucleus of another community. Eventually, still other constellations might form in the Hindu and Moslem worlds, but that possibility belonged to the more distant future.[8]

Regions constitute the best areas for international cooperation since their member states share in common what is undoubtedly the supreme national interest of each of them, that is to say, survival. However, the bond of strategic necessity need not be, and in some cases is not, the only one which binds them together. It may be reinforced by a common history, language, political tradition or cultural heritage.[9]

Apart from the fact that regional organizations facilitate international cooperation, there is another compelling reason

[6] *U.S. War Aims*, pp. 129–133.
[7] *Ibid.*, pp. 89–90.
[8] *Ibid.*, p. 65.
[9] *Ibid.*, pp. 86–87.

to encourage their growth. Lippmann maintains that rivalry between nations is compounded by their search for allies. The uncertain and transient nature of foreign alignments and friendships exerts an unstabilizing effect on international relations. The remedy for shifting alliances is to stabilize them, and regionalism seeks to do just that. Each state in the region, Lippmann suggests, should recognize that it belongs to one and only one larger strategic neighborhood with whose members it must coordinate its military defense and foreign policy. The world should know that the allegiance of this particular state is not open to bids.[10] In *U.S. War Aims* Lippmann observed that the issues of war and peace in the postwar period would hinge upon the policies which the two great powers, the United States and the Soviet Union, pursued with respect to their alliances. They could have peace if they used their alliances to stabilize the foreign policies of their allies. They would have war if either of them reached out for allies in the orbit of the other.[11]

Lippmann argues that since the region is primarily a strategic system, it is axiomatic that its members must outlaw war among themselves. This "rule of reason" has long characterized Canadian-American relations. But when in the twenties Britain would not suffer a strong France, and the two great English-speaking democracies busied themselves with containing each other's naval power, the Western world committed follies for which it had to pay an exorbitant price. Writing in 1944, Lippmann submitted that in the future it would be equally foolish for, say, Holland, Belgium and Norway to spend their energies on building defenses against Britain and France. The weaker states in the regional family could become secure only by taking their places in the defensive system to which they belonged. Their contribution "to

[10] *U.S. War Aims*, p. 140.
[11] *Ibid.*, p. 135.

the common defense against attack from outside is the surest guaranty of their independence and their moral equality within the community."[12] The lesson of experience dictated that, instead of limiting each other's armaments, regional powers would have to agree upon minimum contributions which each, according to its means and resources, would make toward their common security. Since, in combat, regional forces would operate as a combined force, they must be planned and designed accordingly. It would, for instance, be necessary to maintain combined staffs, intelligence services and military planning boards.[13]

Nor could the members of a regional organization have divergent foreign policies, since all would be involved if any one of them went to war with an extra-regional great power. Therefore, they must have frequent consultations in order to reach agreement on measures which might possibly lead to war. This did not mean that foreign policies should be completely identical in scope and substance. Canada and Brazil would not have the same kind of European connections as France. But it did mean that no state, let us say, in the Atlantic Community should make or renounce a major commitment in the outside world without consulting the others. Powers in the regional family, great and small alike, must change their old habits of acting independently in foreign affairs so that they could present a united front to the extra-regional states on all substantive issues. It was the non-observance of this principle which placed the dominions in the Commonwealth in a dilemma at the outbreak of World War II: to fight or not to fight on the side of the mother country in a war which they had no share in bringing about. But in the postwar period, wrote Lippmann, the dilemma could not be resolved within the Commonwealth.

[12] *Ibid.,* p. 70.
[13] *Ibid.,* p. 71.

"The United States, the other American republics, France, the Low Countries, Norway, and others as well, cannot be left out in framing the policies which Great Britain and the dominions adopt."[14]

The need to evolve and formulate a common military and foreign policy would require what might be called "organic consultation"—

something more elastic than a formal treaty of alliance, and something much less than political federation—a network of agreements and understandings that, as a matter of right, there will be a habitual exchange of information and views in the ordinary routine of foreign offices, the war offices, and the departments and agencies which regulate international commerce.[15]

Lippmann defended this somewhat loose apparatus for regional consultation and coordination on the ground that the Atlantic Community could not become an empire ruled from one capital. It must remain an organization of free states which were bound together only by a realization of their common interests. He conceded that this freedom weakened them in their dealings with military empires: it had brought them perilously close to destruction at the hands of Germany and Japan. Yet they must retain this freedom, for it "is their moral passport among the peoples of the earth, the guaranty that they will not unite for aggression and domination. They can unite only in self-defense."[16] In regard to the Soviet

[14] Ibid., p. 76.
[15] U.S. War Aims, pp. 76–77.
[16] Ibid., p. 78. It will be noticed that Lippmann's design of the machinery which is to effect intra-regional cooperation closely follows the classical British pattern. "The forms of association with which the British are familiar are the Commonwealth and the 'combined' agencies of the second world war. . . . The form of cooperation that has grown up between the independent members of the Commonwealth is loose and informal, and at the same time close, in some ways resembling cooperation between two departments of a single government. It is based on a continuous and voluminous exchange of telegrams on all aspects of external

orbit, Lippmann expressed the hope that Stalin would keep his wartime promises to pursue a democratic foreign policy, which meant genuine respect for the independence of other states and non-intervention in their internal affairs.[17]

Some writers on the subject maintain that regionalism necessarily leads to the hegemony of a great power over its small neighbors. We have noted above Lippmann's assertion that a regional community must remain an association of free states. As the argument in *U.S. War Aims* proceeds he elaborates, and in the process somewhat modifies, his position. Regional powers, he says, must act the good neighbor toward one another. He defines the "good neighbor" relationship as being one in which the small states and the leading great power of the neighborhood become allies in peace and war. The great power provides that security from external aggression which no small state can provide for itself. The small state reciprocates by making available strategic facilities, such as bases, needed for common defense. In addition, it takes all possible steps to ensure that it does not permit on its territory spies, intriguers and saboteurs working to injure its great neighbor. Lippmann believes that if the small state makes this "critical" contribution to the common defense of the neighborhood, its independence and prosperity will become a vital interest of the great power. For then its usefulness to the community increases in direct proportion to increments in the health and vigor of its national life. There

---

affairs, a few standing committees mainly for the elucidation of information which cannot be clearly conveyed by telegram, and conferences at the ministerial or official level convened as occasion may require for consultation and the exchange of views, but without the power to take binding decisions. This is a form of cooperation which the British understand and which they prefer in matters where close day to day planning is not required." Henry L. Roberts and Paul A. Wilson, *Britain and the United States: Problems in Cooperation*, pp. 138–139.

[17] *U.S. War Aims*, pp. 142–144.

would be no reason for the great state to subjugate and rule the small state, because the more independent the latter is, and therefore the more conscious it is of its independence, the more jealously it will guard itself against the enemies of the region, who are *ipso facto* the enemies of the leading member of the regional family. Therefore,

when we say that we are the champions of the rights of small nations, we must particularize. We must add that they can now assure their rights only by a general acceptance of the duties of the Good Neighbor Policy. We must not, as many do, identify the rights of small nations with their right to have an "independent" foreign policy, that is to say one which manipulates the balance of power among great states.[18]

In a previous chapter we have seen that Lippmann advocates a complex balance-of-power system composed of great states possessing more or less equal power, each heading a group of states in a region or a sphere of influence. He urges that these regions, these "historic communities of states," should also be the constituent members of the universal society.[19] In *U.S. War Aims* he proposed that regional organizations should settle the issues that were local to them, and should take to the world organization only those matters that had a global significance.[20] As a rule, they should consult "at the higher level after they have consulted at the lower levels, deliberating not as disparate sovereign states but as communities which have in the end a common interest."[21] According to the Wilsonian dogma, a dispute, say, between

[18] *U.S. War Aims,* p. 84. For a similar view of the rights and obligations of small states in a regional organization, see Carr, *Nationalism and After,* pp. 57–58.

[19] *U.S. War Aims,* p. 193.

[20] Regionalists generally take this position. See, for instance, Professor Arnold Brecht, "Regionalism within World Organization," in *Regionalism and World Organization: A Symposium* (Washington: American Council of Public Affairs, 1944), p. 23.

[21] *U.S. War Aims,* p. 193.

America and Panama should be settled collectively by an assembly of mankind. Yet North Americans would not wish to have it settled that way. They would invite Mexico and Brazil to participate in composing the dispute. But they would resent Russian or Chinese intervention in the matter. They would do so because, whereas Mexico and Brazil belonged to the same neighborhood and therefore had a stake in its peace and tranquillity, Russia and China would be outsiders.[22] If the latter were to have a hand in settling the dispute, as they would if it were taken to the universal society, the American-Panamanian dispute would at once become entangled with all other international disputes. How the Soviet Union voted on it would depend on how the United States voted on some Russian-Iranian dispute. Thus, what started out as a negotiable and soluble local issue would end up as an insoluble global issue.

Lippmann concedes that the great power in the region may pressure a weak neighbor into accepting settlements which are not completely just and fair to the latter. But there is no reason to think, he submits, that the small state would get any more justice from the world organization which is bound to be under pressure from not one but several great powers. Worse still, the world organization may not be able to settle

[22] *Ibid.*, p. 188. Taking substantially the same position as Lippmann does, Professor Shotwell observes that "in the field of security, regional organizations might constitute a first line of defense against local wars arising out of the quarrels of neighboring nations because they would be based upon the direct interest of each state in both its own immediate safety and in its intercourse with nations close at hand. . . . Nations close at hand have a more immediate interest in maintaining a good neighborhood than those at great distances from the locality in which disturbances are threatened." James T. Shotwell, *The Great Decision* (New York: The Macmillan Company, 1944), p. 215.

Lippmann is correct in assuming that in an American-Panamanian dispute Americans would call upon Mexico and Brazil, rather than China and Russia, to come in as mediators. But it does not follow that the Panamanians would wish to do the same.

the issue at all, in which event the small state would lose, for all practical purposes, the whole rather than a part of its claim. The unsolved issue would become "an open sore, one among many, infected with the virus of global war."[23]

In the postwar period, Lippmann has reiterated the same thesis. In 1949 he wrote:

These [regional] blocs, and not the fifty-odd separate, sovereign, and theoretically equal states, are the members of the U.N. That is not what the Charter says. . . . But that is what the organization has become—what in the view of some of us it was always bound to become. . . . For a world organization designed to operate by the collective action of more than fifty states as different in size, power and internal structure as the Soviet Union and Yemen . . . is an abstraction and a fiction. It never could hope to deal with the real conflicts of mankind. They can be dealt with only by the great historic communities of nations that have developed through vital necessity and by common tradition over long periods of time. The function of a world organization is to promote agreement among these communities.[24]

The critics of regionalism object that it would lead to the development of gigantic constellations which would fight titantic wars.[25] In *U.S. War Aims* Lippmann implied that the dread of mutual devastation would render war relatively useless as an instrument of national policy. The justified fear that nothing would be gained and nothing decided in a war, which would nevertheless cripple the belligerents, would further dissuade the great powers from resorting to it. Of course, no one could be perfectly certain that they would never fight. But one could say that

[23] *U.S. War Aims,* p. 189.
[24] T and T, April 11, 1949.
[25] See, for instance, Arthur C. Millspaugh, *Peace Plans and American Choices* (Washington, D.C.: The Brookings Institution, 1942), pp. 52–53. It should be noted that the objection has lost much of its force in the 1960's, since war between nuclear powers cannot be anything but titantic, irrespective of whether we accept or reject regionalism.

to stabilize the alliances and military establishments of all states is to remove the most provoking forms of interference and intervention which, because they menace the vital security of great states, are a cause of great wars.[26]

Concluding his argument in *U.S. War Aims*, Lippmann observed that regionalism alone provided an escape from the inadequacies of the nation-state and the impracticability of a world state. It mitigated the "horrid antithesis" between fanatic nationalism and romantic internationalism. For regionalism did not call upon peoples to give up their local loyalties for the sake of a world patriotism.

No one is asked to transfer his allegiance from his own country to a new cosmopolitan fatherland. As he is a good patriot, so he is a good neighbor, and by being a good neighbor he is loyal to the laws, the usages, and the requirements of the universal society.[27]

We must build the universal society not on the basis of visionary sentimentalism but on the secure and stable foundations of reality, beginning with the nation-state and the historic communities of states.

The foregoing statement of Lippmann's views on regionalism, as he develops them in *U.S. Foreign Policy* and *U.S. War Aims*, would indicate that he envisaged intra-regional cooperation vast in scope. Members of the regional community had to have a common foreign policy, a common military policy, and a common commercial policy in relation to the outside world. It should be noted that in contradistinction to several contemporary advocates of regionalism, he did not call for the political union of states in a region. In fact, he opposed the idea of a federal union for Europe after the war. He expected common policies to emerge from "frequent consultation" between member governments. It would become

[26] *U.S. War Aims*, p. 191.
[27] *Ibid.*, pp. 193–194.

the "ordinary routine" of foreign offices, war offices and agencies concerned with international commerce to have "as a matter of right" a "habitual" exchange of information and views. The duty to consult and the right to be consulted would be established by a "network of agreements and understandings."

Considering that foreign affairs, defense and international economic relations together constitute by far the most important part of the functional jurisdiction of a modern state, it seems that in *U.S. War Aims* Lippmann proposes to confer upon the regional community the benefits of common governance without giving it the apparatus of a common government. It is somewhat surprising that at this time he considered voluntary cooperation between separate sovereignties, and forced cooperation in a military empire, as the only alternatives, and did not seriously consider the possibility of one or more federal unions.

Some of these gaps in Lippmann's theory of regionalism disappear if, alongside his advice that states in the regional community should be free, we consider his exhortation that they must act the good neighbor in their relations with one another. In these relations, as we have noticed, the small state renounces in favor of the great power in the region its right to pursue an independent foreign and military policy. It also undertakes to combat forces working on its territory against the big neighbor. These hostile elements need not be of foreign origin. If its own citizens, press or officials begin to agitate against the great power, it should restrain them. The small state in this scheme of things becomes a willing satellite of the leading state in the region. Lippmann says that small states can assure their rights only by accepting the duties of the good neighbor. Does he mean that if they do not discharge these duties, the great power may rightfully coerce them into doing its will? He does not rule out coercion, for as we have noted he concedes that might would make right in certain spheres of intra-regional relations, such as the settlement of disputes between the great power and its small neighbors. We may then conclude that Lippmann's "region" is a version of what is commonly known as a sphere of influence.[28] He might protest that it is a partnership. Yet if we consider that the junior partners in this enterprise do not make but merely carry out policy, and that they can be compelled into compliance, which must mean that they lose even their "moral equality" if they choose not to "cooperate," it would be a mere euphemism to describe the relation as a partnership.

It will be seen that the theory of regionalism which Lippmann developed in *U.S. War Aims* was readily applicable to the proposed Soviet orbit. This region was to consist of Russia and a relatively small number of East European states.[29] The latter were to discharge the duties of the good neighbor, and the Soviet Union, in turn, was to give them security, a foreign policy and autonomy in internal affairs. The same might also be said of the United States in relation to Latin America. However, it is not quite clear how Lippmann intended to apply the good neighbor principle outside the Soviet orbit and the Western Hemisphere, especially

[28] The phrase, it is true, was characteristically used to describe the hegemony of great European powers over some of the less advanced countries of Asia and Africa. During the 1930's, however, its connotation was extended by popular usage "to cover the relations between small European states and great powers seeking to control their foreign policies without the formality of an alliance or protectorate. Austria and Hungary were thus said to be within the Italian sphere of influence early in 1934." Frederick L. Schuman, "Spheres of Influence," *Encyclopedia of the Social Sciences* (New York: The Macmillan Company, 1937), Vol. XIII, p. 297.

[29] "The boundaries of the Russian orbit," wrote Lippmann, "are not clearly defined. But it certainly extends from Prague to Vladivostok, from Eastern Europe to the shores of Eastern Asia, and its heart is the Soviet Union." It should be made clear that China was not included in the proposed Russian orbit, for there was to be a separate Chinese orbit. *U.S. War Aims*, pp. 89, 92–93.

to relations between the great Western powers. He could not have believed that the United States would dictate policy to the British Empire or vice versa. One would think that he viewed the problem of regionalism with regard to the Atlantic Community on two planes. On the one hand there were the subdivisions, so to speak, of this large community— the Inter-American System, the British Commonwealth of Nations and Western Europe—where great powers would preside over the foreign and military affairs of their junior partners. On the other hand, there was the association of the great powers themselves. They would act toward one another as equals. Cooperation between them would be voluntary, sustained by a realization of common interests and facilitated by consultation and exchange of views. With or without the aid of joint planning boards, they would turn out common military and foreign policies, which each would pass on to its "good neighbors." The Atlantic Community was then something of a super-region—an association of regional communities.

With most writers on the subject the regional organization is a useful but definitely subordinate adjunct of the world organization. It is intended primarily to deal with local disputes, and thus to lessen the work load of the parent organization. Lippmann's regionalism, on the other hand, does not derive from or depend upon the universal society. The regions are not the satellites of the general international body: they are rather the pivots around which the latter revolves. They, and not the individual nation-states, are its constituent members. They would live on even if the world organization disintegrated. Nor are regional organizations in Lippmann's scheme of things primarily concerned with the settlement of local disputes. For normally there would be no such disputes, war between the members of a region being outlawed. Regional planners and authorities would be concerned primarily with fortifying the region against possible aggression from other regions.

It should be stated here that regionalism was a subject much discussed in American, British and European official circles during 1943–1944, when Lippmann was writing his *U.S. Foreign Policy* and *U.S. War Aims*. Led by Sumner Welles, a group of men in the State Department were pressing for a postwar world order based on regional organizations, which would work under the "ultimate control" of a supreme council composed of the four great powers and seven regional representatives.[30] Winston Churchill took a position which bore some remarkable similarities to Lippmann's thesis. In his public statements as well as in his confidential messages to President Roosevelt, he insisted that

it would be better to start by building up purely regional organizations which could collaborate if need arose, but which should remain autonomous for an indefinite time, or at least until it was clear whether a supreme international authority could be successfully set up over them.[31]

At a luncheon at the British Embassy in Washington on May 22, 1943, Sir Winston outlined his plan to a group of

[30] Welles records: "Personally, I had come to believe that . . . the new world organization [should rest] upon a foundation of regional organizations. . . . Only if these regional systems proved unable to compose disputes or to restrain an aggressor would the supreme universal authority be required to intervene. In that manner each state in every region, no matter how weak it might be, would be required as well as enabled to contribute in proportion to its resources the assistance needed in maintaining regional, and world, peace. . . . The supreme executive agency of the organization should be composed of eleven members, seven of these representing regional systems, each of the seven members to be elected periodically by all the states comprising the region which he represented. The remaining four members were allotted to the United States, the Soviet Union, Great Britain and China." Sumner Welles, *Where Are We Heading?* (New York: Harper and Brothers, 1946), pp. 23–24. Also see, by the same author, *Seven Decisions that Shaped History* (New York: Harper and Brothers, 1950), Chapter VII.

[31] Sumner Welles, *Seven Decisions that Shaped History*, p. 172.

American Senators and high-ranking officials, including Senator Connally, Secretary Stimson, and Under Secretary of State Welles. He favored the creation of three regional organizations, one each for the Western Hemisphere, Europe and Asia. The world council, he thought, should consist only of Great Britain, Russia and the United States, but if necessary it could be enlarged to include China and the representatives of the regional organizations. "The central idea of the structure was that of a three-legged stool—the World Council resting on three Regional Councils."[32] Churchill went on to observe that the organization of world security did not preclude special friendships between like-minded nations. He told his guests that he

could see small hope for the world unless the United States and the British Commonwealth worked together in fraternal association. . . . I looked forward therefore to an extension of the common use of bases for the common defence of common interests. . . . I made two further suggestions, both of which carried warm assent. First, that after the war we should continue the practice of Combined Staff conversations, and, second, that we should by constant contact take whatever steps were necessary to ensure that the main lines of our foreign policy ran closely together.[33]

At this time, several Western European states also conveyed to the State Department their views on postwar international organization, which in most cases were regional rather than universal. Sumner Welles recalls that

the governments of the occupied countries of Western Europe leaned definitely to that kind of an Atlantic community of nations that Mr. Walter Lippman has so eloquently urged upon us. The basic concept was that the nations of the Western Hemisphere

[32] Winston Churchill, *The Hinge of Fate* (Boston: Houghton Mifflin Company, 1950), p. 804.
[33] *Ibid.*, pp. 806–807.

and of Western Europe that are primarily concerned in the Atlantic should join together in a league for the maintenance of peace in the Atlantic, both south as well as north, and that this Atlantic community of nations should become one of a series of communities, all of which would tend to create a new balance of power—a balance between continents.[34]

The Atlantic Community

For fifty years, albeit with noticeable interruptions, Lippmann has expounded and publicized the thesis that the countries located on the shores of the Atlantic constitute a community, sharing a common heritage of socio-political traditions and foremost strategic interests. It would be instructive to follow the train of his thought on the subject; it should give us an insight into the nature of the Atlantic Community as he conceives it, and indicate the conditions under which it may be expected to live and grow in the thinking of Western men.

In an unpublished address at Philadelphia on May 6, 1949, Lippmann asserted that "the existence of the Atlantic Community was first discerned in this country during the anxious months of decision and deliberation which preceded our entrance into the First World War."[35] Some writers had proclaimed the desirability of fortifying the "Atlantic System" long before the fateful shot was fired at Sarajevo. However, Lippmann's statement is correct insofar as it relates to his own writings. In December 1915 he noted that Americans were haunted and made ashamed by their indecision and inaction in the supreme crisis of their lives. The cause of their painful uneasiness lay in the failure of the administration to formulate a positive policy in regard to the current war, in the

[34] *Where Are We Heading?*, pp. 26–27.
[35] Quoted in Norman D. Palmer and Howard C. Perkins, *International Relations* (Boston: Houghton Mifflin Company, 1953), p. 789.

essentially negative injunction of President Wilson that the nation remain neutral in thought as well as in act. Yet at the end of 1915, Lippmann himself had nothing to offer as a substitute for passive neutrality. He concluded his remarks with the observation that no one could say "whether it was humanly possible for Mr. Wilson to give our neutrality a positive meaning."[36] A month later he hinted that the British command of the seas had a bearing on American vital interests. The United States, he wrote, could not formulate a meaningful foreign policy without making up her mind whether she would support or oppose British sea power or make a working arrangement with it. Her guaranties for Pan-America were bluffs and her military plans were empty guesses unless she knew where Great Britain would stand in relation to them. He submitted:

The administration is at a cross road where it must decide . . . the supreme issue of our foreign policy for years to come. On the courage and insight that inspire that decision may depend our own safety and the peace of the world. . . . Its policy toward Great Britain will be a crowning disaster unless that policy is determined by a vision of the Anglo-American future.[37]

It will be seen that Lippmann was not yet ready to urge unequivocally that Washington join forces with London in order to prevent the control of the seas from passing into the hands of illiberal Germany. He left it to the imagination of his readers whether the proposed Anglo-American entente should take effect forthwith or after the war. He was clearer when addressing the American Academy of Political and Social Science in 1916:

Our security from invasion exists so long as no potential enemy

[36] Walter Lippmann, "Uneasy America," New Republic, Vol. 5, No. 60, (December 25, 1915), p. 196.
[37] Walter Lippmann, "Washington Notes," New Republic, Vol. 5, No. 65, (January 29, 1916), p. 335.

can command the seas against us. . . . Had the Allies lost command of the seas, the suffering of America and most of the neutral world would have been enormous.[38]

The "potential enemy" was obviously none other than Germany. Lippmann went on to say that if the administration had any "wisdom and humanity" it would seek the friendship of the British Empire, which encompassed one-fourth of the human race. In the course of the same address he made a statement which might well be regarded as the forerunner of his thesis regarding the Atlantic Community.

The British Isles, Canada, Australia, New Zealand, South Africa and the United States must share and preserve the command of the seas. . . . It is in the power of the United States and Great Britain to establish such an area of security that the unaggressive nations will be drawn towards them. . . . All larger schemes, such as those for a League of Peace with Permanent Courts of Arbitration and Conciliation must rest, it seems to me, on the unity and supremacy of sea power concentrated in the hands of the liberal powers of the West. They may be workable, but they will be workable only if the British Empire, the United States, France, Pan-America, and ultimately Germany are knit together, their economic conflicts compromised, their military resources pooled in a league of the West.[39]

[38] Walter Lippmann, "What Program Shall the United States Stand for in International Relations?," *Annals of the American Academy of Political and Social Science,* Vol. 66, No. 155 (July 1916), p. 68.

[39] Lippmann, "What Program Shall the United States Stand for in International Relations?," pp. 69–70. Writing about a year earlier, George Louis Beer had made a somewhat similar proposal. Germany, he said, wanted to establish a political and cultural hegemony over the world. Many Americans realized that England was fighting their battles, and that were she to fall the responsibility to defend the cause of liberty and freedom would devolve upon them. Professor Beer went on to advocate an alliance between the United States and the British Empire. Peace plans such as the establishment of an international police force or the constitution of a United States of Europe were impracticable because "they either are not in line with the normal course of evolution or have no point of contact with existing institutions." The British Empire was the logical point of departure for developing a world community. As a first step in

The Anglo-American entente was the core and the guiding force of this league of the West, which must be organized in order to fulfill the vision of a world in which autonomous, yet interdependent, democracies acted as the guardians of under-developed peoples.[40] And then on February 17, 1917, Lippmann wrote his famous and oft-quoted article in the *New Republic*.

We do not hesitate to say—we have believed it and said it since the beginning of the war—that if the Allied fleet were in danger of destruction, if Germany had a chance of securing command of the seas, our navy ought to be joined to the British in order to prevent it. The safety of the Atlantic highway is something for which America should fight.

Why? Because on the two shores of the Atlantic Ocean there has grown up a profound web of interest which joins together the Western world. Britain, France, Italy, even Spain, Belgium, Holland, the Scandinavian nations and Pan-America are in the main one community in their deepest needs and deepest purposes. They have a common interest in the ocean which unites them. They are today more inextricably bound together than most even as yet realize. But if that community were destroyed we should know what we had lost. We should understand then the meaning of the unfortified Canadian frontier, of the common protection given Latin America by the British and American fleets. . . .

A German victory on the high seas would be a triumph of that

that direction, the Empire should be reorganized "in the interest of civilization . . . on the principle of an organic political system." And "if, further, the United States . . . enters into an alliance with England, the logical outcome in time would be political union with the vast commonwealth of Britons, Irishmen, Canadians, South Africans, Australians, East Indians, Egyptians and other peoples." Beer, "The War, the British Empire, and America," *The Forum*, Vol. 53, No. 5 (May 1915), pp. 565–566. Professor Beer repeated this thesis in an address to the American Academy of Political and Social Science in 1916. See "America's International Responsibilities and Foreign Policy," *Annals*, Vol. 66, No. 155 (July 1916), pp. 71–91. Also see his "America's Part among Nations," *New Republic*, Vol. 5, No. 55 (November, 1915), pp. 62–64.

[40] *Annals*, Vol. 66, No. 155, pp. 64–65.

class which aims to make Germany the leader of the East against the West, the leader ultimately of a German-Russian-Japanese coalition against the Atlantic world.[41]

Three significant points emerge from the evidence noted above: the strategic interests of the Atlantic powers were so interrelated as to make them all a community for purposes of defense; its nucleus was the combined power of the United States and the British Empire; this community of Western states should serve mankind by protecting and promoting the interests and welfare of its underdeveloped sections. This was the core of Lippmann's thesis as he developed it up until the end of World War I, and, as we shall find in the following pages, it would seem to have remained intact through the years.

We may pause here to examine Lippmann's assertion that the Atlantic Community was discovered in the months preceding America's entry into World War I. It is true that a great deal was written during 1915–1916 on the interest of the United States in the safety of the Atlantic highway, her stake in the British supremacy on the seas, and the dangers to the security of the Western Hemisphere inherent in a German victory in Europe. But as we have indicated, several distinguished scholars and public men had written on these subjects, some of them long before the war broke out. It would seem appropriate to acknowledge them briefly, not only to set the record straight but also to indicate a possible source of Lippmann's inspiration.

Writing in the British *National Review* of January 1913,

[41] Walter Lippmann, "The Defense of the Atlantic World," *New Republic*, Vol. 10, No. 120, pp. 59–61. Six days before Lippmann's article appeared in the *New Republic*, Professor Albert Bushnell Hart had published in the *New York Times* an open letter to President Wilson strongly urging intervention on behalf of the Allies. He wrote: "You realize, of course, Mr. President, that if the Germans should by any chance destroy the British fleet, New York would be the first objective after London." "Please, Mr. President," *Times Magazine*, February 11, 1917, p. 2.

David Lewis Einstein, a scholar and diplomatist, predicted
that a war between Germany and Great Britain for supremacy
in the world was about to break out. American policy in this
conflict should, he said, be one of preserving the balance of
power in Europe on which her security had always depended.
Significantly, he assured his readers that a British victory in
the impending war would leave the European balance of
power essentially unaltered. But the same could not be said
of a German victory. Therefore it would be blind folly for
America to let Britain fall, a blunder she must later rue.

An Anglo-German conflict would thus affect the United States
at various points and in various ways. . . . However considerable
the responsibility incurred, however great the bait offered, it
would hardly be wise statesmanship to remain passive if England
should by any series of disasters be crushed. . . . The disintegration
of the British Empire would be a defeat for America by the errec-
tion of a power supreme on land and sea.[42]

In 1910, Mahan noted that Germany meant to force the
admission of her influence, capital, commerce, engineering
and culture to the countries of Asia, Africa and Latin
America. The sea power of Great Britain, which was a liberal
and satisfied state, was the only check on Germany's advance
for world domination. It followed, argued Mahan, that the
continuation of British supremacy was a national interest of
every other state. Accordingly, he came out for an Anglo-
American entente.[43]

In two letters written in 1905, Henry Adams advocated an
"Atlantic System" which bears considerable resemblance to
Lippmann's Atlantic Community. Writing from Paris to
John Hay on May 3, 1905, Adams said:

[42] David Lewis Einstein, "The United States and Anglo-German
Rivalry," *The National Review* (London), Vol. 60, No. 359, p. 749.
[43] Alfred T. Mahan, *The Interest of America in International Conditions*
(Boston: Little, Brown and Co., 1910), pp. 114–115.

We want our Atlantic System—which extends from the Rocky Mountains, on the west, to the Elbe on the east, and develops nine tenths of the energy of the world—to control France and Germany as far as it goes. Germany tries, and has always tried . . . to maintain a continental system like Napoleon's independent of ours. . . . All Western Germany is American, Atlantic and anti-military. We need only to work with it, and help it to what it thinks it wants; and above all, to remove, as far as we can, the inevitable friction with France and England.[44]

Again, writing some three months later to his friend Elizabeth Cameron, he observed:

We have got to support France against Germany, and fortify an Atlantic system beyond attack; for if Germany breaks down England or France, she becomes the centre of a military world, and we are lost.[45]

In March 1894 Sir George Clark advocated a naval union between Great Britain and the United States. The intelligence services of both countries, he pleaded, should exchange information and ideas as to the construction and armament programs necessary to protect their interests at sea. He also recommended the constitution of an Anglo-American council of four members from each country, with the president appointed alternately by each for a term of five years, to deliberate on matters of common interest and to help resolve any issues that might arise between them.

To such a body, meeting once a year, would be referred by joint consent, all questions . . . of mutual arrangement; and the misunderstandings which the interchange of diplomatic notes inevitably promotes, together with the friction on the manufacture of which some newspapers thrive, would cease. . . . The sub-

[44] Henry Adams, *Letters of Henry Adams 1892–1918*, ed. Worthington C. Ford (Boston: Houghton Mifflin Co., 1938), pp. 447–448.
[45] *Ibid.*, p. 461.

stitution of personal conference for smart despatch-writing would mark an era in the relations of the two nations.[46]

Lastly, we may take note here of Andrew Carnegie's passionate plea for a reunion of Great Britain and the United States so as to form a new nation—the "Reunited States." The proposed new state, he said, would be unassailable on land and sea alike. It would dominate the world, and rid mankind of the curse of war. It would act as the arbiter of international disputes, saying to any disputants who threatened to draw the sword:

> Hold! I command you both;
> The one that stirs makes me his foe.
> Unfold to me the cause of quarrel
> And I will judge betwixt you.

There would be no need any more for nations to maintain standing armies. The military power of the "Reunited States" would be so overwhelming, and its humanity, wisdom and moral authority so great, that "all would acquire the habit of settling disputes by an appeal to this supreme tribunal, the friend of all, the enemy of none."[47] Carnegie admitted that it might all be a dream. But, if so, it was a dream nobler than most realities. "If it is never to be realized, none the less it should be realized, and shame to those who come after us if it be not."[48]

[46] Sir George Clark, "A Naval Union with Great Britain: A Reply to Mr. Andrew Carnegie," *North American Review*, Vol. 158, No. 448 (March 1894), p. 365.

[47] Andrew Carnegie, "A Look Ahead," *North American Review*, Vol. 156, No. 439 (June 1893), pp. 693–694.

[48] *Ibid.*, p. 710. Carnegie's article provoked several others to write on the subject. Mahan approved in principle the idea of an Anglo-American union or alliance but felt that the time was not yet ripe for such a step. "Possibilities of an Anglo-American Reunion," *North American Review*, Vol. 159, No. 456 (November 1894), esp. 555–560. In the same issue of the *Review*, Lord Charles Beresford accepted Carnegie's idea as being ultimately desirable, but objected that it was not immediately

In the interwar period, one finds, Lippmann not only omitted to mention but actually repudiated the lesson he had preached to the American people in 1917. Year after year in the eventful thirties he told his readers of the approaching war in Europe, at the same time reassuring them that it would not touch them if only they remembered that it was none of their business. Let us take a few instances of this incredible change in Lippmann's view of America's "destiny." During 1931–1932 he emphasized that the issues of war and peace in Europe hinged on whether the frontiers fixed at Versailles were to be maintained or revised. The greatest obstacle to revision was the French fear of renewed aggression by an enlarged, still vindictive Germany. The problem of European peace was then the problem of French security. The only conceivable solution, said Lippmann, lay in the re-creation of an Anglo-French entente. "That alone could relax the rigidity of the French position. Hand in hand with Great Britain the French would feel safe enough to be liberal."[49] Significantly enough, Lippmann did not urge Washington to underwrite or join an Anglo-French understanding.

From 1933 onward, Lippmann wrote time and again that Nazi Germany was preparing for war.[50] The threat of Hitlerian aggression, he argued, could be met only by the organization of superior force. Herr Hitler was a man who "respects force, and Europe will be a safe place so long as there is a force which he respects."[51] He exhorted Britain and France and their allies to stand together and present a united front to Germany. But from this united front against the

---

practicable. He went on to say that "were it possible for this happy dream to be converted into reality, the English-speaking nations could control the future of the world, insure perpetual peace and prosperity, and maybe advance the advent of the millennium." p. 570.

[49] T and T, February 19, 1932. Also see October 24, 1931.

[50] Ibid., March 16 and May 12, 1933.

[51] Ibid., June 11, 1935.

impending Nazi aggression the United States was to be
absent. Americans, wrote Lippmann, desired to see all war
abolished, but what they wanted still more was to remain
out of those wars which could not be prevented. "Only a
military commitment which changed the balance of forces"
in Europe could cause war-bound Germany to alter her
course, and "no one in America has the smallest intention
of making such a commitment."[53] It should be noted that
Lippmann was not merely describing the isolationist sentiment, that myopic indifference to European politics which
swayed American opinion in the thirties. He left no doubt
that he himself approved the popular view of America's
interests and responsibilities in relation to the coming catastrophe. In the aforementioned article he declared:

Once we admit that at the present time Europe is moving not
towards peace and disarmament but towards more armaments and
the possibility of war, our main business is to take a course which
is least likely to involve the United States in a dangerous entanglement. *As long as Europe prepares for war, America must
prepare for neutrality.*[54] [Italics mine.]

During 1935 Lippmann continued to repeat the thesis that
America's vital interests, not being involved in the fate of
Europe, dictated aloofness from the troublesome affairs of
that continent. In an article in *Foreign Affairs,* he observed
that both Britain and the United States were concerned with

[53] *Ibid.,* May 17, 1934.
[54] *Ibid.* Lippmann went so far as to outline a program designed to prevent American neutrality from developing into belligerency. As a first
step, he urged, the country should abandon the traditional doctrine of
neutral rights in war, for experience had shown that "during a war of the
great powers the choice is to go to war or let 'neutral rights' be unen-
forced." Other suggested measures included a strict embargo on the export
of munitions to belligerents and adjacent neutrals; closure of American
ports to armed vessels, including armed merchantmen; forbidding enlist-
ments on American soil and fund-raising for war relief; stoppage of all
foreign loans to belligerents; etc.

the rise of aggressive imperialism in Germany. Then why did they not cooperate more effectively in order to protect themselves and maintain peace in the world? Lippmann's answer not only explained his own isolationism during this period but incidentally exposed what must be regarded as a serious weakness in that chain of common interests which is supposed to hold together the Atlantic Community. He wrote:

While in general their outlook and the desiderata of their policies are the same, their most immediately pressing needs are not identical. . . . Their vital interests have different foci. They are threatened in different degree from different quarters. The result is that the paramount interests of one Power are only secondary interests of the other. And it is this difference in importance that makes difficult a cooperative diplomacy.[55]

British statesmen rightly projected their strategic frontier into the Low Countries and the Rhineland. The first line of American defense, on the other hand, was drawn not in Europe but at the Panama Canal. Since the vital strategic interests of the two nations were widely separated by geography, the United States did not, and could not, join the United Kingdom in maintaining the status quo in Western Europe.[56] The only contribution which Americans could make to the cause of world peace was to help others economically by improving their own economy and society.

By devoting our efforts to a recovery in America we can, by promoting recovery elsewhere, relieve the political tension. By proceeding with our own social reconstruction we can, by its example, hearten the supporters of freedom and peace throughout the world.[57]

As Europe steadily moved toward war, Lippmann assured his countrymen that "in these historic movements" the

[55] Walter Lippmann, "Britain and America," *Foreign Affairs*, Vol. 13, No. 3 (April 1935), p. 365.
[56] *Ibid.*, p. 366.
[57] T and T, February 2, 1935.

United States was not a participant. The intevention of 1917 had conclusively proved that in the very nature of things this country could not usefully participate in the affairs of Europe. Americans, therefore, "must not mislead the world by seeming to promise what the nature of their position makes it impossible for them to fulfill."[58] Borah the Isolationist could not have far outdone the Walter Lippmann of 1933–1936.

It was in 1937 that Lippmann once again saw a connection between American security and British sea power. He rediscovered the truth that America could not sit back in a war that threatened to turn the world topsy-turvy by crushing the mistress of the seas. He found it both interesting and enlightening that the sharpest critics of Wilson's unneutral diplomacy had, by writing the "cash and carry" provision into the neutrality legislation, inadvertently struck an "economic alliance" with Great Britain and her allies and imposed an embargo on trade with Germany and her allies in a future war. For whereas Britain and her partners had the cash and the ships to buy in the American market and carry the purchase home, Germany and her partners were short of cash and ships alike.

Surely it is extraordinary that . . . twenty years later by the deliberate act of his critics, the greatest decision of Wilson's life, the decision that *the deepest American interest is somehow organically connected with Britain, is vindicated and ratified. It is as if some kind of overriding necessity in the very nature of the world as it is,* had compelled men to reinforce the British connection when they thought they were severing it.[59]

He went on to explain that the whole idea of American isolation or neutrality rested on the assumption that the world as a whole would continue to remain orderly under the "final authority" of a sea power controlled by liberal, humane and

[58] *Ibid.*, January 23, 1936.
[59] Walter Lippmann, "Rough-Hew Them How We Will," *Foreign Affairs,* Vol. 15, No. 4 (July 1937), p. 590 [italics mine].

democratic peoples. Lippmann was now convinced that even if the United States wanted merely to live and let live, she could stay out of a European war only so long as Great Britain, whose power and influence made for order in the world, was not in mortal peril.

In the final test, no matter what we wish now or now believe, though collaboration with Britain and her allies is difficult and often irritating, we shall protect that [Anglo-American] connection because in no other way can we fulfill our destiny.[60]

From here on Lippmann returned to the Atlantic Community, emphasizing its significance and its relation to America's vital interest and destiny in several newspaper columns and magazine articles.[61] He discussed the subject at length in U.S. Foreign Policy and U.S. War Aims, and it would seem appropriate to outline his thesis as he postulated it in these two works.

In U.S. Foreign Policy, Lippmann maintained that the geography of military power had transformed the nations of Western Europe, the British Empire and the Americas into one strategic neighborhood. For instance, the positions which the United States must defend were "exposed salients"— Greenland, Alaska, the bulge of Brazil and the Philippines, all of which were nearer by sea and by air to some great power in the Old World than they were to this country. Again, America could not develop and effectively employ her air power without the use of advanced bases overseas. It was

[60] Ibid., p. 594.
[61] See, for instance, T and T, May 11, 14 and 18, 1940 entitled "Wake Up America"; "War or Measures Short of War," T and T, November 29, 1940; "America and the World," Life, Vol. 8, No. 23 (June 3, 1940); "The Weapon of Freedom," Life, Vol. 9, No. 18 (October 28, 1940); "Acquisition of the British Naval Bases," Congressional Digest, Vol. 20, No. 1 (January 1941); "The Atlantic and America," Life, Vol. 10, No. 14 (April 7, 1941); "Awareness of the Danger," Time, Vol. 37, No. 17 (April 28, 1941); "America's Great Mistake," Life, Vol. 11, (July 21, 1941).

impossible to build, supply and defend such bases in Europe and Asia without sea communications, which must pass through the North Atlantic highway. On one side of that passage lay Canada and Newfoundland, and on the other side the British Isles. It followed that the security of the northern approaches to the American continent was inextricably related to the sea and air power of Britain. It was necessary to build and maintain strong sea and air bases on the bulge of Brazil in order to guard the approaches to South America in the South Atlantic. Brazil could not construct or maintain these bases without the aid of the United States. But there were no land communications with Brazil—which meant that the defense of South America as it faced the Atlantic must depend on sea and air communications. And here again,

we find the British power founded on the United Kingdom and projected to Gibraltar and to Bathhurst and Freetown in West Africa, and to Capetown in South Africa. The British Isles command the northern entrance to the Atlantic. Gibraltar commands the Mediterranean entrance. Capetown commands the southern entrance from the Indian Ocean. The Falkland Islands command the southern entrance from the Pacific Ocean around Cape Horn. Thus the region we must defend can be attacked only from the region over which Britain commands all the approaches by sea.[62]

The British and American vital interests were also linked in Canada, the greatest of the British Dominions, whose defense was inseparably bound up with the defense of the Western Hemisphere. The United Kingdom, therefore, must go to the defense of the United States, whose fall would deal a shattering blow at the British Commonwealth and Empire. Likewise, America must go to the defense of Great Britain or countenance the "mortal risk" of a hostile power establishing

[62] *U.S. Foreign Policy*, p. 124.

itself in the strategic approaches to the Western Hemisphere.

France is another member of the Atlantic Community. Her fall in 1940 conclusively proved that she belonged to the same defensive system in which the American republics lived. It exposed Spain and Portugal to possible German invasion and domination. It also gave Germany naval and air bases from which she besieged Britain and inflicted heavy losses on American shipping. The fall of France also opened up the threat of a possible German invasion of South America from bases in French West Africa extending from Casablanca to Dakar. It followed that the security of France was a vital interest of the United States, as was the security of the American position a vital interest of France. The same was true, for similar reasons, of the Low Countries, which were the outer bastions of Britain and France. Norway and Denmark were also members of the same strategic system: when they fell, Britons and Americans at once knew that another breach had occurred in their defenses. The Danes and the Norwegians, like the Dutch and the Belgians, in turn knew that only a victorious Anglo-American combination could liberate them. Thus the course of events in the two world wars should have convinced anyone who would learn from experience that the Atlantic Community was "no figment of the imagination." It was a reality.

Lippmann discussed the subject again in U.S. *War Aims,* in which he listed all the members of the Atlantic Community. They were Argentina, Australia, Belgium, Bolivia, Brazil, Canada, Chile, Columbia, Costa Rica, Cuba, Denmark, the Dominican Republic, Ecuador, Eire, Greece, Guatemala, Haiti, Honduras, Iceland, Italy, Liberia, Luxembourg, Mexico, the Netherlands, New Zealand, Nicaragua, Norway, Panama, Paraguay, Peru, the Philippines, Portugal, Salvador, South Africa, Spain, Sweden, Switzerland, Uruguay and Venezuela in addition to the United States, Great Britain and

France, which were great military powers. For obvious reasons, Lippmann did not admit Germany to this community of Western states. However, he expressed the hope that after the German people had been thoroughly pacified, the Atlantic Community would "come to include Germany and perhaps all of Europe to the borders of the Soviet Union."[63]

Lippmann submitted in *U.S. War Aims* that the identity of interests of the members of the Atlantic Community was not confined to the needs of their mutual and interdependent security. These nations shared the common traditions of Western Christendom. Their moral codes, their legal and political institutions, though different in detail, had a common foundation and a common source. In politics, they adhered to the principle that "the state exists for man, and not man for the state; that the state is under the law, not above it; and that the individual person has inalienable rights."[64]

In the post-World War II period, Lippmann has often endorsed America's vital connection with the Atlantic Community in practically every article and book that he has written on American foreign policy. The following statement represents his position well:

we shall defend not only our own country but the great community from which we sprang and to which we belong. Its peace and security are our peace and security. . . . [We shall not] degrade ourselves and disgrace ourselves by seeking our own security at the expense of the civilization to which we belong.[65]

Nor has Lippmann abandoned his thesis that the power of the Atlantic Community must be wielded to promote the rule of liberty and law in the world. In 1949 he wrote:

[63] *U.S. War Aims*, p. 192; see also p. 80. The Atlantic Community consisted of 42 states with a population, as of 1940, of 522 million (p. 85).

[64] *Ibid.*, p. 87.

[65] T and T, September 14, 1950. For a more recent expression of the same view see T and T, November 2, 1961.

Our friends in Western Europe should try to understand why we cannot and must not be maneuvered, why we dare not drift, into general opposition to the movements for independence in Asia. They should tell their propagandists to stop smearing these movements. They should try to realize how disastrous it would be to them, and to the cause of Western civilization, if ever it could be said that the Western union for the defense of freedom in Europe was in Asia a syndicate for the preservation of decadent empires.[66]

What is the nature of the Atlantic Community if, as Lippmann insists, it is not a figment of the imagination, but a living and enduring reality? We have seen that it is not a super-state. The principal evidence of its existence lies in the fact that certain nations have twice opposed, with varying degrees of vigor, a state which set out to rule mankind, and are now arrayed, again with varying degrees of enthusiasm, against another state which seeks to conquer the world. Lippmann maintains that these nations now stand together, as they did in the past, in order to safeguard their security, which they have found to be interdependent. The Atlantic Community is then a strategic system. Herein lies its greatest strength and also its principal weakness. For what can unite a group of sovereign states more firmly than the knowledge that their peace and security are indivisible? And yet, what will keep them united in the period between wars, in peacetime when there is no specific threat to their survival, when sporadic incidents, though they sow the seeds of a future conflict, seem all too trifling to call for the concerted action of forty-two states or even of the great powers among them? A strategic system must, by its very nature, become relatively inactive when war is nothing more than a remote possibility.

Then what is the significance of the Atlantic Community in peace time? It would appear that whereas in war the Community is, with its combined staffs and agencies, a

[66] *Ibid.*, January 12, 1949.

military alliance with a tangible and fully operative organization, in peace it is not much more than an idea, a hypothesis, or a thesis remembered by a few "wise men"[67] of the West but forgotten by most. The number of these "wise men" must be very small indeed, for, as we have seen, Walter Lippmann, who is admittedly one of the greatest and the most vocal advocates of the Atlantic Community, forgot it in the interwar period. When peoples and governments in the Atlantic world relearned the lesson that in the hour of peril they had, in spite of their numerous differences, a common destiny, and when they translated this notion into organs of joint endeavor to plan and prosecute their fight against a common foe, they broke and conquered the lawless power of Nazi Germany. But this idea of a common destiny, though it delivered them from the cataclysm of Hitlerian aggression, returned to the consciousness of these men of the West at a staggering cost in blood and treasure. Their forgetfulness did not cost them their lives, but it wrought revolutions in the power relation between states, and it changed, indeed mutilated, the face of the West. Lippmann himself has often observed during the post-World War II period that the Atlantic Alliance tends to loosen and weaken whenever the threat of war with the Soviet Union recedes. In recent years he has repeatedly noted and criticized the current French policy of expelling the influence of the "Anglo-Saxons" from Western Europe. It may well be that the Atlantic Community cannot become a constantly operative factor in international politics unless it acquires a form and an organization, which men can see and recognize—which they can grow to love and cherish.

The concept of the Atlantic Community as a defensive

[67] Lippmann once wrote that even though the nations constituting the Atlantic Community had, at times, competed and fought with one another, "the wisest of their leaders" had always known that "when the issue was life or death, they would stand or fall together." T and T, April 7, 1949.

system is obviously predicated on certain assumptions regarding development in the art of warfare. Lippmann based his thesis on the assumption that sea power was an irresistible weapon of war. One may readily grant that the defense of the Atlantic states was interdependent in the age of naval blockades. But it is problematic whether it will continue to be interdependent in the age of intercontinental guided missiles. Again, as a strategic system the Community may remain relatively inactive and may even disintegrate if, because of a nuclear stalemate, its enemies stick indefinitely to the techniques of economic and propaganda warfare.

When the bonds of strategic necessity break or loosen, can the bonds of devotion to a common faith and a common philosophy of life hold intact the fabric of unity among the Atlantic powers? Lippmann has often referred to these bonds, though, significantly enough, he has not emphasized them as much as the "vital connections" of mutual security. It is generally accepted without question that the members of the Atlantic Community adhere to a democratic way of life. This is obviously an unwarranted generalization. For more than half the states in this Community flagrantly violate the democratic principle in their political practice. Some openly hold it in contempt. Even France, a key power in the Atlantic Community, is currently ruled, according to Lippmann, by an "old king" who is a dictator, not a constitutional monarch.[68] It is fortunately true that the most powerful of the Atlantic states, together with some middle-sized and small powers, are firmly committed to the traditions of democracy. But it cannot be said that the commitment goes far and deep enough to counteract in peace time the divisive influence of immediate national interests.

It should also be borne in mind that the preservation of democracy in these countries is not as demonstrably inter-

[68] T and T, March 1, 1962 and May 17, 1962. Also see *Western Unity and the Common Market* (1962), pp. 22–23.

dependent as is, or was, their defense. Now that the conduct of French national affairs rests in the hands of a dictatorship, non-communist but a dictatorship nevertheless, it is by no means certain that the average American or the average Australian sees in the subversion of French democracy, which never made sense to him anyway, a threat to his own Bill of Rights or institutions of representative government. In fact, he may be pleased at the departure of a national assembly which had become paralyzed by its perpetual and irreconcilable dissensions.[69] It would appear that adherence to a more or less similar way of life, unaided by the mutuality of vital and concrete national interests, cannot always preserve the unity even of the democratic states in the Atlantic Community.

And yet there is truth in the assertion of Walter Lippmann, Henry Adams and others that the Atlantic Community must develop, prosper and maintain its solidarity if the tradition of liberal democracy is not to die out, if the free world is not to be reduced to the hopeless position of a progressively shrinking island in a vast and ever-expanding sea of tyranny. One may ask whether new relations cannot be forged between the members of this family of Western states so as to hold them together even when the connections of strategic necessity become ineffective or altogether obsolete.

[69] It should be remembered that many democrats in the West were once enchanted by the fact that railway trains in Mussolini's Italy had begun to run on time. Others were vastly impressed by the "triumphant struggle" of fascism "against the bestial appetites and passions of Leninism." Charmed by the "gentle and simple bearing" of Signor Mussolini, no less a democrat than Winston Churchill told the press in Rome that Italian fascism "had rendered a service to the whole world" by showing that "there is a way of fighting the subversive forces which can rally the mass of the people, properly led, to value and to defend the honour and stability of civilized society. She [Italy] has provided the necessary antidote to the Russian poison. Hereafter no great nation will be unprovided with an ultimate means of protection against cancerous growths . . . " *The Times* (London), January 21, 1927, quoted in Virginia Cowles, *Winston Churchill: The Era and the Man* (New York: Harper and Brothers, 1953), pp. 271–272.

VI

A European System: Europe and the Atlantic Community

EVERY NOW AND THEN THROUGH THE CENTURIES, INDIVIDUAL
Europeans have proclaimed the cultural and spiritual unity of
Europe, and have called for its political integration and unification. But the spirit, the religion, the culture, and the socio-
political traditions and institutions of Europe have long
since broken the demarcation lines of geography and spread
far and wide. As a result, Europe is spiritually linked with
lands and peoples thousands of miles away. And though it is
the source and the fountain of Western civilization, it is not
the whole but only a part of what is known as the Western
world. Then what shall be the political relation, if any, of
Europe to these other communities which share with it a
common way of life? Should they all organize themselves
into a larger community? And if so, should it be a super-
state or a loose and flexible organization? In either case,
should the several states of Europe enter this larger community independently, or should they join it as an organically
united whole? Should they join it at all? Might they not
themselves unite but make no binding commitments with the

non-European parts of the Western world, and lead their lives competing or cooperating with the latter as the occasion and their own vital interests may demand? And finally, should all or some of the several states of Europe unite even among themselves? These are difficult questions, and, as we shall see in the following pages, they have baffled Lippmann.

In *U.S. War Aims,* Lippman wrote that even though the idea of European unity had much to commend itself, it would not be furthered by the political unification of the Continent, which "in our time certainly . . . would be a great evil."[1] In the first place, Europe could not be federated because it was not a clearly definable geographic and strategic entity.[2] No one could say categorically what the boundaries of this federation would be. But more importantly, argued Lippmann, Europe *should not* form a federation or a separate strategic system. For if it did, it could not escape German domination. Germany would inevitably be the strongest military state, the strategic center, and the hard core of a European federation. Could anyone doubt that Germans, who were industrially advanced, militarily seasoned and by far the most highly disciplined and industrious people on the Continent, would "dominate the federation as Prussia dominated the federal German Reich after 1871? No blueprint can provide against the very nature of things in Europe."[3] The

[1] *U.S. War Aims,* p. 125.

[2] This is one of the common, though minor, objections to the federation or any regional organization of Europe. It refers to the uncertain nature of the relation of Russia, and also of Great Britain, with Europe. Specifically, the question is whether these two powers are in or out of Europe. Most Europeans insist that Britain is and should be treated as European, while Russia is not and should not be so treated. On their part, the British tend to resist their inclusion in, and the Russians to resent their exclusion from Europe. See in this connection, Ross J. Hoffman, "Europe and the Atlantic Community," *Thought,* Vol. 20, No. 76 (March 1945), pp. 28–29.

[3] *U.S. War Aims,* p. 126. The fear of German domination in the post-war Europe was voiced by other writers during and after the war. How-

proponents of a European federation were bound to end up with precisely what the war was being fought to prevent—a German Europe. And if that was not what they wanted, they must not talk of federating Europe until Germany had become thoroughly pacified and had ceased to menace the freedom and independence of her non-German neighbors. First and foremost, Europe needed security against the recurrence of German aggression, which could be provided only by organizing the Atlantic Community and the Russian orbit.[4] Then, while the peoples of Europe were secure, they could form an economic and cultural "federation."

> Then the other agencies of government that are concerned with commerce and welfare can and should bind the civilian life of the Continent together in matters affecting tariffs, commercial policy, money, transportation, public utilities, social security and the like.[5]

After the war, the Soviet Union rejected the idea of regional systems based on the "good neighbor" principle, and unceremoniously established an outright dictatorship in its own orbit. The Cold War, which began even before World War II had come to an end, closed the door on Soviet-American cooperation in protecting Europe against future German aggression or in sponsoring its economic and cultural unity. Lippmann agreed that under the circumstances the states of

---

ever, some writers hinted at the unwisdom of overemphasizing the postwar German menace, and suggested that greater threats to the peace and security of Europe would emanate from another quarter—a victorious Russia. See Robert Strausz-Hupé, *The Balance of Tomorrow* (New York: G. P. Putnam's Sons, 1945), p. 266.

[4] Lippmann argued that if Great Britain and the United States were to aid the states of Western Europe in containing Germany, then they must all coordinate their military systems so as to organize the Atlantic Community. Similarly, the states of Eastern Europe must coordinate their military systems with that of the Soviet Union in order to check Germany from the east. *U.S. War Aims*, p. 128.

[5] *Ibid.*

Eastern Europe should disengage themselves from the Soviet orbit. But obviously Russia would not willingly let go of them. Moreover, they could not regain their independence merely by detaching themselves from the Soviet Union. They could not return to a Europe where they might once again groan under the heel of German domination. Lippmann observed that the only way to liberate them was to provide a place where they could go, to create "something else to which they can attach themselves. That something . . . can be only a framework for continental Europe."[6] He conceded that the Western powers could not have established such a framework without Russian consent. But they should certainly have begun to build in Western Europe a system which could eventually embrace the whole of Europe. Then,

instead of pushing and picking at the Russian orbit, we should have been pulling the people of Europe away from it, pulling them not into a British-American orbit but into the orbit of Europe itself.[7]

In 1947 he proposed that the American contribution to European recovery should not take the form of aid to individual nations. Rather, this country should request the governments of Europe to draw up a general program of production and exchange, imports and exports so as to arrive at a consolidated deficit for as much of Europe as could agree to a common plan. Not only would this amount to less than the total of individual deficits, but it would be a "refreshing innovation" for the United States to aid not this or that government, but Europe. The proposed *modus operandi*, said Lippmann, would also serve as an "inducement to the unification of Europe."[8] During this period, he wrote

[6] "A Year of Peacemaking," *Atlantic Monthly*, Vol. 178, No. 6 (December 1946), p. 38.
[7] *Ibid.*
[8] T and T, May 1, 1947. About two weeks earlier, Lippmann had ad-

several articles urging the resumption of trade between Western and Eastern Europe, which, he maintained, would not only speed up European recovery but would also help end its economic division and keep the door open for its unification.[9]

Lippmann emphasized that Europe must be "independent" and master of its own destiny. Its people could not rehabilitate their economic and political life unless they were able to talk out their differences and work out their common problems without first having to seek the approval of Washington or Moscow. "The family life of Europe is not likely to be restored if mother-in-law Russia and Uncle Sam are all over the house all the time."[10] He also noted that Europeans were becoming increasingly opposed to policies which sought to make them the stakes of Soviet-American diplomacy and their homes the battlefield of another war. They were determined, indeed "destined," to align themselves neither with Russia nor with America, but to mediate between them and prevent the catastrophe of a third world war.[11]

Germany was, of course, the heart of the European problem. Lippmann maintained that Europe could neither unite nor regain its independence so long as the Red Army was encamped at the Elbe. That army would not retire behind its frontiers until a German peace treaty had been agreed upon and signed. Washington should therefore give top

---

vocated a European economic union to save the Continent from the economic and financial collapse for which it was heading. *Ibid.*, April 12, 1947. According to Herbert Luethy, this was "the first public premonition of things to come." *France against Herself* (New York: Frederick A. Praeger, 1955), p. 352.

[9] T and T, November 10, 11, 13, 1947 and January 19, 1948. Lippmann's insistence on the resumption of East-West trade was based, as was his general emphasis on the economic unification of Europe, on the assumption that the economies of the agricultural East and the industrial West were complementary.

[10] T and T, June 24, 1947.

[11] *Ibid.*, June 19, 1947.

priority to obtaining a settlement of the war, providing for the withdrawal of all occupation forces from the Continent and for the decentralization of Germany, which, having been neutralized as between the United States and the Soviet Union, should take its place in an independent and un-committed European system.

The decentralization and the neutralization of Germany were both prerequisite to European unity. Europeans, East-ern and Western alike, would dread and shun a system in which Germany had become united under a centralized government. Therefore Germany must be decentralized so that the individual German states would not be big enough to overawe and dominate their non-German neighbors. There were also other reasons which dictated this policy. The Ger-man people could not regain national unity, as they must understand it, without recovering the Eastern territories which they had lost to Poland as a result of the war. The Poles would be loath to leave the Soviet orbit and become the next-door neighbors, in a European system, of a revita-lized, reunited and centralized Germany whose government must demand and press for the return of the Eastern prov-inces or lose the confidence of its electorate. The institution of a centralized government in a united Germany was thus incompatible with and inimical to the unification of Europe. Nor should the Western powers encourage the establish-ment of such a government in West Germany, for it too would have its gaze fixed on the lost territories, and would therefore tend to make a deal with the Soviet Union in order to regain them.

There can be no German settlement which is tolerable by re-establishing the sovereign power of a central German government in a truncated area and dedicated to the unity of Germany. The annexations in the east of Germany demand a radical decentraliza-tion of Western Germany.

The truncated area will have to be decentralized, not unified, and the German states which are in it will have to take their places within a larger European system and a European economy. Not German unity, but European unity, not German self-sufficiency but European self-sufficiency, not a Germany to contain Russia but a Germany neutralized as between Russia and the West . . . should be the aims of our German policy.[12]

What did Lippmann mean by the "decentralization" of Germany? His insistence that Germany should not be unified, and that the separate German states should individually enter a European system, would indicate that he opposed not only the re-creation of a centralized Reich but even a federal structure of government for that country. Since the proposed "European system" was not to be a federation of Europe, one must conclude that Lippmann meant to vest the separate German states with the customary attributes of national sovereignty. He proposed, then, to abolish Germany as such, and to create instead a dozen or so Germanies. In sum, he recommended, as the German Social Democrats called it, the dismemberment of Germany.[13]

It should be noted here that during the war, and also in the early postwar period, there were many who, like Lippmann, wished to see Germany dismembered. At the Teheran Conference in November 1943, President Roosevelt proposed, to the delight of Marshal Stalin, that after the war Germany should be divided into seven regions, five of which should be self-governing and autonomous, and two—Kiel and its canal and Hamburg; the Ruhr and the Saar—should be administered in "trust" by the United Nations.[14] Sumner

[12] The Cold War, pp. 49–50.

[13] See, for instance, Carlo Schmid, "Germany and Europe," Foreign Affairs, Vol. 30, No. 4 (July 1952), p. 532. It may be noted here that the Social Democrats denounced political decentralization per se, and equated it with dismemberment.

[14] Cited in Winston Churchill, Closing the Ring (Boston: Houghton Mifflin Company, 1951), pp. 400–403.

Welles, to mention only one distinguished American writer and statesman, consistently opposed the reconstitution of a united Germany under a central government, which in his opinion would certainly make a deal with the Soviet Union and thus extend the border of the Soviet system to the shores of the Atlantic.[15] In France, General De Gaulle and his followers took a position which closely paralleled that of Lippmann. Giving the "Gaullist view" on the German question, Jacques Soustelle wrote:

After 1945 there was but one possible policy to be followed toward Germany—the one advocated by the Provisional French Government under the leadership of General De Gaulle. It favored the rebirth of the German states—Baden, Wurtenberg, the Palatinate, etc.—and sought to make it possible for each of them to develop its own political and economic existence so that they could be incorporated in a federated Europe as distinct states, not as "Germany."[16]

The common denominator of these proposals was the underlying desire to weaken Germany. It was born of the conviction that Germans were possessed of an irresistible and incorrigible urge to dominate Europe, and that given the opportunity, which reunification under a central government would allegedly provide, they would make still another attempt to establish their hegemony. It should be noted here that even though the fear of German domination was widespread, certain sections of European opinion never accepted the thesis that the principal task confronting postwar Europe was to "contain" Germany, or that the best way to do it was to dismember her. The governments of the United States and the United Kingdom favored a decentralized Germany.

[15] Sumner Welles, "Justice for Peace," *Washington Post* (January 8, 1947); "German Policy: Dangers in Unification Now," *ibid.*, November 4, 1947; "Western Germany: Shadow of Rearmament," *ibid.*, November 16, 1948.
[16] Jacques Soustelle, "France and Europe: A Gaullist View," *Foreign Affairs*, Vol. 30, No. 4 (July 1952), p. 546.

But to them, as to the Popular Republicans in France, decentralization meant federation. Accordingly, they encouraged the establishment of a federal republic in West Germany, which would be decentralized enough to make it possible for the state governments to block the wishes of the central government at Bonn.[17] The French socialists would go even further and give Germany a strong rather than a weak central government. They proceeded on the assumption that imposing upon the people of Germany a regime which they did not like would only arouse in them a nationalistic desire to have a government of their own choosing.[18] Furthermore, they maintained that after the war Russia, not Germany, posed the real threat to the independence of Europe. Commenting on the Gaullist thesis, the influential Le Monde observed:

In theory it would be simple to meet this alleged threat by resuscitating the ancient German principalities. In fact, present-day Germany is too conscious of her national unity to submit to such a fragmentation—except under the pressure of force. But this is an absurd solution, for Germany is no longer the principal threat to France in a world in which all of Europe is contested ground between the United States and Russia. The real danger overhanging Europe is the alternative between subjection to the Soviet police state or dictation by American capitalism. This danger faces France and Germany as well as all nations of the Continent.[19]

Germany must also be neutralized, for neither the West nor the Soviet would countenance its inclusion in the rival coalition. The West could not permit Germany to become

[17] Peter Nettl, "Economic Checks on German Unity," Foreign Affairs, Vol. 30, No. 4 (July 1952), p. 557.
[18] Rene Courtin, "French Views on European Union," International Affairs, Vol. 25, No. 1 (January 1949), pp. 19–20.
[19] Quoted in Robert Strausz-Hupé, "France and the Future German State," The Yale Review, Vol. 38, No. 2 (December 1948), pp. 323–324.

allied with Russia, for such an alliance would advance the military frontier of the Soviet orbit to the Rhine and pave the way for a rapid sovietization of the rest of Europe. Likewise, the Kremlin would never withdraw its forces from Europe to facilitate German and European unification, if it seemed that a reunited Germany would enter the anti-Soviet camp. Thus, Germany's alliance with either side of the fence would close the door on European unity. In *The Cold War,* Lippmann denounced the administration's attempt to arouse the sentiment of German unity in order to turn the German people against Russia and to win them over to the Western side. He warned that the policy-makers in Washington would surely lose Germany to Stalin if they incited the Germans to want something which only the Russian dictator could give them. He implied that in exchange for an alliance, Germany would ask the West to liberate Eastern Germany and the lost provinces by force, if necessary, in order to restore her national unity.[20] The Western powers could obviously not pay the prohibitive price of a war with the Soviet orbit for a West German alliance. The Germans would then see no gain in allying themselves with the West; they would turn to the Soviet. The West should therefore try not to make an ally

[20] Lippmann has clearly stated this point in several articles. In 1950 he wrote that Germans would not go back to the army except to fight for "German perspectives," to liberate East Germany and regain the lost provinces. The French insistence that German troops should have no autonomy stemmed "not from the ancient fear that a German army would march against Paris; it stems from an accurate and contemporary realization that a German army would wish to march, and to drag along with it all the rest of us, against Konigsberg and Warsaw. The Soviets take the same view of German rearmament, and so do their satellites." T and T, December 4, 1950. Also see *ibid.,* October 27, 1953.

Many Frenchmen would verify Lippmann's testimony. Members of the Socialist Party (SFIO), and an active minority of M.R.P., feared that Germany's admission to NATO would bring a new "dynamism" into that organization and might turn it into an instrument of conquest. See International Relations Group Committee, University of Pennsylvania, Philadelphia, "United States-European Tensions," unpublished manuscript, 1952, pp. 106–107, nn. 60, 66.

of the Western part of a divided Germany but to neutralize the whole of Germany in order to forestall the catastrophe of a Soviet-German alliance.

For if Germany is to become allied on either side of the diplomatic conflict, the precedents of history and the logic of the situation tell us that when she is strong enough to be a useful ally to any one, she will become the ally of Russia.[21]

Lippmann concluded that if the Soviet Union agreed to evacuate Europe on the aforementioned conditions—the neutralization of a decentralized Germany and the withdrawal of all occupation forces from the continent—the division of Europe would end, and Eastern Europe would be enabled to take its natural and rightful place in a European system. But if the Kremlin rejected these terms, the United States would gain immensely in popularity and prestige by advocating them.

For having made ourselves the champions of the unity of Europe, the unity of Germany, the liberators of the continent from the burden and oppression of alien armies, all the elemental forces of nationalism, pride and hope, all the deep instincts of all peoples against foreign domination, will gather in our cause. Time will work for our diplomacy.[22]

In January 1948, John Foster Dulles and Bernard Baruch proposed that as many nations of Europe as were willing to do so should organize themselves into an economic, political and defense union. The United States, they suggested, should guarantee this union against possible Russian aggression. Lippmann opposed the proposal, saying that it would divide rather than unite Europe. The security of Europe, he explained, depended not on the defensive power of the European states, which at the time was negligible as compared

[21] *The Cold War,* p. 48.
[22] T and T, November 17, 1947.

to the military might of the Kremlin, but on the balance of power between the United States and the Soviet Union. The proposed union would thus add nothing to the security of Europe, but by requiring its nations to identify themselves, openly and publicly, as the opponents of the Soviet Union, it would certainly increase their sense of insecurity. Moreover, it would inevitably divide them into two camps—the proponents and the opponents of an American-sponsored anti-Soviet defense union. Last, it would distract their attention from the urgent task of postwar "economic reconstruction and reunion in Europe."[23]

Lippmann's opposition to a "United States of Europe," which found expression in *U.S. War Aims,* persisted through 1947. It is true that he repeatedly called for the "unification" of Europe, and supported or opposed policies as they seemed to help or hinder the project of "European unity." But by such phrases as "a united Europe," "a unified Europe," and "an all-European system," he did not mean political unification. He did not mean even economic unification, if that should be equated with the creation of supra-national agencies to direct and deal with the economic affairs of the Continent. He meant that the states of Europe should trade and cooperate with one another, as they saw fit, unhampered and unrestrained by the non-European great powers, especially the Soviet Union; that the Red Army should go home and, since it would not go until and unless the other occupation forces also left, they should all leave Europe, restoring it to the Europeans; that in order to facilitate the withdrawal of the Red Army, and eventually to break up the Soviet orbit, without at the same time exposing the people of Europe to a renewed threat of German domination, Germany should be neutralized and decentralized; and finally that Europe thus "united" should pull itself out of the Cold War to develop

[23] *Ibid.,* January 22, 1948.

and perfect its "unity." One might say that up to about the end of 1947, Lippmann's concept of European unity lacked positive content. It meant, essentially, the restoration of the *status quo ante bellum* in Eastern Europe—the nullification of Soviet control over Europe east of the Elbe. It meant not so much unity as the end of a division which had been imposed by the Red Army.

In 1948, Lippmann reversed his earlier position and declared that only the political unification of Europe, not mere cooperation between its separate states, could bring about a settlement of the war and the rehabilitation of its dislocated and devastated economies. Commenting on Winston Churchill's suggestion in January 1948 that the West bring matters to a head with the Soviet Union and, through the channels of secret diplomacy, negotiate a settlement, Lippmann observed that the disorder and the disunity of the Western democracies made it impossible for them to negotiate with the Kremlin from a position of strength. In order to bring matters to a head successfully, it was indispensable that

the unity of Europe should not be a mere aspiration but should be effectively begun and growing. It is after, not before, Western Europe has agreed to unite,—after, not before Britain and America have made up their minds about Germany—after, not before the adoption of the Marshall Plan is assured—that matters can be brought to a head with the Soviet Union. To bring them to a head before there is unity would merely destroy the chance of attaining unity. Yet without European unity neither the European recovery program nor a settlement [with Russia] can be achieved. Let us hope then that Mr. Churchill will use his great influence to persuade the British Government to take a bold constructive initiative in *forming the United States of Europe*.[24] [Italics mine.]

This time Lippmann was undoubtedly advocating the political unification, a federation, of Europe. He explained that

[24] *Ibid.*, January 27, 1948.

even though the work of unification would have to begin in the West, the "United States of Europe" must eventually include the whole of Europe. Germany should enter the proposed federation as a decentralized state. Lippmann realized that the Soviet Union would oppose the federation of Europe, and would, at any rate, refuse to permit the states of Eastern Europe to join it. But apparently he hoped that after the threat of a reunited and centralized Germany had been removed, the satellites would see no advantage in clinging to the Soviet Union. As trade and cultural relations with the West increased, their political ties would once again become European, and not exclusively Russian.[25] In the end, no matter what the Soviet Union desired, they would find the "United States of Europe" much too attractive to remain out of it for long.

In February 1948 Lippmann wrote an article that more or less knocked the bottom out of his own earlier argument that it was both possible and desirable to effect economic collaboration between the countries of Europe without establishing their political unity. Commenting on a proposal of the Senate Foreign Relations Committee for the creation of a European customs union, he observed that in the absence of a common government, the proposed union would meet the certain opposition of deeply entrenched vested interests which had long benefited from the existing tariff walls. But even if it survived the attack of these protectionists, it could not overcome the indifference or the hostility of national governments preoccupied with their sovereignty and security. Americans should therefore make it perfectly clear that they were immensely interested in the constitution of a "United States of Europe," which, said Lippmann, would ensure prosperity and security to Europe and bring peace to the world.

[25] *Ibid.*, February 2, 1948.

There will be no war if Europe recovers not only from the economic devastation of the last war but also from the political weakness which followed it. A strong Europe, which can be had only by uniting Europe, is indispensable to the security of all—including the Russians and ourselves—security against the menace of a world war.[26]

Taking note of Ernest Bevin's call for a united Europe, Lippmann wrote in February 1948 that the work of unification should begin with the political union of Britain, France and the Benelux countries. They were highly civilized and politically mature democracies, possessing vast and rich territories in Africa. Their union would constitute the hard core, the nucleus, around which a larger union of Europe must be built.[27] This was the last of a series of articles supporting the political union of Europe which came from Lippmann's pen. Two months later we find him wavering between a united and independent Europe on the one hand, and the Atlantic Community on the other. In April 1948 he saw that the project of a European federation was likely to collapse on the rock of British unwillingness to join it. The British, he said, were in a dilemma. They had called for a federation of Western Europe, which they desired to promote and join. But they also wanted to preside over the Commonwealth, which they could not do were they to enter a federated Europe. Apparently, this complication reminded Lippmann once again of the Atlantic Community. The old nation-state system, he wrote, was breaking up under the pressure of changes and problems which the war had brought in its train. The new relations which the logic of necessity had forged between the United States and the nations of Western Europe pointed to a "new order of things," to the coming of a "new political society" comprising Europe, the British Common-

[26] *Ibid.*, February 16, 1948.
[27] *Ibid.*, February 26, 1948.

wealth and the Americas. In a passage which merits lengthy quotation, he said:

The [British] dilemma can be resolved only by the construction of a large political community which includes the British Commonwealth, the inter-American system, and a European federation with its African dependencies and colonies. In this larger community, it would be unnecessary for the British to choose between Europe and the Commonwealth. In this community, Great Britain and France could at long last become united in peace, not merely allied in war. In this community alone is there hope of solving the German problem, which is becoming progressively more snarled up. . . .

Dire necessity and extreme peril compel and invite us to undertake the formation of this great Western political society. . . . Everywhere men are asking to what high and useful project they may dedicate themselves. . . . The union of the peoples of the Western tradition is this project, this idea, and this purpose. Free and civilized men cannot quiver and quake for ever about Communism . . . or degrade themselves in witch-hunting and a morbid concern with the demonology of Moscow. Nor can they live forever and exclusively on the calculations of dollar deficits, and predictions about long-range bombers and atomic bombs, and resounding declarations about how much better liberty is than tyranny. They need also great constructive ideas which enlist their energies and give meaning to their lives.[28]

Was Lippmann in this impassioned statement urging the forty-two states of the Atlantic Community to merge themselves into a super-state? Admittedly, he used language which would lend itself to varying interpretations. Yet one should think that in calling for "the construction of a large political community," for "the formation of a great political society," Lippmann was referring to something more than a loose and formless system of cooperation among the governments of the West. The new political society was to replace the old

[28] *Ibid.*, April 26, 1948.

nation-state system. Then it must provide itself with the customary institutions and apparatus of government—perhaps a federal government with limited functional jurisdiction—but government nevertheless. Again, the free and civilized men of Western Europe could not have stopped calculating their dollar deficits if they were not entering the unified economy of a single state in which dollars and pounds and francs would all give way to a new common currency.

But even if the foregoing interpretation is correct, even if on April 26, 1948 Lippmann did advocate the political union of the nations in the Atlantic Community, the fact is that three days later he reversed himself. On April 29, 1948 he advised the White House to tell the Kremlin that Americans looked not to war but to a negotiated settlement in which Europe would become a buffer between the United States and the Soviet Union.[29]

Thus, the first quarter of 1948 saw a radical, albeit temporary, change in Lippman's views on some of the major problems of American foreign policy. Whereas up to the end of 1947 he had maintained that a settlement with the Soviet Union must precede the political and military reconstruction of Europe, in the period under review he came to accept the official American position that the West must build up a position of strength before it could negotiate with the Soviet with any hope of success. He altered his view of the "destiny" of Germany and of Europe. By advocating Britain's participation in a United States of Europe, he implied that Western Europe, and eventually the whole of Europe, would become an active partner of the United States in the Atlantic Community. Again, by saying that only in the larger political community of the West could the German problem be solved, he inevitably implied that, far from being neutralized, Germany was to become an integral part

[29] *Ibid.*, April 29, 1948.

of a Western coalition. By implication again, he also accepted the possibility that Europe might remain divided indefinitely.

Through 1948, Lippmann continued to vacillate between
an independent Europe, uncommitted as between Anglo-
America and the Soviet Union, and a Europe which was a
principal and indispensable member of the Atlantic Community. In May 1948 he wrote that even though Europe
was not as yet ready or willing to federate, its people were
almost unanimous in desiring to see their continent become
a great power in the world, independent of both Moscow
and Washington. They wanted to be a power "in their own
right to decide the fate of Europe and the destiny of the
world."[30] But in October 1948 the negotiation of the Atlantic
Pact once again indicated to him that the nations of the
Atlantic world were one community for war and peace, and
that they could wage neither war nor peace unless they
equipped themselves with a system of unified defense and
common diplomacy.[31]

Through 1949 and afterwards, we were still to find a Europe detached from the Soviet-American tussle, and the
Atlantic Community, comprising Western civilization, competing for Lippmann's allegiance and support. Yet we were
able to perceive a definite swing toward an independent and
uncommitted Europe. We could also notice the hint of an
attempt to reconcile such a Europe with the Atlantic Community, and as a result we could see the latter descending
from the high pedestal of a super-state back to the position
of a shapeless, formless, yet ultimate reality.

During 1949–1950 Lippmann wrote several articles advocating the establishment of a neutral belt to interpose
between the Western and Soviet coalitions. He maintained

[30] *Ibid.*, May 11, 1948.
[31] *Ibid.*, October 28, 1948.

that in keeping the two camps physically separated, this neutral borderland would reduce the danger of war between them. On the other hand, its inclusion in one or the other coalition would bring them in dangerously close contact with each other and thus increase the possibility of conflict.[32] The proposed buffer would also make it possible for the satellites to detach themselves from Russia without having to join an anti-Russian coalition. But most important of all, the neutral zone would provide a place for Germany. For "the only solution of the German problem," wrote Lippmann, "is to invite her to take her place in a widening zone of buffer nations not actively participating in the world-wide conflict of the great powers."[33] In 1950 he predicted that in the years to come an increasing number of states would want to keep out of the struggle between the United States and the Soviet Union, since they were both equally capable of devastating them in the event of war.

The only alternative to an indecisive war in which they can hope for no security against devastation from both sides is the progressive neutralization of a great buffer belt from Scandinavia to the Mediterranean. . . . They cannot be the frontier posts of a military system which cannot insure their security in case of war. They must do something else. That something else is to disalign themselves . . . no matter what their ideological sympathies, and to seek security in as much neutrality as the balance of power among the great nations enables them to maintain.[34]

Germany was the core of the proposed buffer belt. Lippmann emphasized that the world could have no peace so long as that country was divided at the Iron Curtain into two states —one a satellite of the West and the other a puppet of the Soviet. The alternative to the existing volatile situation in

[32] *Ibid.*, January 18 and March 10, 1949.
[33] *Ibid.*, February 15, 1949.
[34] *Ibid.*, January 12, 1950.

which the two camps faced each other in the heart of Europe lay in making a reunited, neutralized Germany the nucleus of a buffer belt, including Austria, Switzerland, Italy, the Scandinavian countries, Yugoslavia and Greece. Lippmann explained that the prospect of neutrality would meet the true wishes of the people who would compose the buffer belt. Therefore, "were we to make it our purpose . . . we would make ourselves convincingly, as alas we are not today, the champions of peace and national freedom" in Europe.[35] Moreover, the development of such a buffer around Germany was inevitable, for the Germans were too great and dynamic a people to live as satellites or to remain divided for long.[36] In the interest of its own survival and independence, this "widening zone" of neutral states would resist absorption into either military system; there was no danger that one day it might join hands with Russia.

In recommending the creation of a large neutral borderland revolving around a reunited Germany, Lippmann apparently brushed aside the thesis that history had endowed the Germans not only with a domineering disposition but also with those other qualities—military experience, industrial skill, diligence and discipline—which made German domination of Europe inevitable. And if he did not, then we must conclude that he reconciled himself to the prospect of German domination—economic and cultural, if not military—of the proposed buffer belt.

In the Schuman Plan, Lippmann saw the cure for the seemingly irreconcilable dissensions between France and Germany, and the means by which Europe could achieve and retain the position of a great and independent power. In May 1950 he wrote that if the plan materialized "then in the Franco-German partnership there will come into existence

[35] Ibid., March 16, 1950. Also April 10 and 11, 1950.
[36] Ibid., April 17, 1950.

the nucleus of a European power—of that 'third force' which is so indispensable to the stabilization of Europe and to peace in the world."[37] Lippmann discounted the belief held in certain quarters that the Franco-German partnership envisaged in the Schuman Plan would become the nucleus of a West European system. This, he said, was impossible, because Germany could never relinquish "her national unity or her organic connections with Eastern Europe." The virtue of this partnership lay precisely in its potential to stir up and hasten the movements for German and European unity.[38] Lippmann explained that allied with each other Germany and France would gain enormously in stature and prestige among the nations of Europe. Their combination would acquire a tremendous negotiating power, and Germany, as a result, would find it much easier to arrive at a mutually agreeable settlement with Eastern Europe.[39] But if these two leading nations of Europe did not cooperate, the Continent would have to go without its postwar reconstruction. In addition,

Its nations will become the satellites or the clients of the non-European powers. And at the worst its cities and its lands will be

[37] *Ibid.*, May 11, 1950. The "Third Force" is a favorite slogan of French neutralists. They denounced the Atlantic Pact as "a total renunciation of the policy that Franch adopted at the time of the liberation—to be the arbiter, a meeting ground for conciliation, an intermediary zone placed between the two blocs. The Pact means the end of what might have been a great French postwar policy." Alexander Worth, "Where the French Score," *New Statesman and Nation*, Vol. 38, No. 958 (July 16, 1949), p. 64.

[38] T and T, May 15, 1950.

[39] *Ibid.* Far from facilitating the reunification of Germany, the Schuman Plan did, according to Carlo Schmid, create a "grave obstacle" to it. The territorial jurisdiction of the Plan cannot be extended without the consent of all the six members of the Coal and Steel Community. This means, says Schmid, that a united Germany must either agree to remaining split into two economic systems or else permit the powers represented on the High Authority to dictate the conditions under which Germany will be reunited. Schmid, *op. cit.*, pp. 540–541.

the battlefields where nothing can be decided certainly except that European civilization will be ruined.[40]

Lippmann went on to advise that acting independently and separately France and Germany could exercise little influence in a world where the United States, the Soviet Union and the British Commonwealth were the leading powers.

The fourth great power, which is waiting to be born, is the Commonwealth of Europe. It will be born when France and Germany have formed a lasting partnership. . . . To this nucleus will adhere the surrounding countries that are free to do so. The others [Eastern Europe] will know where they can go when they are free again. . . . Because the European Commonwealth opens up to the people of Europe the prospect not only of a material improvement but of their greatness and of their historic mission, it will provide a great reason for their loyalty.[41]

This time Lippmann included even France in his "neutral borderland," leaving only Great Britain and the United States to constitute the Western Coalition. For it is clear that if the proposed Commonwealth of Europe were to admit the "surrounding countries," including ultimately the Soviet satellites, then it was none other than the familiar "neutral and independent" Europe referred to above.

Lippmann's views on Western plans and projects for West European defense further reveal his commitment to the idea of an "all-European system," and provide valuable insights into his position on the relations of Europe with the rest of the Western world. In his *Isolation and Alliances* (1952), he maintained that the decision to incorporate a rearmed West Germany into the Atlantic alliance had put Western statesmen in the "wholly untenable position" where their

[40] T and T, May 25, 1950. The advocates of a neutral Europe would wholeheartedly endorse Lippmann's position. See Robert Barrat, "A Neutral Europe," *Commonweal*, Vol. 52, No. 10 (June 16, 1950), p. 245.

[41] T and T, July 6, 1950.

strategic interests and planning seemed to contravene the German desire for national unity. The Red Army would not evacuate Germany, which meant that Germany would not be reunited, except as the result of a general agreement between the occupying powers to withdraw. But if the British, French and American forces together with the Red Army did leave Germany, then Western military plans and strategy would have to be radically revised. Lippmann warned that

the military system of our alliance . . . will rest on quicksand, if in a country like Germany we cannot support the irreducible minimum national interests of the German people. We are unable to do that so long as our military interests are founded on the partition of Germany.[42]

Western declarations in support of the reunification of Germany did not sound convincing because the West had not formulated and proposed a plan which would, under known conditions, lead to the evacuation of Germany. Lippmann suggested that the United States should agree to withdraw from Germany, simultaneously with the other occupying powers, on the condition that a reunited Germany enter a "European system," which meant

first of all, a reconciliation between united Germany and France, a reconciliation which is so thorough that it can be sealed by a Franco-German alliance within which Germany and France would be bound to concert their foreign policy in Europe. Until France and Germany are fully at peace the forces of the Atlantic Community must keep watch on the Rhine. For a European system can exist only if at the heart of it there is Franco-German partnership. Without that partnership Europe cannot be united. With that partnership, a preponderance of the interest and weight of the European continent will be on the side of a European system.[43]

[42] *Isolation and Alliances*, p. 52.
[43] *Ibid.*, pp. 53–54.

Lippmann went on to propose that France and Germany thus united should then open negotiations with Poland to fix the German-Polish frontier, provide for the relief of the expellees, and conclude an economic treaty. Only when all three of these powers—France, Germany and Poland—had reconciled their differences and reached an understanding, could one speak "with any seriousness about the unity of Europe or, as I should prefer to call it, a European system."[44]

Lippmann has often opposed the political integration of Western Europe as a means of increasing its contribution to Western defense. He has taken the position that Europe must be protected and made secure in order that its nations may work for unity. In other words, instead of asking West Europeans to unite and thus increase their military potential, the United States should shield them from aggression by maintaining a favorable balance of power with the Soviet Union, while they endeavor to overcome their emotional, constitutional and other reservations to a politically united Europe. In 1950 he warned that if European unity and NATO, which was a military alliance directed at the Soviet Union, became identified with each other in the public mind in America and abroad, then Europe would never be united. One could not possibly exclude Austria and East Germany from a united Europe. And yet it was certain that Russia would never permit them to join an anti-Russian coalition. The Western powers should therefore aim at creating an all-European system, which must be loose so that it could accommodate nations with different social systems. The development of such a system would show the Europeans what Europe could be "if it were no longer partitioned, no longer occupied, no longer helpless and satellite—and yet were not once again to fall under the threat of domination by the most dynamic of the European nations."[45]

[44] *Ibid.*, p. 55.
[45] T and T, December 24, 1951; also January 3, 1952.

This was the beginning of Lippmann's battle against the EDC. He carried it on with increasing vigor in the following months and years—on the grounds, first, that it would freeze the division of Europe at the Elbe,[46] and second, that by imposing on the unwilling French a German army in a larger West European military establishment it would sharpen rather than mitigate Franco-German differences.[47] In other words, it would defeat the two indispensable conditions of European unity. He advised the United States to undertake "a great diplomatic effort" for reviving the movement toward Franco-German reconciliation and partnership in the business of Europe.[48] If necessary for achieving this objective, the EDC and NATO should be scrapped. For "while there may be alternatives to EDC, there is none to Franco-German partnership."[49] Lippmann even suggested that the West European economic, political and military system should be converted into an all-European system.[50] The United States, on her part, should concentrate on the Atlantic Community, which was a "far greater thing, more reliable and more deeply founded than any of the hastily contrived pacts of recent times."[51]

[46] German socialists took the very same position. In the article cited above, Carlo Schmid argued that the integration of West Germany in the Western military system would certainly jeopardize German reunification. It was futile, he observed, to expect the Russians "to renounce the East German potential in order that this potential may be fitted into a political and military pact which the Russians must feel is directed against them." Schmid, *op. cit.*, p. 544. In this thesis, the German Social Democrats had the support of the Bevan Laborites in Britain. See "Paved with Good Intentions," *New Statesman and Nation* Vol. 42, No. 1085 (December 22, 1951), pp. 723–724.

[47] The EDC did indeed embitter Franco-German relations in that it aroused a widespread fear in France that a German army would reign supreme in Europe and would eventually become the instrument of German hegemony. See *United States-European Tensions*, Part II, pp. 103–104, nn. 50, 55. Also see *New Statesman and Nation*, Vol. 43, No. 1094 (February 23, 1952), p. 201.

[48] T and T, January 8, 1953.

[49] T and T, December 17, 1953. The Gaullists shared Lippmann's view

In 1955 Lippmann wrote that the Russians were moving toward the position that the issue of German unification could be solved only within the framework of a general security system in which both Eastern and Western Europe could participate. They seemed to favor negotiations for the creation of a neutral belt which should include some if not all of the satellites. He commented:

There is no good reason why we should shrink from the negotiation, why we should not seek such a negotiation. . . . The idea is of capital importance to those who want to free Eastern Europe. Eastern Europe cannot be freed by war, and the Kremlin would not release [its countries] to go and join NATO. The only way is that they should be able to enter a community of neutrals. Our reaction should not be to reject it but to ask that it should be widened.[52]

It would seem incredible that Lippmann should have been willing to barter away the EDC and a going concern such as NATO for a vague and loose entity—the European system. However, his readiness to dispense with these organizations makes sense when we consider it alongside his conviction that the security of Western Europe from Soviet aggression depends not upon its own military power but upon the nuclear deterrent power of the United States, upon the maintenance of an over-all balance of power between the United States and the Soviet Union. Western Europe does not and cannot make a significant contribution to the Western side of this balance.

The Atlantic Pact, according to Lippmann, had merely

---

on the importance, and also on the ways and means, of mending Franco-German relations. See Jacques Soustelle, "France and Europe: A Gaullist View," *Foreign Affairs*, Vol. 30, No. 4 (July 1952), pp. 547–548.

[50] T and T, September 15, 1953.

[51] *Ibid.*, February 16, 1953.

[52] T and T, May 17, 1955.

legalized an existing reality, to wit, that an attack on any nation west of the Soviet orbit would be deemed an attack on the United States. The physical presence of American troops on the continent gave Europeans the needed assurance that America's promise to defend them would be honored the moment they were attacked. Its principal objective was to bolster the morale of Europe and to give it that sense of security which it needed to work constructively for its unity and independence "as a new great power" on a par with the United States and the Soviet Union.[53]

There was something hollow and unconvincing in the official view of NATO. He explained:

It is a long time since any one has really believed, if any one ever believed it, that the security of Europe and of the Atlantic Community depends upon being able to win a defensive battle on the German ground between the Rhine and the Elbe rivers.[54]

The essence of NATO lay in

a North American guaranty to go to war if there is a Soviet military aggression across the frontiers of the members of the NATO alliance. . . . Upon this fundamental guaranty there has been erected a superstructure . . . on the assumption that if the Soviet Union decided for a war of aggression it would use the Red Army to invade and conquer [Western Europe]. This as-

[53] T and T, January 3, April 14, May 3, 1949. See also *ibid.*, August 10 and 24, 1950; December 18, 1951; June 3, 1952.

It is interesting to note here that Lippmann's view of the Atlantic Pact as a North American guaranty to defend Western Europe was almost literally adopted by the *New Statesman and Nation* in its issue of July 14, 1951. It noted: "What has deterred the Kremlin from launching war during the last two years when it had overwhelming military superiority? . . . It is clear that the deterrent must have been the threat of a long war with the West in which, as Stalin once remarked to Roosevelt, America's vast industrial potential would always win. In short, insofar as a military deterrent is important, the Atlantic Pact, which is in fact an American guarantee of Western Europe, is the effective force, not the size of any particular European country's armaments." Vol. 42, No. 1062, p. 32.

[54] T and T, August 18, 1955.

sumption was adopted before the Soviet Union had developed serious nuclear power of its own. . . . On this assumption, which was most strongly held in the bad days of the Korean War, the NATO powers decided to build up a large European army which was to include strong West German forces. The troubles of NATO have been wholly concerned with this army superstructure. Neither the French nor the Germans, the nations presumably most interested in the NATO army, seem to be taking it very seriously.[55]

Lippmann went on to explain that France and Germany did not take this army superstructure seriously because no one in these countries, or for that matter anywhere else, believed that in spite of the abundance of nuclear weapons on both sides the next great war would begin with the invasion of Western Europe by the Red Army.

In the early 1960's Lippmann is still very much concerned with the problems of Germany's place in Europe. He tends to the view that these problems can be solved best by creating a "European system." The Common Market, he says, has always rested on the premise that "West Germany must be reconciled with France, and that a new political community must be created which controls German sovereignty and recognizes tacitly that the unification of Germany is impossible."[56] The present union in Europe would eventually become a political entity capable of exercising equal influence with the super-powers. If the current prosperity of Western Europe can be combined with a "far-sighted over-all central European arrangement," it will attract and influence the countries of Eastern Europe enormously.[57]

The United States is, of course, outside the European community. But she must consider how she and the rest of

[55] *Ibid.*, May 1956.
[56] T and T, October 3, 1961.
[57] *Ibid.*

the non-communist world—especially Australia, Canada, New Zealand and Latin America—will adjust to the Common Market. The "clue to policy," according to Lippmann, may lie in the formation of economic and political communities which can represent their member nations in dealing with the outside world. The United States, Canada and Latin America could be one such community. Japan, Australia, New Zealand and the Philippines might be another.[58]

In the several articles written on the subject during 1961 and early 1962, Lippmann nowhere specifically refers to the need for a German-Polish reconciliation. But he seems to see an all-around acceptance of the present division of Germany which would accomplish the essential objective of the German-Polish reconciliation he has advocated so often in the past. The policy of German reunification, he says, was always insincere, always a "shabby hoax."[59] The Soviet Union opposed it, and so did the Western powers. "Although it is never openly avowed, the whole of Europe, West and East, from France to Poland and Czechoslovakia, is deeply committed to the partition of Germany."[60] The attitude of West Germany herself toward the question of her national reunification, says Lippmann, is ambiguous. She has learned to live comfortably without reunification. But neither West Germany nor the other Western powers are willing to acknowledge, sign and seal the partition of Germany because they fear that the German public opinion will then demand the withdrawal of West Germany from the Atlantic Alliance. "Dr. Adenauer and General De Gaulle are haunted by the fear that one of Dr. Adenauer's successors may do once again what the Germans have so often done in the past—make a deal with the Russians at the expense of the West."[61]

[58] Ibid.
[59] T and T, October 31, 1961.
[60] Ibid., September 12, 1961.
[61] Ibid., September 12, 1961; also September 19, 1961.

The possibility of a German-Russian "deal" is, according to Lippmann, still very real. In a recent statement, which merits lengthy quotation, he observed:

We have many reasons for supposing that the German nation will move in some variant of its historic national policy. It will move, that is to say, toward one of those accommodations with Russia which have for two centuries followed its many wars with Russia. Recent events in West Germany support this hypothesis. The Free Democratic Party, which is conservative and nationalist, . . . has never lost sight of Germany's interest in the East. The West German ambassador in Moscow, Dr. Kroll, is an avowed believer in a Russo-German rapprochement, and that he was scolded by the minor officials in the Foreign Office but upheld by Dr. Adenauer is, to say the least, a straw in the wind.

There is little doubt, it seems to me, that the purely Western policy of Dr. Adenauer is going to give way to a more Bismarckian policy. The problem for the West is how its ties with West Germany can be maintained against an abnormal and dangerous pull towards the East. Reunification, the rectification of the Eastern frontiers, the opening of vast markets in Russia and China will exert a strong pull on German policy.[62]

Lippmann advises Germans that while they need not formally renounce their national reunification as an ultimate aim, they will have to wait a long time for it and "a lot will have to be done first in order to make it possible in the end."[63] In the meanwhile, they should reconcile themselves to the fact of partition and forego unification as an active and im-

[62] T and T, November 21, 1961.

[63] Ibid., September 19, 1961. Lippmann recalls a conversation in 1958 with a high-ranking West German official, who maintained that during the past fifteen years or so the two Germanies had grown so far apart that it was now idle to talk about their reunification. The ideological, religious and political obstacles to uniting the Protestant and socialist East Germany with the conservative and Catholic West were enormous. The subject of reunification should therefore be approached very gradually. The already existing trade relations between the two German states should be expanded and their level raised so that eventually they might form a confederation. Lippmann added that this happened to be also Mr. Khrushchev's proposal,

mediate objective. The effect of such a policy, he observes, will be profound in Poland and elsewhere in Eastern Europe, where "the fear of a revived and rearmed Germany seeking its lost territories is, next to the Red Army, the most powerful fact which binds the satellite empire to Moscow."[64] With the removal, or reduction, of that fear, the tension in Eastern Europe will decline and a spirit of independence may arise.[65]

Connected with the question of German reunification is the issue of Berlin. Lippmann believes that the present Western policies with respect to West Berlin make the future of that city bleak. By raising the wall between East and West Berlin, Mr. Khrushchev has demolished the hope that the Atlantic Alliance might one day reunify Germany and restore Berlin as its capital.[66] West Berlin is no longer the escape hatch and the show window it once was. It is now not even a good place for intelligence work. It does not any more threaten the security of East Germany and it does not attract East Germans as a symbol of German unity.[67] The decline in the importance of West Berlin will destroy the morale of its people. In the present atmosphere of uncertainty about its future, West Berlin is a doomed and dying city. In order that young men may plan their careers and others may invest their savings there, they must have some basis for confidence in its future.[68] It is not enough to guarantee access to the city to the West. West Berlin will flourish only if it is free and if it has a function to perform in the coming years. The status quo, says Lippmann, cannot prevail for ever. "Sooner or later,

but he had first heard it from this German official, whose record of loyalty to the West is impeccable. "The idea," he noted, "was bound to take hold because it fits so exactly the reality of the German situation." T and T, September 26, 1961.

[64] T and T, September 19, 1961.
[65] *Ibid.* Also T and T, January 11, 1962.
[66] T and T, September 7, 1961.
[67] *Ibid.*, October 17, 1961 and April 3, 1962.
[68] *Ibid.*, September 12, 1961 and January 11, 1962.

the freedom of West Berlin will have to be guaranteed in an international covenant which makes it an international city under the specific protection of the Great Powers, the general protection of NATO and the Warsaw Alliance, and of the United Nations."[69] Having become an international city, West Berlin should become the headquarters of the organs of the United Nations, and a great international center for the study and pursuit of arts and sciences and sports. This will be a good future for West Berlin, "far better than to be a dying city kept alive by subsidies and by the dubious assumption that the United States and its allies will always be willing to live on the brink of a thermonuclear war."[70]

It will be seen that the connotation of Lippmann's "European system" has not remained constant through his expositions of it at different times. Sometime he has represented this European system as an ever-widening neutral belt with Germany at its core. He has first included France in this neutral belt and then excluded her. At times he has conceived his European system as a United States of Europe—a genuine European federation. At other times he has looked upon it as a loosely connected group of sovereign states, which are well disposed toward one another and which cooperate as their common needs and interests may require.

But these are occasional deviations from a pattern of which the following are the distinguishing features: a pacification of Germany which convincingly removes the danger of her once again trying to dominate Europe; the withdrawal of foreign armies, especially the Red Army, from Europe; the eventual emergence of Europe as a great and independent power of equal rank with the United States and the Soviet Union.

The pacification of Germany is the central and the con-

[69] *Ibid.*, April 3, 1962.
[70] *Ibid.*, October 10, 1961.

trolling part of this pattern. Her reconciliation with Poland means her reconciliation to the loss to that country of her eastern territories. Her reconciliation with France is necessary so that France may restrain her domineering propensities, so that France and Germany together and not Germany alone may negotiate with Poland and the Soviet Union, so that Germany may not make a "deal" with the Soviet Union. At one time, Britain's participation in a European system was necessary because France would not hold hands with Germany except in the reassuring presence of Britain. The European system must eventually be an "all-European" rather than a West European system because whereas the latter may be established even without a thorough pacification of Germany, the former cannot be. Western Europe cannot or should not be federated because West Germans, unsublimated by pacification, can enter the armed forces of a federated Europe, and because West German businessmen and industrialists may become the leaders of a West European economy. A federated Europe will be a German Europe.

It would appear that Lippmann's concept of a European system, insofar as it revolves around the pacification of Germany, is essentially negative. His relative indifference to the effective political unity of Western Europe, let us say in the form of a federation, which might eventually include a part or whole of Eastern Europe, constitutes a weakness in his blueprint for the Europe of tomorrow. There was a time when Eastern Europe was free, when the Iron Curtain did not divide Europe at the Elbe, when the German menace did not exist, and when there was no NATO. What was Europe then? Was it, in the power-political sense, anything more than a conglomeration of great and small sovereign states, which spent their lives fearing, fighting and weakening one another? Spain, France, Austria, Prussia, Britain and all the rest were great powers in their turn and time. But history has not known a great politico-military power called Europe. Then how can we expect that Europe as such will become a great power, on a par with the United States and the Soviet Union, merely by re-creating the past with respect to its "independence"? To seek the greatness of Europe without seeking to weld its separate states into a single political unit may be a slogan, but it cannot be the objective of rational policy.

One begins to wonder whether the problem of German domination is at all soluble. If the Germans are indeed so dynamic, resourceful and clever as they are said to be, then perhaps it is in the nature of things, as Lippmann put it in *U.S. War Aims,* that they should dominate Europe. This need not mean that they would subjugate Europe. For why would the far greater number of non-German deputies in a European federal legislature ever sanction a move which sought to bestow special privileges upon the German-speaking citizens of Europe? It may be that Germans will occupy a position of pre-eminence in a European arrangement. Possibly the number of Germans who, by virtue of initiative and hard work, manage to get at the helm of affairs in a federated Europe will be somewhat larger than the number of their French counterparts. But perhaps that is just as well. Perhaps by offering stiff competition, by raising the price of "success," they will give some of their "dynamism" to their fellow Europeans. One may even ask why the Germans should not play a leading role in Europe if, according to the hypothesis, they are endowed with the qualities which make for leadership. It seems that basically the question about Germany is not whether she will dominate Europe, but whether she accepts and means to promote and defend the way of life which Europe must unite to preserve.

The positive content of Lippmann's concept of a European system may be stated as follows: Europe was bled white in the last war. Its decline became all the more conspicuous by the rise of the United States and the Soviet Union to unprecedented heights of power. For the first time in centuries, the great powers of Europe found themselves virtually excluded from the controlling position which they had hitherto occupied in world affairs. Ironically enough, the states of Europe became the stakes of Soviet-American diplomacy. Being a tempting prize for any would-be conqueror, Europe because of its weakness threatened to plunge mankind into the disaster of another war. Europe must rise to its feet again and fill with its own power the vacuum which threatened to make it the battlefield of the great non-European states. Western policy should therefore aim at restoring Europe to the position of a great power. Only a united Europe could fill this position, for no single state in it was even potentially a power comparable to the United States or the Soviet Union.

In order to encourage the movement of independence in Eastern Europe, and also to embarrass the Soviet Union, Anglo-America should, *inter alia,* free their European allies of their commitments and obligations to the Western alliance, promote Franco-German reconciliation and friendship, and thus help create a united and independent West European system which, it was to be hoped, would one day become an all-European system. They could well afford to undertake this program, because they did not need the assistance of Western Europe in balancing the power of the Soviet Union.

Once Europe, or just Western Europe, had achieved unity and the status of a great power, it could decide, much more meaningfully than it could in the existing state of its weakness and disunity, the question of its relation to the rest of the Western world. It might join a "League of the West," or a political union of the Atlantic Community. But even if it chose to retain its "neutral and independent" position, it would continue to be a member of the Western family. It could never become indifferent to the fate of the American and British nations. The Wilsons and Roosevelts of Europe must answer the call, if in a crisis Anglo-America needed their assistance. To preserve its own existence, even if not to rescue the outlying segments of its civilization, the Old World must come to redress the balance of the New—the balance which guarded its own independence and security. In this frame of reference, Lippmann's independent Europe was still very much a member of the Atlantic Community.

The Franco-German reconciliation which Lippmann had advocated for years as a prerequisite to European unity, independence and greatness has finally come about. At his press conference on May 15, 1962, President De Gaulle of France expressed the view that Europe should be organized and led by a Franco-German combination. He maintained also that Britain, being an "island," did not belong to Europe, and that the United States was destined eventually to withdraw from it. Europe should become a great power in its own right, strong enough to come to terms with the Soviet Union. It would extend from the Atlantic to the Urals. In Paris on January 22, 1963 President De Gaulle and Chancellor Adenauer signed a Franco-German treaty of friendship, committing the two countries, among other things, to consulting with each other on all important matters of foreign policy before deciding them. Lippmann interprets the treaty to mean also that West Germany will contribute money, technology and manpower to the creation of a military force which will be under French leadership and control and which will be independent not only of NATO but also of the other states in the West European community.[71]

De Gaulle's design for Europe, says Lippmann, is a "formidable conception of policy." In the Common Market, France and Germany have created a rich and dynamic

[71] T and T, January 24, 1963.

economy which is superior to that of Britain and the Commonwealth and is at least equal to that of the United States. Politically, these two countries are the core of a new great world power. While Germany cannot, under her treaties, make nuclear weapons, she can aid France in developing the nuclear striking force which De Gaulle wants so much to have. But Lippmann is now far from pleased with these developments. He has criticized De Gaulle's policy in *Western Unity* and the Common Market (1962) and in a number of subsequent articles in the New York *Herald Tribune*.

De Gaulle does not fear Soviet aggression against Western Europe. He knows that the United States has achieved, and will do her best to maintain, a decisively favorable balance of nuclear power vis-à-vis the Soviet Union. He takes it for granted that this country will continue its commitment to defend Western Europe until the latter is strong enough to deal with the Soviet Union on equal terms, regardless of what France may do. In the meantime, he feels, there is no need to "woo us" or "to reward us for doing what we have to do."[72] Western Europe is already robust economically. Prophetically, De Gaulle envisions the day when it will not need American military protection. He is acting "as if the future, which is probably coming, has already arrived."[73]

Lippmann argues that the United States cannot welcome a "Gaullist Europe," which means a restrictive and exclusive Franco-German community, whose aim will be to establish a Franco-German, or entirely French, hegemony over Europe.[74] Moreover, De Gaulle's ambition to assume the leadership of Europe is irreconcilable with the American need to "retain the ultimate power in nuclear affairs."[75]

[72] T and T, February 14, 1963.
[73] T and T, January 31, 1963.
[74] *Western Unity and the Common Market*, Chap. 3. Also T and T, January 17, 1963.
[75] T and T, May 24, 1962, February 14 and 21, 1963.

A Franco-German Europe, says Lippmann, is an "optical illusion," which will disintegrate when the two "old kings" who have produced it depart from the scene. For a closed Franco-German community not only violates the vital interests of the United States; it also contravenes the vital interests of West Germany. The Gaullist design is based on the premise that the division of Germany will continue. De Gaulle does not want the Germans to stray away from the Franco-German combination, either to work with Americans and the British in finding a solution to the problem of Berlin or to follow Dr. Kroll toward a larger Russo-German deal.

The hard line that France takes about Berlin and the Soviet Union is founded, we must be sure to understand, on a basic French national determination not to have to live with a large reunited Germany. At bottom the hard policy is directed not against the Russians but against those Germans who want to make an opening to the East. Its purpose is to make any departure from the present position seem un-German and unpatriotic.[76]

A restricted Franco-German Europe hurts German interests also because it jeopardizes the American military commitment in Europe. The United States cannot concede to France a leading position in making decisions about war and peace so long as it carries ultimate responsibility for Western defense. Secondly, the United States needs a large low-tariff trading area in order to earn the foreign exchange for financing its military and civilian commitments abroad. If the European Economic Community becomes a "close, restrictive and exclusive society," then this country "cannot earn the cost of defending that community on the ground in Europe."[77] Then this restrictive society must pay for its own defense. Then Americans, with their dollar deficits and with their increasing responsibilities in the Western Hemisphere, Asia

[76] *Western Unity and the Common Market*, p. 32.
[77] *Ibid.*, p. 38.

and Africa, cannot go on "subsidizing the local and tactical defense of the European continent."[78] It is not without reason that many European leaders and governments—Jean Monnet, M. Spaak, Dr. Hallstein, Dr. Erhard, the Netherlands government, leading German industrialists, the Free Democratic Party and also the Social Democrats in Germany, and "the leading spirits of the present Italian coalition"—also oppose a Franco-German Europe.[79]

Lippmann urges the Germans to blast the idea of a Gaullist Europe. They can do so by insisting that the Common Market should include Britain and somehow accommodate the Commonwealth. The Common Market should also include other European states, and it should establish a partnership with the United States. The "grand project" of building an enlarged Common Market along these lines is in "the manifest destiny of the West." The real interests of Germany do not lie in promoting Gaullist grandeur. They run

with the Atlantic Community and with a wider European society, open enough to be an attraction to the European peoples on the other side of the Iron Curtain. To promote this wider community is the way to save Berlin, it is the way to reunite Germany, it is the way to unite Europe, it is the way to confront peaceably and successfully the Soviet Union.[80]

Lippmann's criticism of the so-called Gaullist Europe is not easy to understand. The objectives he attributes to De Gaulle—the creation of a Europe which extends from the Atlantic to the Urals, which is independent of both "Uncle Sam" and "Mother-in-law Russia," which is strong enough to be the master of its own destiny, of which the core and the leading force is a Franco-German combination

[78] Ibid., p. 38.
[79] Ibid., p. 25. Also see T and T, January 17, 1963.
[80] Western Unity and the Common Market, p. 32.

—are the very same which Lippmann himself has endorsed and advocated times without number throughout the post-World War II period. It may be that France does not want to have to live with a reunited Germany, and that therefore De Gaulle does not want West Germany to "stray away" in search of "openings to the East." But then, according to Lippmann himself, no country in Western or Eastern Europe wants to live with a reunited Germany. The Western policy of German reunification has always been a "shabby hoax." Germany not only cannot be reunited in the foreseeable future, it need not be reunited. De Gaulle wants the "Anglo-Saxons" to leave Europe to the Europeans. Lippmann too has advocated such a course of action many times in the past. De Gaulle wants to develop a nuclear force which will be independent of the American nuclear power. But how, in the nuclear age, can Europe become a great power equal to the United States and the Soviet Union, which Lippmann has so often urged it to become, without developing independent nuclear force?

There is merit in Lippmann's argument that an independent French nuclear striking force will be both useless and dangerous for the West because it will be inadequate for defending Western Europe against the Soviet Union, because it could start a war but not finish it. It would have been in keeping with Lippmann's advocacy of an independent and united Europe to propose that the United States help France, or an organically united Western Europe of which the "core" is a Franco-German combination, become a great nuclear power capable of deterring aggression, and then withdraw from the responsibility of defending Western Europe. But such a proposal Lippmann has not made.

De Gaulle does not want a federated Europe. He would rather have a loose system of cooperating sovereign states. Barring one or two occasions, Lippmann himself has not been a warm advocate of a federated Europe. His own European system is a loose arrangement. Indeed, De Gaulle's design for the Europe of tomorrow is almost an exact replica of Lippmann's "European system."

Lippmann objects that the Gaullist Europe is restrictive. In *Western Unity and the Common Market,* he himself observes that De Gaulle is thinking of a Europe which extends from the Atlantic to the Urals. Then in what way is it restrictive? It is restrictive because De Gaulle does not welcome Britain into the Common Market. He does not welcome the Commonwealth—which consists not only of countries that are part of Western civilization but also of others in Asia and Africa. But above all, De Gaulle wants to seize from the United States the position of leadership in Europe and the power of deciding its fate, of directing its destiny.

Lippmann has once again swung toward the Atlantic Community. His *Western Unity and the Common Market* would appear to be a repudiation of his earlier position with respect to a "European system." However, such a judgment should be tempered with the following considerations. His arguments in favor of a European system were made mostly in the context of a situation where the possibility of a European power challenging the position of the United States as the leader of the West was remote. Western Europe then did not have an independent negotiating power, vis-à-vis the Soviet Union, which would be based on its own military power. For a position of strength in negotiation, it depended on the United States. With the prosperity that the Common Market has brought to France and Germany, with the development of French nuclear power supported by the alliance with Germany, the possibility of that challenge has become real and imminent. Lippmann does not like it. In his view, French rivalry with the United States threatens to disrupt the Atlantic Alliance, of which the essence is an American readiness to defend Western Europe against Soviet agression. It threatens also to break up the Atlantic Community, which is not only a strategic system but is also a bond of mutual understanding that the Western world has a common destiny. In this community, serious rivalry between a European power and the United States is inadmissible.

We have noted above that even in his advocacy of a European system, Lippmann had believed that his united, independent and great Europe would never become indifferent to the fate of the American and British nations, that it would answer the call if Anglo-America needed it. It would appear that in Lippmann's present view Anglo-America now does need Europe, especially the Common Market. The case of Britain's need is patent. The United States needs access to the markets of Western Europe to bolster its "fading economic pre-eminence."[81] Indeed, she needs a "great open low-tariff area," to include the entire Western world and even parts of the Orient—Japan and the Philippines.

Lippmann's opposition to a "Gaullist Europe" may be due also to his fear that the Franco-German combination is aiming really at the hegemony of Europe. This fear stems probably from his assessment that the present French and German governments are both authoritarian rather than liberal and democratic. In all seriousness, he observes that since France does not have a hereditary monarchy, the question of succession to De Gaulle is fraught with the possibility of large-scale disorder in that country after the General's retirement. France's return to a system of genuine democratic government is problematic. Although West Germany has made a spectacular economic recovery, she has not yet had a chance to mature politically. The present Franco-German combination is thus a combination of illiberal forces which cannot be trusted with the leadership of Europe.[82] It seems

[81] *Western Unity and the Common Market*, p. 3.
[82] *Western Unity and the Common Market,* Chapter 3. See also T and T, January 17 and February 5, 1963.

that in Lippmann's mind there lurks also the fear that in a Franco-German combination Germany, and not France, may emerge as the more dynamic power, and that Western Europe may get not Franco-German but wholly German leadership. Hence the need for Britain's presence in any West European economic and political arrangement. But Britain now is not the power that she once was. She may not counterbalance the influence of a Franco-German "axis." The power and the influence of the United States must be added to those of Great Britain in order to prevent the Germans, or Franco-Germans, from leading Western Europe in directions of their choosing. A West European system must therefore give way to the Atlantic Community.

Curiously enough, it is now the Atlantic Community, and not the old familiar European system, which will solve the problem of Berlin, reunite Germany, and unite Europe. It will be seen that Lippmann has now returned to the position which he had taken briefly in 1948. The problems of German and European unity can be solved only through negotiating the related issues with the Soviet Union. The West should conduct these negotiations from a position of strength, which is supplied principally by the United States. The actual reunification of Germany and of Europe may take a long time, perhaps a generation or more. During this period, there may occur developments which will dictate a change in the present Soviet policy. The exact nature of these developments cannot be foreseen. But the West will pull through this long haul and take advantage of favorable situations as and when they arise only if it stands united and maintains its position of strength, which can best be done by promoting the Atlantic Community.

It follows from Lippmann's opposition to the development of an independent French nuclear force that in his view the primary responsibility for Western defense should continue to rest with the United States. The leading role in planning the strategy of war and peace should therefore also remain with this country. The Atlantic Community, consisting of the entire Western world and associated in a friendly way with the non-communist Asians and Africans, should confront the communist world as long as it may be necessary to contain it, to reduce its influence, to disrupt it, even to reform it and to convert it to a liberal way of life as future events and developments may permit.[83] Over this grand coalition for the defense of the non-communist world and for the uplift of mankind the United States should preside, with Great Britain as the next ranking member.

It appears that the decisive reason that has swung Lippmann away from his European system and returned him to the Atlantic Community is the prospect of active rivalry between a European center of power and the United States. In advocating a great, independent and united Europe, built around the core of a Franco-German partnership, he should have foreseen such rivalry. Perhaps he did. But now that the rivalry threatens to become real and significant, he finds it to be detrimental to both the United States and the West as a whole. It would appear to follow, then, that Mr. Lippmann's forceful and continuous advocacy of a "European system" over the last decade and a half has been misplaced. It is possible that at a future date, under another set of cir-

[83] More than once Lippmann has expressed the hope that communist Russia might one day become liberal and democratic. According to him, Mr. Khrushchev is leading the forces of modernization in Russia, forces which are changing the character of the Soviet state, "changing it from a Byzantine despotism into what might be described as a Western state in the very early phases of its development. . . . The same practical circumstances which brought the West its liberty . . . are present in the Soviet Union. A complex society cannot be made to work without a large measure of personal liberty and personal incentive and popular consent. . . . Although everything moves faster than it used to move, we must not forget how long it took for our free institutions to grow from their beginnings in the Middle Ages." T and T, February 13, 1962.

cumstances, Lippmann may once again advance and support the idea of an independent and united Europe. But it is clear that in his mind this idea is feasible and desirable only in the context of a basic harmony of interests among the Western powers. When the independence of Europe, which in the final analysis means its right to go its separate way, becomes incompatible with the essential unity of the Western world, then, in Lippmann's view, the concept of a "European system" must yield to the larger concept of the Atlantic Community.

How does Lippmann's position on the postwar evolution of Europe fit in with his views on regionalism? The foregoing should establish that in his opinion the nation-state should give way to a larger and more inclusive unit of political organization to afford security and stability, peace and prosperity to the peoples of the world. While his basic commitment to the principle of regionalism has remained unimpaired, he has changed his wartime proposal for postwar regional organization in some important respects. In *U.S. War Aims* he allotted, so to speak, Eastern Europe to the Soviet orbit. But since the Soviet Union has failed to act like a good neighbor, he now holds that Western policy should aim at eventually pulling the states of Eastern Europe out of the Soviet "strategic system." In order to create a place where the satellites may find peace and security, he favored the evolution of Europe into a separate region. But even then he did not exclude the possibility that at some future date Europe might choose to coordinate, or even integrate, its military and foreign policies with Anglo-America, in which case the Atlantic Community would become a super-region.

The preceding pages will also confirm our conclusion in a previous chapter that Lippmann would like to see the Western world, under liberal Anglo-American leadership, establish and maintain a clearly favorable balance of power vis-à-vis the communist world. Under the aegis of this liberal and preponderant Western power, mankind may march towards creating a good life on earth.

It is not enough for the West to maintain a preponderance of military power to ensure the final triumph of liberty over tyranny. It must also offer mankind something which warms the heart and elevates the soul. But before they can offer it, the men of the West must possess it. They must show that they have not only the desire but also the ability to lead the world in creating the good society. Do they have the ability? Lippmann tends to think that they are in grave danger of demolishing, by their own unwisdom and neglect, the citadel of liberal democracy which their forefathers had built through the centuries. A study of Lippmann's concept of liberal democracy will be the concern of our next chapter.

VII

The Public Philosophy: A Theory of Government

THE UNITED STATES EMERGED FROM WORLD WAR II NOT ONLY
as the mightiest power on earth, but also as the guarantor of
Europe's liberty and the guardian of Western civilization.
Gone forever are the days of aloofness from the "mischievous" entanglements of foreign friendships. With aston-
ishing eagerness and fervor, Americans in the postwar period
have looked for allies and taken them wherever they have
found them. About twenty-five years ago, President Roosevelt
pledged his administration to shun political commitments
abroad which might involve the United States in "foreign
wars."[1] Today, under the North Atlantic Alliance, "a quarter
of a million American soldiers, drafted from home in time of
peace, are sprawled across Europe in bivouac and barrack.
. . . These men are the flesh of America's pledge that Europe's destiny is ours."[2] This revolution in American outlook
testifies that in the current conflict between the Free World

[1] Address in New York on August 14, 1936. See *Roosevelt's Foreign
Policy 1931–41: Franklin D. Roosevelt's Unedited Speeches and Messages*
(New York: Wilfred Funk, Inc., 1942), p. 102.
[2] Theodore H. White, *Fire in the Ashes: Europe in Mid-Century* (New
York: William Sloane Associates, 1953), p. 7.

and international communism the stakes are no less than life
and death. And while free men everywhere forego the good
things of life in order to spare the billions needed for the
defense of freedom, it would indeed be a calamity if they
lost the battle by sheer mismanagement of their affairs at
home and abroad. In Lippmann's view this is not merely a
theoretical possibility; it is a real danger, to which he has repeatedly called attention.

Lippmann's *U.S. Foreign Policy* (1943) is a long criticism
of the manner in which Americans have conducted their
foreign relations. During the greater part of the nineteenth
century, he said, they did not formulate a foreign policy
because they did not need one. But in this long period of
relative peace they also forgot the nature of foreign policy,
and lost the art of shaping it. When the twentieth century
thrust upon them the status and the responsibilities of a great
power, they did not know what to seek in their foreign affairs. As a result, for nearly fifty years they remained without
an intelligent, coherent or generally accepted foreign policy.
Lippmann found "the spectacle of this great nation which
does not know its own mind" both humiliating and dangerous.[3] Five years later he observed that the history of American foreign relations in the present century was one of "repeated declarations and repeated disappointments."[4]

In *The Public Philosophy*, Lippmann charged that since
the turn of the century the Western democracies had all
mismanaged their foreign affairs. Twice in a generation the
brute forces of despotism had threatened the defenders of
liberty and found them unprepared to meet the challenge.
During the interwar period, democratic leaders and statesmen
placidly watched the clouds of a second war rise from the

[3] *U.S. Foreign Policy*, pp. 3–6.
[4] Walter Lippmann, "Philosophy and United States Foreign Policy,"
Vital Speeches, Vol. 45, No. 8 (February 1, 1948), p. 243.

smoke and ruin of the first. They drifted with the current of events rather than attempting to govern and control its direction. They won the war again. But, once more, they lost the peace.

Could it be denied that they were sick with some kind of incapacity to cope with reality, to govern their affairs, to defend their vital interests and, it might be, to insure their survival as free and democratic states?[5]

Other writers share Lippmann's view that the democracies have failed to discern and protect their vital interests. Some of them tend to see in the democratization of policy-making a major reason for the failure of Western diplomacy in recent times. They point to a "golden age" in the conduct of foreign affairs, when the masses as well as their elected representatives were virtually excluded from the antechambers where matters of high policy were deliberated and decided. The "right" of the people to know all the "facts" was severely limited, and the principle of the system was that the vital issues of war and peace were the concern of the executive department. In the words of Sir Harry Johnston,

In those days, a country's relations with its neighbours or with distant lands were dealt with almost exclusively by the head of the state—Emperor, King or President—acting with the more or less dependent Minister of State, who was no representative of the masses, but the employé of the monarch. Events were prepared and sprung on a submissive, a confident, or a stupid people. The public press criticized, more often applauded, but had at most to deal with a *fait accompli* and make the best of it. . . . [In England, for instance] the foreign policy of the Empire was shaped by a small camarilla consisting of the Sovereign, two Cabinet Ministers, the permanent Under-Secretary of State for Foreign Affairs, and perhaps one representative of *la plus haute finance.*[6]

[5] *The Public Philosophy*, pp. 5–6.
[6] Sir Harry Johnston, *Common Sense in Foreign Policy* (New York: E. P. Dutton and Co., 1913), p. 1.

The case of the United States was somewhat different. Congress has always had the right to be consulted in matters such as the declaration of war and the ratification of treaties. But one should add that the framers of the Constitution did not intend this right to operate as an instrument of democratic control of foreign affairs.[7] In the "golden age," even the Congress of the United States recognized the pre-eminence of the executive in the external relations of the republic. As early as February 15, 1816, the Senate Committee on Foreign Relations, reporting on negotiations with foreign nations, observed:

They think the interference of the Senate in the direction of foreign negotiations calculated to . . . impair the best security for the national safety. The nature of transactions with foreign nations, moreover, requires caution and unity of design, and their success frequently depends on secrecy and dispatch.[8]

On their part, the people of the United States showed, according to Lippmann, a remarkable appreciation and respect for the principle of executive supremacy in matters of war and peace. When World War I broke out, they wanted to remain out of it. But they did not trust Congress, which was in recess, to achieve this objective for them. Describing the situation in *The Stakes of Diplomacy* (1915), Lippmann wrote that most Americans who desired peace also wished Congress to stay at home.

Instead of shouting for the people's representatives to assemble and restrain the autocrat, we knew that the mere act of summon-

[7] W. Stull Holt, *Treaties Defeated by the Senate* (Baltimore: The Johns Hopkins Press, 1933), p. 11.

According to Thomas Jefferson, "the transaction of business with foreign nations is executive altogether," and in the words of John Marshall, "the President is the sole organ of the nation in its external relations, and its sole representative with foreign nations." Cited in Quincy Wright, *The Control of American Foreign Relations* (New York: The Macmillan Company, 1922), p. 21.

[8] L. Larry Leonard, *Elements of American Foreign Policy* (New York: McGraw-Hill Book Company, Inc., 1953), p. 45.

ing Congress would be a threat of war. . . . The prospect of lavish rhetoric and lavish appropriations, of resolutions calling on the Secretary of State to explain this and furnish information about that, the interviews, proposals and speeches which might be let loose, the heat which would be engendered, made those of us who hoped for peace prefer to trust the cool intentions of Mr. Wilson.[9]

Americans discovered that their desire for peace conflicted with their devotion to democratic principles. But they also found that they could not realize the desired objective except by abandoning the pretense that "the people" could conduct and control their foreign relations in a positive manner.[10]

In *The Stakes of Diplomacy*, Lippmann not only accepted but also justified the exclusion of the masses from the formulation of foreign policy. He maintained that while the democratic method of making decisions might work in domestic affairs, it was inherently inappropriate to the conduct of foreign relations. The two realms of governmental activity stood on somewhat different footings. Lippmann explained that in their relations with one another nations acted as sovereign entities, unrestrained by a common higher authority. They settled their differences either by the quiet give-and-take of negotiation and compromise or by war. In either case, it was manifestly necessary that a nation should speak with one voice and act as one person in its dealings with the "foreigner." Public debate of the issues involved would make it impossible for a government to maintain that "unity of design" or the "secrecy and dispatch" which were so important to success in foreign affairs. No wonder then that "the most advanced republics are autocratic in the management of foreign affairs. They are autocratic because democracy can never deal with an affair that is 'foreign.' "[11]

[9] *The Stakes of Diplomacy*, pp. 16–17.
[10] *Ibid.*, p. 25.
[11] *The Stakes of Diplomacy*, pp. 45–46. Alexis De Tocqueville anticipated Lippmann on this point by almost eighty years. Writing with special

Lippmann also argued that the masses were unable to think rationally about the intricacies of their relations with other states. For one thing, events on the scene of international politics moved too fast for the common man to comprehend their meaning and significance, with the result that popular sentiment on the crucial questions of war and peace was generally out of gear with objective developments.[12] The emergence of the media of mass communication did not improve the situation, for the new magnates were usually more interested in selling their product than in enlightening their audience. They undoubtedly made and molded public opinion, but paradoxically enough they were also afraid of it. They preferred to cater to the wishes, fears and prejudices of their readers, however unreasonable and ill-founded these might be. Moreover, their material had to be dramatic in order to be newsworthy. Editors and commentators could not declare in time of peace that "goodwill between France and Britain is on the increase," or shout about "the aggression that will not take place, or announce with joy the markets that are not coveted."[13] It was difficult to say good things, however true, about the foreigner. Ignorance and distrust of his manners and motives made him a handy villain against whom public feeling could be easily aroused. One should also remember, said Lippmann, that most people did not think about foreign affairs at all. "It would be sheer hypocrisy to pretend that any large section of the American people is informed, or interested or thoughtful about international relations."[14]

---

reference to the United States, he observed: "Foreign politics demand scarcely any of those qualities which are peculiar to a democracy; they require, on the contrary, the perfect use of almost all of those in which it is deficient." *Democracy in America*, trans. Phillips Bradley (New York: Alfred A. Knopf, 1945), Vol. I, p. 234.

[12] *The Stakes of Diplomacy*, pp. 28–29.

[13] *Ibid.*, p. 55. See also *A Preface to Politics*, pp. 196–197.

[14] *The Stakes of Diplomacy*, p. 20.

It should follow from the foregoing evidence that in 1915 Lippmann definitely favored "autocratic" management of foreign affairs. But the "golden age," when this view reigned supreme, came to an end with the outbreak of World War I. This was a new kind of war. The "progressive" nations had become "capable of sacrifices so irrationally great that the bleeding victor would faint upon the corpse of his victim."[15] Governments had to ask their peoples for unprecedented exertions to wage this hyperbolic conflict. They obtained the needed support, but at the cost of democratizing foreign affairs—the issues of war and peace and national existence.

In substance they ceded the executive power of decision over the strategical and the political conditions for concluding the war. In effect they lost control of the war. . . . In fact, the powers which were ceded by the executive passed through the assemblies, which could not exercise them, to the mass of voters who, though unable also to exercise them, passed them on to the party bosses, the agents of pressure groups, and the magnates of the new media of mass communications.[16]

Lippmann wrote these lines in 1955. In 1917 he was by no means an unhappy witness to the developments which uprooted the traditional ways of thinking on the conduct of foreign affairs. Even if we make the generous assumption that he did not literally accept Wilson's idea of "open covenants, openly arrived at," there can be no doubt that he welcomed the democratization of foreign affairs and expected public opinion to play a beneficent role in maintaining and promoting world peace and order.[17] However, as we have seen earlier, Lippmann's flirtation with Wilsonianism was

[15] Hoffmann Nickerson, *The Armed Horde,* cited in *The Public Philosophy,* p. 11.
[16] *The Public Philosophy,* pp. 12–13.
[17] It should be noted here that the official commentary on the Fourteen Points, which the Allies accepted as the basis of their discussions in October 1918, was written almost wholly by Lippmann.

brief. It turned into an acute distrust of public opinion as a guide to public policy. In 1955 he would still have the internal and the external affairs of a state managed in a democratic manner. But in the course of these four decades he had radically altered his concept of the democratic process itself. He would now consider it the very essence of liberal democracy to exclude the masses from the making of high policy on both domestic and foreign issues. This fundamental change in his political philosophy did not occur overnight. It matured over a long period of time, beginning in the twenties and continuing through the thirties and on into the post-World War II period. Let us trace its course.

In his *Public Opinion* (1922), Lippmann delivered an all-out attack on the theory of "government by the people." He rejected as unfounded the "dogma" that God had stored in the breast of every man the knowledge which was needed to manage public affairs. Not all men, he said, were reasonable, informed, and educated enough to discern and pursue even their own interests.[18] There were also other reasons why "the people" were not happily placed to form valid opinions on the affairs of state. In the first place, they suffered from a well-nigh universal limitation: they received and considered facts in the context of their own desires, hopes and fears, prejudices and stereotypes. The "stereotypes" traveled "from the edge of [their] vision into the center"[19] and blinded them to the true nature and significance of the evidence under review. They were further confounded by the fact that in dealing with the affairs of state they dealt with "unseen reality." They had to form opinions on events which took place in a distant and unfamiliar context, not at their doorstep. Nor did they get all the facts. The press merely gave

[18] *Public Opinion* (New York: The Macmillan Company, 1922), pp. 255–256.
[19] *Ibid.*, p. 111.

them scattered incidents and episodes.[20] In talking to the great public, political leaders and government officials gave out carefully selected facts, couched in a language and placed in a setting calculated to placate and appease rather than dispel and discourage popular prejudices.[21] In sum, the people lacked the intelligence on which sound opinions must be based. One should also remember that they were not always interested in the myriad questions that engaged the attention of their government at any given time, with the result that on very many issues a "popular will" or a "public opinion" simply did not exist.[22] Lippmann went on to say that the fallibility of popular thinking on public affairs was not a passing phenomenon.

There is no prospect, in any time which we can conceive, that the whole invisible environment will be so clear to all men that they will spontaneously arrive at sound public opinions on the whole business of government. And even if there were a prospect, it is extremely doubtful whether many of us would wish to be bothered, or would take the time to form an opinion on "any and every form of social action," which affects us. . . . We cannot ourselves inspire or guide all these acts, as the mystical democrat has always imagined.[23]

Lippmann also rejected the view that the "will of the people" should find expression in governmental policy and action. The theory, he said, wrongly assumed that "self-expression" was the highest interest and the consuming passion of men.[24] In fact, it was merely one, and for that matter not the most intensely felt, of human desires. Men sought self-government not as a vehicle of self-expression but as the instrument of satisfying their various needs. They sought

[20] *Ibid.*, p. 364.
[21] *Ibid.*, pp. 199–203, 248.
[22] *Ibid.*, p. 313.
[23] *Ibid.*, p. 314.
[24] *Ibid.*, p. 310.

it most when they did not get what they wanted, when conditions were bad. The democratic theorists tended to forget that "mankind was interested in all kinds of other things, in order, in its rights, in prosperity, in sights and sounds and in not being bored."[25]

It was therefore not at all surprising that "the people" ruled nowhere except in the realm of theory. In the world of reality there was always a king, a captain, a boss, a party leader, however chosen, who governed the people. The public, as a group, could neither think nor act. It could do "little more than assent or dissent."[26] It was rarely, if ever, that the masses of men cooperated in any complex affair except through a central machine managed by a very few people. Lippmann wrote:

If you take any particular institution, be it a legislature, a party, a trade union, a nationalist movement, a factory, or a club, the number of those who govern is a very small percentage of those who are theoretically supposed to govern.[27]

The people's representatives in national assemblies did not fare much better. Lippmann observed that while the executives had steadily gained, legislatures had lost in prestige all over the world. The reason for their decline was not far to seek. A congress of representatives was essentially "a group of blind men in a vast, unknown world."[28] Even if the districts sent to Congress their wisest men, as the theory of American democracy implied, the sum of local impressions which would result from the exchange of views between

25 *Ibid.*, pp. 311–312.
26 *Ibid.*, p. 227.
27 *Ibid.*, p. 228. Lord Bryce made a similar observation in his *Modern Democracies*: "No one can have had some years' experience of the conduct of affairs in a legislature or an administration without observing how extremely small is the number of persons by whom the world is governed." Vol. II, p. 542. Quoted in *Public Opinion*, p. 228.
28 *Public Opinion*, p. 288.

them did not furnish an adequate base for national policy in domestic or foreign affairs. The representative, like his constituents, lacked pertinent information on which to base his opinions and judgments. The President and his officials, who were his chief regular source of information, told him only what they deemed expedient to tell.

So bad is the contact of legislators with necessary facts that they are forced to rely either on private tips or on that legalized atrocity, the congressional investigation, where Congressmen, starved of their legitimate food for thought, go on a wild and feverish man-hunt, and do not stop at cannibalism.[29]

As a result, legislative action closely paralleled mass action at least in one important respect: in most cases, the legislator did, or could do, little more than say "yes" or "no" to the bills which were prepared by a few informed "insiders." Many of the measures which he approved or disapproved he did not even understand. One could not blame him for his lack of understanding or for his failure to participate creatively in the making of public policy. For, among other things,

the cleverest and most industrious representative cannot hope to understand a fraction of the bills on which he votes. The best he can do is to specialize on a few bills, and take somebody's word about the rest. . . . And even when [he] really knew a subject, [his] anxieties had only begun. For back home the editors . . . and the women's clubs had spared themselves these labors, and were prepared to view the Congressman's performance through local spectacles.[30]

[29] *Ibid.*, p. 289.

[30] *Ibid.*, p. 291. Legislators everywhere face these difficulties. It is reported that only two members of Parliament understood the Local Government Bill of 1928–1929, and one of these was the minister who presented the bill and "who had been very carefully instructed by the civil servants who drew it up." Gwendolen M. Carter and Others, *Major Foreign Powers* (New York: Harcourt, Brace and Co., 1952), p. 91.

The situation in Congress is no better. According to Senator Ferguson, a normal person would take four to five months to go over the material

Lippmann concluded that given the limitations which beset the public as well as its representatives in legislative assemblies, democracy, as conceived by its theorists, could exist and function only in relatively small, self-contained rural communities, where everyone knew not only everyone else but also the things that should and should not be done. If the people were to manage their public affairs, the environment must be confined within the range of every man's direct and certain knowledge.

The doctrine of the omnicompetent citizen is for most practical purposes true in the rural township. Everybody in a village sooner or later tries his hand at everything the village does. . . . There was no serious trouble with the doctrine of the omnicompetent citizen until the democratic stereotype was universally applied, so that men looked at a complicated civilization and saw an enclosed village.[31]

Democracy was not a practical proposition in highly advanced, industrial societies. It lived a precarious existence, and faced a grim future.

---

which the Republican Senate Policy Committee had urged the senators to read before they could vote "intelligently" on the Marshall Plan. Robert A. Dahl, *Congress and Foreign Policy* (New York: Harcourt, Brace and Co., 1950), pp. 129–130. Dahl sums up the position as follows: "The congressman, short of information and experience, pressed by time, bedeviled by constituents, pressured on all sides, casts his vote for a policy that in a decade's time may ripen into a million casualties." *Ibid.*, p. 139.

[31] *Public Opinion,* pp. 270, 273. In support of his argument Lippmann quotes Aristotle, who in his *Politics* observed that "the citizens of [an ideal] state must know one another's characters. Where this is not the case, the distribution of offices and the giving of decisions will suffer. Both are matters in which it is wrong to act on the spur of the moment; but that is what obviously happens where the population is overlarge." *Politics,* Book VII, Chapter 4. See Barker's translation, pp. 342–343. We may incidentally note here that Aristotle was full of praise for rural democracy, which he considered to be the best kind. What is more, he implied that the mixing of mechanics and day-laborers with the peasants in the same state made it unstable. See Book VI, Chapter I, especially Barker's note on p. 300, and Chapter IV, pp. 308–312.

Lippmann saw a ray of hope in the organization of a "machinery of knowledge." He recommended the creation of intelligence bureaus composed of all kinds of expert fact-finders—accountants, auditors, personnel managers, public administrators—who would distill evidence, isolate and untangle the facts from their biased interpretations and offer them to the public as a basis for judgment. These bureaus, he tentatively suggested, should be attached to all the major departments of a government without being accountable to them. They should have access to the records of the agency concerned, and they should report their findings to an authority named by the enabling act of Congress. The organizations of the kind proposed had more than justified their existence in the sphere of industrial management. Lippmann hoped that they would make the unseen and the invisible in government visible to the people.

Enough has been done to demonstrate, I think, that unseen environments can be reported effectively, that they can be reported to divergent groups of people in a way which is neutral to their prejudice, and capable of overcoming their subjectivism.

If that is true, then in working out the intelligence principle men will find the way *to overcome the central difficulty of self-government, the difficulty of dealing with an unseen reality*.[32] [Italics mine.]

It should be emphasized that the foregoing proposal was supposed to benefit not the people but their representatives. Lippmann did not expect that the findings of the proposed bureaus would significantly affect the ability or the disposition of the public to understand or participate in the processes of decision-making in government. The common man, he feared, would greet with an "anguished yawn" the charts, the statistics, and the reports which the experts had prepared. He

[32] *Public Opinion*, pp. 395–396.

would rather go without an "intelligent opinion" on an issue than read them. Nor could one expect the average citizen to find the time or the enthusiasm to study and analyze these publications. The intelligence bureau was then primarily

an instrument of the man of action, of the representative charged with decision. . . . In so far as it helps them to understand the environment in which they are working, it makes what they do visible. And by that much they become more responsible to the general public. The purpose then is not to burden every citizen with expert opinions on all questions, but to push that burden away from him towards the responsible administrator.[33]

In judging an issue of policy, the average citizen could not do much more than ask whether the relevant facts had been considered and correct procedures followed by the officials concerned. He could not say what the relevant facts were, for he would not know.[34]

In the last chapter of *Public Opinion*, Lippmann gave a hint of the direction which his thinking on government was to take in the years to come. In the following statement of Plato he found a solemn idea possessing an "unapproachable grandeur."

Let me next endeavor to show what is that fault in States which is the cause of their present maladministration, and what is the least change which will enable a State to pass into the truer form. . . . *Until philosophers are kings, or the kings or princes of this world have the spirit and power of philosophy, and political greatness and wisdom meet in one, and those commoner natures who pursue either to the exclusion of the other are compelled to stand aside, cities will never have rest from their evils. . . .*[35] [Italics in original.]

[33] *Public Opinion*, p. 399.
[34] *Ibid.*, pp. 400–401.
[35] Plato, *The Republic*, Book V, 473, trans. Jowett, partially quoted by Lippmann on pp. 411–412.

At this point, however, Lippmann felt that men could neither forget nor live by Plato's idea.[36]

In *The Phantom Public* (1925), which came as a "sequel" to his *Public Opinion,* Lippmann repeated the main argument of the earlier work, albeit more emphatically. The book opened with the following quotation from Lord Grey:

"Government by Public Opinion" . . . is an admirable formula: but it presupposes, not only that public opinion exists, but that on any particular question there is a public opinion ready to decide the issue. Indeed, it presupposes that the supreme statesman in democratic government is public opinion. Many of the short-comings of democratic government are due to the fact that public opinion is not necessarily a great statesman at all.[37]

Lord Grey's distrust of public opinion runs through *The Phantom Public.* This time Lippmann was even surer that the public could not pronounce on the substance of policy. It could only give or deny its support to the executive, which was the appropriate agency to consider and decide upon the intrinsic merits of a question. Lippmann rejected as entirely false the assumption that the people could govern themselves if only they were better educated and informed. However intelligent, educated and wise, the average citizen could never get the facts which the public official, an "insider," possessed. He concluded:

Only the insider can make decisions, not because he is inherently a better man but because he is so placed that he can understand and can act. The outsider is necessarily ignorant, usually irrelevant and often meddlesome, because he is trying to navigate the ship from dry land. . . .

The public must be put in its place, so that it may exercise its own powers, but no less and perhaps even more, *so that each of*

[36] *Public Opinion,* p. 411.

[37] Walter Lippmann, *The Phantom Public* (New York: The Macmillan Company, 1925), p. 7.

us may live free of the trampling and the roar of a bewildered herd.[38] [Italics mine.]

Lippmann went on to say that society should be conceived, not as the sum total of a given number of individuals but as the compound of those adjustments which must be made between their special interests. A good society was that in which the process of adjustment was the least painful or frustrating. Men acted as a public when they took a particular position in regard to the purposes of other men. The goal of public action should be "to promote the conditions under which special purposes can be composed."[39] In the conduct of public affairs Lippmann would put his trust in the

individuals directly concerned [the executive]. They initiate, they administer, they settle. . . . The public intervenes only when there is a crisis of maladjustment, and then not to deal with the substance of the problem but to neutralize the arbitrary force which prevents adjustment. It is a theory which economizes the attention of men as members of the public, and asks them to do little as possible in matters where they can do nothing very well. . . . I set no great store on what can be done by public opinion and the action of the masses.[40]

The argument of *Public Opinion* and *The Phantom Public* may be summed up as follows: "Government by the people" is an unattainable ideal in modern industrial society. The people no doubt have a right to a say in the management of their public affairs.[41] But they cannot themselves act as gov-

[38] *Ibid.*, pp. 150, 155.
[39] *Ibid.*, p. 198.
[40] *Ibid.*, pp. 198–199.
[41] It should be noted that Lippmann does not equate this right with the right of the majority to rule. In fact, he has always deprecated majority rule and pointed to "the inherent absurdity of making virtue and wisdom dependent on 51 per cent of [a] collection of men." *The Phantom Public*, p. 58. Majority rule is not an ethical but merely a practical necessity. See also "Why Should the Majority Rule?," *Harper's*, Vol. 152, No. 3 (March

ernors. Nor can they give positive guidance to those whom they elect to govern, for they do not have the skill, the experience, the time, and above all the information needed to formulate sound policy. The only practical way in which the people can exercise the aforementioned right is by giving or denying their support to an executive according as it succeeds or fails in promoting their interests. In taking this position Lippmann accepts Aristotle's view that in an ideal state "the function of governors is to issue commands and give decisions [that is, to govern]: the function of the governed is to elect the governors."[42] In Lippmann's plea for the constitution of intelligence bureaus composed of "disinterested" experts, and in his tribute to Plato on his injunction that princes should possess the spirit and the insight of philosophers, we can discern the germ of an idea which he more fully developed in his subsequent works, especially *The Public Philosophy*— the idea of government by the enlightened and disinterested elite.

In *A Preface to Morals* (1929), Lippmann again addressed himself to the question of disinterestedness in government. Modern civilization, he said, had depersonalized the relation between the governors and the governed. The loyalty of the sovereign people did not converge upon a personal superior. Moreover, their interests had become immensely diversified. A man now belonged to his place of work, a trade union, a club, a church and several other organizations. Often enough, he was at once a buyer and a seller, a boss and a subordinate,

---

1926), pp. 399–405. In 1928 he wrote that the lovers of liberty were in duty bound to limit the power of majorities. *American Inquisitors* (New York: The Macmillan Company, 1928), p. 11. In *The Method of Freedom* (1934), he observed (p. 76) that the "prevailing opinion is not the opinion which the majority would hold if it understood the question" and made its decision without being influenced by special interests. As we shall see in the following pages, he spoke ever more frequently in the post-World War II period of the "transient majorities" and their "tyranny."

[42] *Politics,* trans. Barker, Book 7, Chapter 4, p. 342.

a wage-earner and a stockholder. Consequently, he could not give his wholehearted allegiance to any one person, interest or institution. These developments, Lippmann maintained, had compelled men to acquire the habit of making their own decisions and judgments instead of looking for orders from a captain or a king, or passively responding to organic loyalties.[43] They had also blunted the "edges of partisanship," and cultivated in modern men and their leaders a certain measure of judicial disinterestedness. The growing new outlook had already found expression in such political and administrative devices as the civil service, which embodied the principle that the business of the state should be managed by persons who were impartial and neutral as between rival political parties and special interests. The tradition of an independent judiciary had a similar origin. But even more significant was the increasing reliance which responsible men in business, government and politics placed in their everyday work on the evidence of technicians, experts and neutral observers.

In 1937, Lippmann found that the judicial temper which he had hopefully ascribed to the public and public men in *A Preface to Morals* was in fact sadly lacking. In *The Good Society* (1937), he complained that the absence of disinterestedness among government officials and members of representative assemblies had corrupted the liberal tradition. Legislators alleged that judges had begun to make law. But they forgot that the judges had merely filled the vacuum created by the failure of legislators to act judicially. They had come to think of themselves "as the lineal descendants of the Caesars, and the heirs of their sovereignty."[44] The complement of the "judicial usurpation" was the "growing dictatorship of the lawmakers."[45] The fact that legislators made the

[43] *A Preface to Morals*, pp. 274–275.
[44] *The Good Society*, p. 288.
[45] *Ibid.*, p. 288.

law, while judges applied it, did not denote a fundamental difference in the nature of their functions. The distinction was merely a matter of practical convenience. For one should remember that "the enactment of a new law is a judgment rendered for certain interests and against certain others."[46]

In applying the principle of disinterestedness to politics, Lippmann arrived at the distinction between politicians and statesmen. A politician, he observed, was a partisan. He worked for a special interest: at worst for his own personal profit, at best for an institution, a party or a constituency. He could not be counted upon to judge impartially among all the interests concerned in an issue. Even when he served "the people," he worked to appease or obfuscate their momentary wishes and opinions. He "accepts unregenerate desire at its face value and either fulfills it or perpetrates a fraud."[47] A statesman, by contrast, sought to protect not only the valid interests of the contenders in a controversy but also the interests of those who had gone unrepresented. He served the living, but also built for the future. With Burke he viewed society not merely as

a partnership in a trade of pepper and coffee, calico or tobacco, or some other such low concern, to be taken up for a little temporary interest and to be dissolved by the fancy of the parties. . . . It is a partnership in a higher and more permanent sense—a partnership in all science; a partnership in all art; a partnership in every virtue and in all perfection. As the ends of such a partnership cannot be obtained in many generations it becomes a partnership not only between those who are living, but between those who are dead and those who are to be born.[48]

---

[46] *Ibid.*, p. 287.

[47] *A Preface to Morals*, p. 282.

[48] Quoted in *A Preface to Morals*, p. 280. This statement of Burke is a favorite with Lippmann. He has quoted it in *The Good Society* (p. 253) and also in *The Public Philosophy* (p. 35). A discussion of the need to "refine" the will of the people will also be found in *The Good Society* (pp. 250–256). In this work Lippmann predicted that the need would increase in the years to come (p. 256).

The statesman did not follow but, rather, led the people. He educated and refined their desire by confronting it with reality. His task was no doubt hard and exacting. But once he succeeded in converting the electorate to his view of their true and enduring interests, he acquired a measure of public esteem and affection which the "ordinary glib politician" could never have. Often he would have to act in advance of his people, giving them not what they happened to want at the time but what they would in the end find to be good. He could not always wait for their consent and approval, for there were many things which men learned to appreciate only after they had actually experienced them.

The capacity to act upon the hidden realities of a situation in spite of appearances is the essence of statesmanship. It consists in giving the people not what they want but what they will learn to want. It requires the courage which is possible only in a mind that is detached from the agitations of the moment. *It requires the insight which comes only from an objective and discerning knowledge of the facts, and a high and imperturbable disinterestedness.*[49] [Italics mine.]

In *The Good Society* Lippmann went on to argue that officials and legislators could not acquire the disinterestedness of a statesman unless they ceased to look upon themselves as Caesars and realized that there was a law higher than the statutes which they enacted in the name of the sovereign people, a law which was superior to kings, parliaments, majorities and mobs. One could find in every civilized society the intuitive belief that there was such a law.

For if there is no higher law, then there is no ground on which anyone can challenge the power of the strong to exploit the weak, there is no reason by which arbitrary force can be restrained. In the absence of a higher law there can be tyranny and there can be anarchy. . . . But a free and ordered society, resting chiefly

[49] *A Preface to Morals*, p. 283.

on persuasion rather than on coercion, on the pacific adjudication
of human conflicts, on the security of known rights and duties ...
is inconceivable in theory and unworkable in practice unless in
the community there is a general willingness to be bound by the
spirit of a law that is higher and more universal than the letter of
particular laws.[50]

It was true that the text and the source of this law were not
clearly set down in black and white. Nor could one deny that
in the nineteenth century the privileged classes had invoked
it to perpetuate the status quo. But it was "philistinism," said
Lippmann, to deny its existence because its content was vague
or because its concept was exploited in the past. Even though
the saints and sages who proclaimed it put it in words which
modern men found confusing, their intuition must nevertheless be treated as a deep insight into the nature of human
affairs.[51] The denial that there was a higher law was "the
cardinal heresy of the modern generation."[52]

Lippmann himself was evidently not satisfied merely with
the assertion that a higher law did exist. For in taunting the
"unbelievers" that they were heretics and philistines, that is
to say unbelievers, he was indeed indulging, as Bentham had
told the earlier proponents of the concept, in "womanish
scolding . . . which is sure to irritate and which never can
persuade."[53] Like them he wanted a definition of the
higher law; he sought to pin it down. And he did come up
with a tentative definition. "The denial," he wrote, "that men
may be arbitrary in human transactions *is* the higher law."[54]
[Italics in the original.] As we shall see in the following pages,
he did not revive this definition when, eighteen years later,
he discussed the subject again in *The Public Philosophy*.

[50] *The Good Society*, pp. 334–335.
[51] *Ibid.*, pp. 337–338.
[52] *Ibid.*, p. 332.
[53] Jeremy Bentham, *A Fragment on Government*, pp. 126–127, cited in
The Good Society, pp. 335–336.
[54] *The Good Society*, p. 346.

In defining the higher law as the denial of arbitrariness, Lippmann equated it with the familiar principle of the "rule of law" or the "supremacy of law." This was not much of a "scoop." But he may have found it necessary to reassert the time-honored dictum of the Anglo-Saxon political tradition that subjects and sovereigns—be they kings, parliaments, majorities, or even "the people"—are alike under the law; at any rate, after 1934 he began to see Caesars, that is to say arbitrary rulers, in the administrators of the New Deal. *The Good Society*, it should be remembered, was a criticism of "collectivism" of the left and of the right. He still saw the need to refine the will of the people. He still did not set great store by public opinion. But now he would not put his trust in the "insiders"—the executive—as he was willing to do in *Public Opinion* and *The Phantom Public*.

We may say that in the mid-thirties Lippmann distrusted the people no more than he distrusted the governors. Accordingly, he did not question their right to veto the policies of the executive. The latter, he seemed to think, should not disregard or obstruct the expressed wishes of the public. As has been mentioned in a preceding discussion, he justified the Senate's rejection of the World Court in January 1935 on the ground that many Americans, at least a third of them, did not want this country to adhere to the Court. The popular will, he said, might conceivably change, but "until it changes those who believe in democratic government must, of course, abide by the results."[55] In the same year, Lippmann conceded that the frequent failure of the Senate and the people to ratify the commitments their government had made abroad caused misunderstanding and bitterness in American relations with foreign governments. But this difficulty, he observed,

is inherent in any truly democratic control of foreign affairs. . . . If it is to exercise control, it must, therefore, be the final judge as to whether it will ratify agreements that have been negotiated. The system is inconvenient and it is confusing. Yet almost certainly it is worth the trouble. Absolutely certainly it will not be abandoned. The only possible remedy for its defects is such a clarification of American vital interests and purposes that no President will negotiate agreements that he is not certain to have ratified.[56]

In the postwar period we find the masses and their representatives once again falling out of favor with Lippmann. He became increasingly concerned about the lack of imagination, firmness and leadership in the conduct of American diplomacy. Up to about the end of 1951, he attributed this weakness largely to the alleged inability of President Truman to lead and control his party and his administration.[57] The failure of the President in this respect created a vacuum of authority which Congress promptly filled. But it employed its inflated authority and influence to corner, embarrass and restrain the administration rather than to improve the conduct of foreign affairs. The Republican opposition relentlessly accused the State Department of incompetence and of being under the "guiding influence of subversives and sexual perverts."[58] It put the Secretary of State in a position where he must spend his time and energy not on determining how best to promote American interests abroad but on how to prove at home that he was neither a communist nor a fellow-traveler. Lippmann noted: "The Secretary of State is treated on Capitol Hill with less courtesy and with smaller regard for the rules of evidence than if he were a convicted horsethief."[59] In this atmosphere of total distrust and hostility between the legislature and the executive it became impossible for the government officials concerned to think constructively

[56] *Ibid.*, June 11, 1935.
[57] *Ibid.*, April 1, 1948.
[58] *Ibid.*, May 2, 1950.
[59] *Ibid.*, March 14, 1950.

or to deal firmly and confidently with the representatives of foreign governments.

In May 1951 Lippmann deplored the declared intention of a congressional committee, which investigated the dismissal of General MacArthur, to examine, and possibly publish, the advice and instructions which the Joint Chiefs of Staff had given the President and the field commanders in Korea. The investigators seemed to accept the theory that in the name of "the sacred right of the people to know all the facts" an officer could compel his lawful superiors to open up all their files to Congress and perhaps to the general public as well. He warned that if this theory became a part of the American tradition of government, it would operate not to enlighten the public but to corrupt and intimidate officials. It would put them all on notice that nothing could be treated as confidential, and that anything they said or signed might one day be published. They would then tend to hide, withhold or distort the truth that was given to the people, the President and Congress. They would write their letters and statements with an eye to eventual publication, addressing them "not to the vital interests of the United States in the long run but to the passions and the prejudices and the ignorance of the moment."[60] About a month later Lippmann complained that while Republican senators charged the administration with incompetence and ignorance, they credited themselves with omniscience. They seemed to take the position that they knew perfectly well what should not have happened in the past and what should happen in the future. If Senator Smith (a hypothetical person) could have his way, he would obtain from the Secretary of State

[60] *Ibid.*, May 1, 1951. Recently Lippmann opposed, on similar grounds, Senator Thurmond's demand to know the names of individual censors who had examined specific speeches to be made by military officers. T and T, February 8, 1962.

a script of everything that the United States Government will ever say for the next five years on the subject of China, Korea, Formosa, Japan and the United Nations. This script having been fully debated and edited by the Senate in open session with television added, would then in its final form be recorded on discs and deposited at the FBI. Mr. Acheson would then resign, and no one would need to be appointed in his place. If, unhappily, it ever became necessary again to stoop so low as to discuss the future of anything in the Far East with any other government, the appropriate disc would be brought out of the FBI and played on the steps of the Senate Office Building.[61]

During the post-World War II period, Lippmann often charged that a breakdown of executive power had occurred in the federal government of the United States. Congress had obtained an unprecedented measure of influence in the conduct of foreign affairs. So had the Army. The opposing political parties and factions rallied around rival generals, who publicly disputed not only the questions of strategy but also the fundamental issues of foreign policy and American destiny. However, as we have suggested above, it was not until about the end of 1951 that Lippmann saw in this decline of the executive power a sign of some inner and deep-seated ailment which had seized the democracies. The crisis was one of Truman's own making. He as well as his top-ranking advisers had lost the respect and the confidence of the nation. His Secretary of State had clearly become *persona non grata* with Congress and the people. "Some day, when he retires," wrote Lippmann, "I hope that Mr. Acheson will write a book explaining how he persuaded himself to believe that a government could be conducted without the support of the people."[62] Truman could have regained popular support by bringing able and trusted men in his cabinet. Instead, he and

[61] *Ibid.*, June 11, 1951.
[62] *Ibid.*, May 21, 1951.

his administration chose to employ scare tactics in order to obtain congressional endorsement of their policies. They assumed that the nation would not take appropriate steps to protect its vital interests unless it was kept in a "condition of perpetual frenzy." Lippmann argued that if this estimate of the American people was at all correct, it was so because the administration had done nothing to inform and educate the people, to tell them the truth about the nature of the issues confronting them, and about the ways and means by which it proposed to deal with those issues. "Instead of leading the people, the administration spokesmen have relied upon the bastard art of manipulating opinion by sloganeering and shock."[63] The nation could not make progress and build for the future unless its leaders treated the people as adult, free men who possessed the ability to make up their minds on issues when these were explained to them, and who would support sound policies if their soundness was demonstrated to them.

Accordingly, during the greater part of the Truman administration Lippmann did not see the need to do away with democratic control of foreign affairs. In January 1949 he wrote an article that stands in marked contrast to the position which he was to take six years later in *The Public Philosophy*. He observed that by occupying the office of the Secretary of State at a time when a Democratic President was at odds with a Republican Congress, George Marshall, a non-political figure of great stature, had prevented the collapse of American foreign policy. But since the 1948 elections had returned Truman to the White House and a Democratic majority to the Capitol, a new Secretary of State, a party man, should be appointed to replace General Marshall. For

it is not healthy in the long run to treat foreign policy as some-

[63] *Ibid.*, October 2, 1950.

thing separate from the normal process of democratic government and of party responsibility. There are no statesmen wise enough, and no experts who are expert enough, to make decisions of life and death when they are artificially insulated from the give and take of general debate. An unavoidable result is to thrust excessive power upon men who are not accountable to Congress or to the people . . . who decide questions of great moment without having to explain or to justify their decisions, without themselves being aware of all the consequences and ramifications of what they decide.[64]

Lippmann went so far as to criticize bipartisanship in foreign affairs on the ground that whereas it did not admit the leaders of the opposition to participation in the decision-making process, it did prevent adequate airing of issues, discussion and debate.[65]

Commenting on the controversy over Truman's right to dispatch troops abroad, Lippmann observed that the issue was one of policy rather than of law. It would have been more sensible for the President to share his "awful responsibility" in this respect with Congress. He should also have remembered that the latter could not give him a blank check in disposing of the armed forces, to maintain which it had to levy huge taxes on the people.

It followed, as night the day, that Congress which had to impose the sacrifices would demand, as its moral right because it was answerable to the people who bear the sacrifices, a voice in the grave decisions where the stakes are life and death.[66]

Lippmann maintained that in excluding Congress from making the political decisions which had dictated the dispatch of troops, the President had certainly violated the spirit if not the letter of the law. The administration, he said, should have

[64] *Ibid.*, January 11, 1949.
[65] *Ibid.*
[66] *Ibid.*, April 5, 1951.

shown the same respect and deference to Congress in this matter as it would in obtaining the ratification of a treaty.[67]

In the summer of 1951 the New York *Herald Tribune* an-
nounced that "Today and Tomorrow" would be temporarily
discontinued, since Walter Lippmann had retired to the country to write a book, "The Image of Man." Lippmann never
published the book, but it seems that during these months he
further developed the ideas which he had stated in his earlier
works, and which culminated in *The Public Philosophy*. He
came to the conclusion that the paralysis of the administration, the growing hostility between the executive and the
legislature, the increasing penetration by Congress into the
domain of the executive, especially foreign affairs, did not
issue exclusively from the personal qualifications of a President or a particular line-up of the parties at the Capitol.
Something much more fundamental had gone wrong. Lippmann noticed a general lack of respect for the spirit and the
intent of the Constitution. The President on the one hand,
and many Congressmen and Senators on the other, were alike
guilty of trying to usurp each other's power and prerogatives.
Senator Taft rightly felt that President Truman had exceeded
his authority when he committed an army to Korea, and again
when he committed another army to NATO without congressional authorization. But Lippmann found it deplorable that
the Senator

should pass over in complete silence the unprecedented usurpation by Congress of the President's powers in the conduct of
foreign affairs. The most clearly identifiable has been the seizure
by the Senate Foreign Relations Committee . . . of . . . the President's constitutional right to recognize governments. But the
usurpation of the President's powers has gone far beyond that.
Congress has invaded and infiltrated not only the making of

[67] *Ibid.,* January 16 and February 13, 1951.

policy, not only negotiation with foreign states, but the very administrative detail of every part of American foreign relations.[68]

The situation did not improve even after the inauguration of President Eisenhower. On March 9, 1953 Lippmann noted that the Republicans were obsessed with the notion that Congress was a coequal branch of the government, and as such had the right to amend any legislation which the President proposed to it. No one denied, he said, that Congress was coequal with the President in making laws and passing resolutions. But the crucial question was whether

the coequal branches of the government become one government at the water's edge. Whether in our relations with other governments, we are one government . . . or whether there are several more or less independent United States governments acting in foreign affairs.[69]

Lippmann wondered whether the Republicans in Congress would ever rise to their new and unfamiliar responsibilities. A few days later he warned that the United States could not meet Malenkov's "peace offensive" unless the administration obtained control over the making of policy. American purposes abroad would surely be defeated if the executive branch continued to be paralyzed and defeated in an indecisive struggle with a few Senators.[70]

As time passed, Lippmann became increasingly pessimistic about the ability of President Eisenhower to control his party in Congress and to exercise his constitutional authority in the conduct and control of foreign affairs. The Republicans, he felt, had set themselves up in Congress as a rival government. Their attitude was exemplified by Senator Mundt during the "Army-McCarthy" hearings in 1954. Justifying the illegal supplying of secret information to Senator McCarthy

[68] *Ibid.*, January 17, 1952.
[69] *Ibid.*, March 9, 1953.
[70] *Ibid.*, March 24, 1953.

by federal employees, Mundt declared: "If I were President Eisenhower or Brownell, I'd do everything I could to stop it. I am down here [in Congress] and I do all I can to get it. That's the way you play the game."[71] Commenting on the episode, Lippmann observed that Senator Mundt's theory of constitutional government seemed to be that "if you are the President, you try to enforce the law. If you are in Congress, you try to beat the law."[72] As a result, the principal problem of Mr. Eisenhower in his relations with Congress had become not how to get it to pass the necessary laws but how to persuade the Republican leaders to let him execute the office of President.[73] More and more, Lippmann spoke of the "usurpation" by Congress of the executive power, of the paralysis of government, and of a derangement of the constitutional balance.

In his travels abroad, Lippmann found a replica of the Washington scene in West European capitals. In May 1953 he observed that the democracies in Europe were preoccupied not with how to solve the grave issues that faced the Western world but with how to create governments which had the will and the power to act. Western Europe was in the grip of a constitutional crisis: it seemed that the method of popular elections had failed to provide governments which could lead and govern effectively. Apart from the peculiar troubles that afflicted each individual government, one fundamental condition of constitutional disorder was common to all of them. It was that the representative assemblies,

being closest to the voters, are exerting their power to invade and to usurp the prerogatives of the executive. Since it is impossible for assemblies to govern a country, they exercise their usurped power by preventing the executive from governing it.[74]

[71] *Ibid.*, June 1, 1954.
[72] *Ibid.*
[73] *Ibid.*, June 14, 1954.
[74] *Ibid.*, May 21, 1953. Lippmann has continued to find, and to criticize, cases of congressional usurpation of the President's powers and prerogatives.

The future of liberal democracy in Europe seemed far from bright. In order to prevent the election of a parliament which would gladly dismiss the institutions of representative democracy, it had been found necessary in Italy to enact an electoral law that made it twice as difficult to elect an opponent as to elect a supporter of the existing government. In West Germany, the weakness of Chancellor Adenauer's government was revealed by the manner in which it obtained the ratification of the EDC. It received no more than a simple majority in the lower house, and for all practical purposes bypassed the upper house. The constitutional disorder in France was proverbial. She "is living under the despotism of an assembly which will not tolerate effective and responsible government."[75] The tyranny of this assembly was illustrated by the fact that in May 1953 it overthrew the government of Premier Mayer barely three hours after it had cheered his announcement about the Big Three conference in Bermuda.[76] The democrats of Europe got no comfort, but only further disillusionment, from the American situation, where President Eisenhower had failed to assert his

legitimate authority, and thus to do his duty, which is to defend the balance of the Constitution, the powers of the Executive, its responsibilities and duties in dealing with foreign affairs, the dignity of the Government, and the rights of individual Americans.[77]

The shaky structure of democratic governments in Europe and the continued decline of the executive power in the United States convinced Lippmann by the middle of 1953

He recently criticized the House Armed Services Committee for seeking to "direct" the President to spend the sums appropriated for building the RS-70. T and T, March 13, 1962.

[75] Ibid.
[76] Ibid., May 25, 1953.
[77] Ibid., May 21, 1953.

that the troubles of democracy sprang from a failure of faith among Western men, from weaknesses which had taken root in their hearts and spirits, or as some other writers have put it, from a breakdown of "vital beliefs."[78] Writing of the coronation of Queen Elizabeth II in June 1953, he observed that in every good society there must be a center of public allegiance which stood above parties, factions and power politics. But it could not remain above the worldly passions of men, and command their loyalty and affection, unless its power and influence were founded in things of the spirit, unless they were associated with laws and truths which were eternal and which were more than "the private and passing opinions" or the wishes and impulses of persons and crowds.[79] Lippmann went on to say that the Free World was in great peril not only because it had to contend with formidable foes but because its popular assemblies had overwhelmed and paralyzed its governments. This state of affairs had been caused by the demagogic popularization of the heresy that

majorities can do no wrong, that there is no higher truth than the transient opinions of contemporary majorities, and that there is no higher law than the ambitions and the maneuvers of the persons they are persuaded to elect. Against this heresy, which must subvert a free society and desecrate its most sacred principles, free men will prevail *when they have learned once again to carry the shield of faith, to wear the helmet of salvation and to wield the sword of the spirit.*[80] [Italics mine.]

In *The Public Philosophy* Lippmann again asserted that the West was threatened by a "massive counterrevolution"

[78] Robert Strausz-Hupé, *The Zone of Indifference* (New York: G.P. Putnam's Sons, 1952), p. 41. Strausz-Hupé also calls it the "alienation of the Social Mind." Three years later, Lippmann described it as the "alienation" of the people from the "public philosophy." *The Public Philosophy*, p. 102.

[79] T and T, June 2, 1953.

[80] *Ibid.*

against the tradition of liberal democracy. The masses in the democracies had acquired a power which they could not exercise. By the same token, elected governments had lost the power to govern. Public opinion had come to dominate the formulation of policy. But instead of giving the policy-makers helpful guidance it had merely chained them to inaction, precisely at those times when positive and active policies were needed to solve the momentous issues that faced the West. Almost invariably during the past half century, the masses had reacted with a solid negative whenever new courses of action were proposed to them. They had answered with the only words that "a great mass qua mass can speak—with a Yes or a No."[81] Lippmann wrote that in matters of war and peace the usual popular answer was No. The rule to which there were few exceptions seemed to be that

at critical junctures, when the stakes are high, the prevailing mass opinion will impose what amounts to a veto upon changing the course on which the government is at the time proceeding. Prepare for war in time of peace? No. It is bad to raise taxes . . . to take men away from their schools or their jobs, to provoke the enemy. Intervene in a developing conflict? No. Avoid the risk of war. Withdraw from the area of conflict? No. The adversary must not be appeased . . . Negotiate a compromise peace as soon as the opportunity presents itself? No. The aggressor must be punished. Remain armed to enforce the dicated settlement? No. The war is over.[82]

Nor could one expect popular control of policy to yield any better results. Rational thinking on foreign affairs called for a specialized knowledge, not to speak of an experienced and seasoned judgment, which the multitude did not possess. The people would then neither understand nor put up with the cold, concrete and qualified terms of reality which must be

[81] *The Public Philosophy*, p. 19. See also *The Good Society*, p. 253.
[82] *The Public Philosophy*, pp. 19–20.

employed to explain complex situations. But the truth inevitably suffered a radical distortion if in communicating it to
the great public

the complex is made over into the simple, the hypothetical into
the dogmatic, and the relative into an absolute. Even when there
is no deliberate distortion . . . the public opinion of masses cannot be counted upon to apprehend regularly and promptly the
reality of things. There is an inherent tendency in opinion to
feed upon rumors excited by our own wishes and fears.[83]

In *The Public Philosophy* Lippmann declared that the rise
of the masses to power in the twentieth century had turned
public men and officials into cowards and hypocrites. Those
who supposedly governed the democracies were insecure and
intimidated men, afraid to speak their minds lest they offend
public opinion. Telling the truth was often imprudent, but
suppressing it was always uncomfortable. As a result, public
men themselves tended to shun the "bitter truth." Their sub-
ordinates in turn discovered that it was safer to be wrong until
it had become "fashionable to be right." Neither the people
nor their leaders realized that the "sovereign masses," like
all other sovereigns, were ill served by flattery. They were
betrayed "by the servile hypocrisy which tells them that what
is true and what is false, what is right and what is wrong, can
be determined by their votes."[84] In this atmosphere, politicians and officials promoted their personal careers either by
seducing and manipulating or by appeasing public opinion.
They rationalized their lack of candor and courage by saying
that in a democracy "public men are the servants of the people."[85] This cowardly misrepresentation and distortion of the
truth had created a vicious circle of mistakes, which sapped
the vitality of the West and threatened its very existence.

[83] *Ibid.,* p. 25.
[84] *Ibid.,* p. 14.
[85] *Ibid.,* p. 27.

304 PHILOSOPHY OF INTERNATIONAL POLITICS

This breakdown in the constitutional order is the cause of the precipitate and catastrophic decline of Western society. It may, if it cannot be arrested and reversed, bring about the fall of the West.[86]

Why does democratic politics today lack the statesmen who, with their wisdom and courage, would break down the vicious circle in which the democracies are caught, free the executive from the bonds of slavish obedience to the masses, and restore the authority and dignity of government? Lippmann's answer is that men in this age have lost touch with the "traditions of civility, the heritage of the public philosophy."

In the "traditions of civility," says Lippman, there is a sound relation between the people and their government, which has been corrupted by the Jacobin revolt against the liberal tradition. The executive formulates policy and proposes it to the representatives of those who must supply the means to carry it out. The governed, acting through their representatives, accept or reject the proposed measures. "The executive is the active power in the state, the asking and the proposing power. The representative assembly is the consenting power, the petitioning, the approving, the criticizing . . . and the refusing power."[87] Both these powers are necessary to the maintence of order and freedom in the state. The government must be able to govern, and the people must be represented to ensure that they are not ruled arbitrarily.

What is the basis for public criticism or approval of a government's measures? Lippmann has categorically asserted in the works reviewed above, including The Public Philosophy, that the people cannot judge the substance of policy. This means that they can only ask, as he observed in Public Opinion and The Phantom Public, whether correct procedures have been followed in formulating and executing

[86] Ibid., p. 15.
[87] Ibid., p. 30.

policies. Perhaps they can also criticize a proposed measure if its cost exceeds their paying capacity or if it hurts their personal interests. Americans who like Swiss watches may object to an increase in the import duty on foreign-made watches on the ground that it would upset their budgets, but not on the ground that it would damage America's position in the Cold War.

In *The Public Philosophy* Lippmann maintains, as he does not in *A Preface to Morals* or *The Good Society,* that there is a vital difference between the functions of the executive and of the representative assembly. Public officials owe allegiance to the law of the land, to the criteria of their professions, and to their own sense of duty. But they do not owe allegiance to the opinions of the electors. The voters elect the ruler but they have no right to command him. "Their duty is to fill the office and not to direct the office-holder."[88] This may sound undemocratic to the popular mind. However, that does not invalidate the principle. This is the principle which governed the election of rulers until comparatively recent times.[89] It applied to popes and also to elected kings. And this must be the principle of election when the electors chose, not someone to represent them to the governors, but the governors themselves. When we move over to the representative assembly we see a different picture. The image of the representative's virtue is like that of the lawyer's. Generally speaking, he not only is entitled but is duty bound to represent the interests and sentiments of his constituents. In doing this he performs an important function, for the voters must be effectively represented in order that they may not be op-

[88] *Ibid.,* p. 52. It will be seen that this is a clearer and more emphatic statement of the thesis enunciated by Lippmann in *The Phantom Public.* See (*Supra,* p. 284.) He repeated it in *The Good Society* (p. 248). "In the English tradition," he approvingly noted, "it was assumed that the people limited the power of their king, and not that the people ruled the state."
[89] *The Public Philosophy,* p. 52.

pressed.[90] This distinction between the functions of the representative and the public official is implicit in the Western system of government even today.

No President or head of a department could afford to admit that he was using his office to further the interests of a client or a pressure group, or even of his party. His acts must be presented as taken in obedience to his oath of office, which means taken disinterestedly and rationally.[91]

The function of a representative[92] corresponds to that of a lawyer, the duty of the executive to that of a judge. It will be noticed that this is a departure from the position Lippmann had taken in his earlier works. The description of a statesman in *A Preface to Morals* was addressed to executives and legislators alike, and so was the plea for disinterestedness in the management of public affairs. In *The Good Society*, the legislator was explicitly urged to cultivate a judicial outlook, since his function was no less judicial in nature than that of the judges. It would appear that by 1955 Lippmann had given up the hope that the average legislator would ever acquire the virtues of a statesman.

Lippmann does not rigidly limit the role of the legislator to representing the interests of his constituents. There are indeed occasions when he is "the holder of one of the great offices of the state—as when he must speak and vote on a declaration of war and the ratification of a treaty."[93] Lippmann implies that on these occasions the representative assembly takes on the character of the executive. But he does not explain how a politician who is used to accepting unregenerate desire at its face value, who does not normally confront the wishes and

[90] *Ibid.*, p. 54.
[91] *Ibid.*, pp. 53–54.
[92] Throughout this discussion, "representative" refers to a member of an elected legislative assembly.
[93] *The Public Philosophy*, p. 54.

interests of his constituents with the wishes and interests of the people in other constituencies, and who does not habitually weigh the rights of the present against the claims of the future, will acquire the courage, the insight and the wisdom of a statesman when on a given day the order of business in the legislature happens to call for the ratification of a treaty rather than the passage of a tax measure. This inconsistency arises probably from Lippmann's desire to accommodate the United States Constitution, which empowers Congress to declare war and the Senate to ratify treaties.

It will be seen that Lippmann's position on the duties and the prerogatives of the executive is almost a direct reproduction of the thesis which Edmund Burke preached to his constituents in Bristol—to his cost no doubt, for he lost the constituency in 1780. Rejecting the current view that a representative should faithfully carry out in Parliament the "instructions" and the "mandates" of his constituents, Burke observed:

Certainly, Gentlemen, it ought to be the happiness and glory of a representative to live in . . . the most unreserved communication with his constituents. Their wishes ought to have great weight with him; their opinions high respect. . . . But his unbiased opinion, his mature judgment, his enlightened conscience, he ought not to sacrifice to you, to any man, or to any set of men living. These he does not derive from your pleasure; no, nor from the law and the constitution. These are a trust from Providence, for the abuse of which he is deeply answerable. Your representative owes you . . . his judgment; and he betrays, instead of serving you, if he sacrifices it to your opinion.

My worthy colleague says, his will ought to be subservient to yours. . . . But government and legislation are matters of reason and judgment, and not of inclination; and what sort of reason is that, in which the determination precedes the discussion; in which one set of men deliberate, and another decide. . . .

To deliver an opinion is the right of all men. . . . But *authorita-tive* instructions; *mandates* issued, which the member is bound blindly and implicitly to obey . . . though contrary to the clearest conviction of his judgment and conscience,—these are things utterly unknown to the laws of this land, and which arise from a fundamental mistake of the whole order and tenor of our constitution.

You choose a member indeed; but when you have chosen him, he is not a member of Bristol, but he is a member of *parliament*.[94] [Italics in original.]

Six years later, Burke was back in Bristol to seek re-election. Addressing an alienated electorate in the local Guild Hall, he defended his conduct as a member of Parliament in these historic words:

I did not obey your instructions: No. I conformed to the instruc-tions of truth and nature, and maintained your interest, against your opinions, with a constancy that became me. . . . I am to look, indeed, to your opinions; but to such opinions as you and I *must* have five years hence. I was not to look to the flash of the day. I knew that you chose me, in my place, along with others, to be a pillar of the state, and not a weathercock on the top of the edifice . . . and of no use but to indicate the shiftings of every fashionable gale.[95] [Italics in original.]

Burke did not reject the thesis that a representative should, as Lippmann puts it, "represent the people to the govern-ment." Indeed, he did represent the citizens of Bristol to the government of the day. He did errands for them, and he presented their petitions to Parliament. But he did it in his own way. He explained his "way" in the course of a speech on presenting to the House of Commons a petition from Bristol, which had urged the government to exercise econ-omy in public expenditure. He observed:

[94] Edmund Burke, *Works* (London: Henry G. Bohn, 1854), Vol. I, pp. 446–447.
[95] *Ibid.*, Vol. II, p. 138.

I cannot indeed take upon me to say I have the honour *to follow* the sense of the people. [Italics in original.] The truth is, *I met it on the way*, while I was pursuing their interest according to my own ideas. [Italics in original.] I am happy beyond expression to find that my intentions have so far coincided with theirs . . .

I am therefore *satisfied to act as a fair mediator between govern-ment and the people.*[96] [Italics mine.]

This is Burke's outline of the representative's virtue. And this is the outline which Lippmann followed in *The Good Society* and *A Preface to Morals,* wherein he insisted that representatives and public officials alike should serve the nation rather than localities. Burke, let us remember, did not put the legislature and the executive on two radically different planes. Nor did he have to, for the Ministers of the Crown are themselves the leaders of the representative assembly.

The people and their representatives are unable to exercise executive power in the final acts of the state, which are the issues of war and peace, security and solvency, order and insurrection. But more than that, says Lippmann in *The Public Philosophy,* they do not even have the right to judge and decide these issues. The true relation between the masses and government is obscured and confused by an inappropriate and misleading use of the phrase "the people." It is wrong to identify the community with the voters. It is likewise wrong to equate it, as Bentham did, with the individuals who compose it at any given time, and to conceive of its interests as being the sum total of their interests. For if Bentham had been right, it should be possible to make a list of the members of a community. Yet no such list can be made, for new members are constantly being born and old members are dying. One must, therefore, view the community as a "corporation" which lives on while individuals

[96] *Ibid.,* Vol. II, p. 66.

come and go, as a stream in which the generations of changing persons are joined together, as a partnership between the
living and the dead and the unborn.[97] The beneficiary of
state action in domestic as well as foreign affairs is this
corporate being, *The People*. It is to preserve this entity that
young men die in battle and old men plant trees under which
they will never sit.

The voters have then no right to decide the issues of life
and death for this community.

The opinions of voters in elections are not to be accepted unquestioningly as true judgments of the vital interests of the community. . . . Because of the discrepancy between The People as
voters and *The People* as the corporate nation, the voters have no
title to consider themselves the proprietors of the commonwealth
and to claim that their interests are identical with the public
interest. A prevailing plurality of the voters are not *The People*.
The claim that they are is a bogus title invoked to justify the
usurpation of the executive power by representative assemblies
and the intimidation of public men by demagogic politicians.[98]

It should be remembered that the voters do not equal even
the living population, and therefore have no right to speak
for the community even in the Benthamite sense.

Lippmann confronts the doctrine of popular sovereignty
with the principle of virtual representation. Those who do
not vote because they are ineligible, or cannot because they
are too old to go to the polls, or those who are still unborn,
"are presumed to be represented by someone like the Pope,
the King, the Parliament, speaking in their name."[99] This
principle is rooted in the Western political tradition. We

[97] *The Public Philosophy*, pp. 32–35.
[98] *Ibid.*, pp. 32, 33–34.
[99] *Ibid.*, p. 37. Here again we can see a parallel with Burke who was a
believer in the principle of virtual representation. Writing to Sir Hercules
Langrishe on the subject of Irish Catholics, he observed: "Virtual representation is that in which there is a communion of interests, and a sympathy
in feelings and desires, between those who act in the name of any description of people, and the people in whose name they act, though the trustees

cannot ignore it or reject it. It may sound incongruous to modern ears that the Pope should represent the people. But it is no less incongruous, says Lippmann, that they should be represented by an aggregate of voters who have "diverse, conflicting self-centered interests and opinions."[100] It will make no difference if we bring a larger percentage of the eligible voters to the polls. For experience shows that in all matters, and especially in foreign affairs, "public opinion becomes less realistic as the mass to whom information must be conveyed and argument must be addressed, grows larger and more heterogeneous."[101]

The doctrine of the "sovereignty of the masses" is barbaric, says Lippmann, in that it is founded on the Jacobin theory of unlimited rights. It claims rights but proclaims no corresponding responsibilities. In the traditions of civility, there are no absolute rights; they are accompanied by corresponding duties and obligations. Nor can the rights of the individual be considered "natural," immutable and inviolable. For rights derive from the state; they are creatures of the law, "and have no other validity except as they are ordained by law."[102] The purpose of the laws which establish the right, let us say, to private property or the freedom of speech, is not to satisfy this or that instinct of the primitive man but to promote "the grand ends of civil society," which comprehend the peace and security of individuals. The absolutist notion of the individual's rights leads to their in-

---

are not actually chosen by them. This is virtual representation. Such a representation I think to be, in many cases, even better than the actual. . . . But this sort of virtual representation cannot have a long or sure existence, if it has not a substratum in the actual." Burke, *op. cit.*, Vol. III, pp. 334–335.

[100] *The Public Philosophy*, p. 38.

[101] *Ibid.*, p. 39.

[102] *Ibid.*, p. 119. On this point see also "The Indispensable Opposition," *Atlantic Monthly*, Vol. 164, No. 2 (August 1939), pp. 186–190; and *The Good Society*, pp. 243–246. For a similar view, to wit, that in civil society all rights are the creation of law, see Burke, "Reflections on the Revolution in France," *Works*, Vol. II, pp. 331–335.

tolerable abuse—which, in the end, inevitably arouses a counterrevolution. Such a revolution is already on the march in the West. It threatens to overwhelm the traditions of civility and to open the door to totalitarianism. In the sphere of government, it has brought about a "derangement of powers" between the governors and the governed; it has devitalized the executives and incapacitated them to govern wisely.

The doctrine of popular sovereignty threatens the citadel of liberty from two sides. It preaches the heresy that the people are sovereign, that their wishes are law, and that they are the final arbiters of what is right and what is wrong, what is true and what is false. It hides from them the abiding truth on which the institutions of liberal democracy were founded, that there is a law which is higher than the authority of the sovereign people, and that there is a mode of discovering the truth which is superior to their will as expressed in popular elections. Since what the people in the democracies have come to believe is basically untrue, and since the truth is hidden from their eyes, a vacuum has come to exist in their lives. They have lost an indispensable source of guidance and support, and with it their peace of mind.

There is a . . . radical disconnection between the notions of their minds and the needs of their souls. They have become the "lonely crowd" that Riesman has described. They are Durkheim's anomic mass. Their "true hallmark is neither poverty nor humble birth but is the consciousness—and the resentment that this consciousness inspires—of being disinherited." They are, as Karl Jaspers says, men dissolved into an anonymous mass because they are "without an authentic world, without provenance or roots," *without, that is to say, belief and faith that they can live by.*[103] [Italics mine.]

[103] *The Public Philosophy*, pp. 111–112. The works to which Lippmann refers in the above quotation are as follows: David Riesman, *The Lonely Crowd*; Emile Durkheim, *Suicide*; Arnold J. Toynbee, *A Study of History*,

The anguish which results from their present disconnection with their heritage is further accentuated by their inability to exercise that sovereignty to which they hold the title. Though they hailed the enfeeblement of the executive power as a victory for the forces of freedom, they are already turning away from it.[104] This is understandable. For while it is possible to govern without giving the people full representation, it is not possible to go on for long without a government that is able to govern. When the masses find that they have to choose between getting representation in an assembly which is incompetent to govern and being governed without such representation, they are sure to choose "authority, which promises to be paternal, in preference to freedom which threatens to be fratricidal."[105]

How can the mounting danger of a totalitarian counter-revolution be averted? Only by returning to the traditions of civility, to the public philosophy, says Lippmann. And what, one may ask, does the phrase "public philosophy" mean? It means that there is a law that is higher than the will of both the governors and the governed. It is the law of reason. It is also known as the natural law.

It will be recalled that in *The Good Society* Lippmann defined the higher law as being the denial that men may be arbitrary in their relations with one another. In *The Public Philosophy* he identifies the "higher law" with natural law in the usual, orthodox meaning of the term.[106] The natural law comprehends, but also goes further than, the rejection of arbitrariness. It means a commitment to the principle of rational determination. It means that by rational, sincere

Vol. V, p. 63; and Karl Jaspers, *The Origin and Goal of History* (London: Routledge and Kegan Paul, 1953), pp. 127–128. Citations given in *The Public Philosophy*, pp. 111–112.

[104] *The Public Philosophy*, p. 110.
[105] *The Public Philosophy*, pp. 60–61.
[106] *Ibid.*, pp. 104–108.

and disinterested inquiry we can discover the right and wrong and the reality of things. It is natural in the sense that its dictates are not the commands of a sovereign power but the discoveries of a rational mind. It is natural also in the sense that it is universal: when rational men address themselves to a given problem, they will all come to the same conclusion.

Let any human being have enough information and exert enough thought upon any question, and the result will be that he will arrive at a certain definite conclusion, which is the same that any other mind will reach under sufficiently favorable circumstances. . . . There is then to every question a true answer, a final conclusion, to which the opinion of every man is constantly gravitating. He may for a time recede from it, but give him more experience and time for consideration, and he will finally approach it. . . . This final opinion then is independent, not indeed of thought in general, but of all that is arbitrary and individual in thought; is quite independent of how you, or I, or any number of men think.[107]

The rational method is the "ark of the covenant of the public philosophy." It is a principle of everlasting value. "There is no set of . . . laws or constitutional guarantees which are unchangeable. What is unchangeable is the commitment to rational determination."[108] Lippmann adds that the public philosophy is not a body of actual laws enforceable in courts. It is rather a way of looking at things.

What is the significance of the postulate that men should act rationally? Taken by itself, it sounds axiomatic, almost commonplace. But it becomes pregnant with momentous implications when we remember that in Lippmann's view the ability to think rationally and reason disinterestedly is rare

[107] This is a statement of C. S. Peirce which Lippmann approvingly quotes. Ibid., p. 133.
[108] Ibid.

among the masses. Then it points to the location of governing power in the good society. It proclaims on the one hand that the people and their representatives do not have an inherent and immutable right to rule the state and, on the other, that those who do rule must follow "right reason," which is the law of nature. Like the men who founded the institutions of liberal democracy, they must be well versed in the traditions of civility, the public philosophy. These men were rational and they were free.

They were rational because they comprehended the moral order of the universe and their place in it. They were free because in that moral order they had a personal moral responsibility to perform their duties and to exercise their corresponding rights.[109]

Lippmann would entrust the conduct of public affairs to men who are subject to the law of reason, which is not only a method of arriving at propositions on issues of policy but also an ethical standard of judgment, a norm of conduct. His governors will be acquainted with the principles of good life, which consists in the "government of our appetites and passions by the reasons of a second, civilized and, therefore, acquired nature."[110] They will exercise what Thomas Aquinas called "a royal and politic rule" over their "irascible and concupiscible" powers. They will discharge their duty under the law as did Socrates, who refused to escape from the prison on the ground that it was more right for him to undergo his sentence. He was a true citizen of Athens, and he would not cheat the law, least of all for his own personal advantage. For

if Athens was to be governed, it must be by citizens who by their second natures preferred the laws to the satisfaction of their own

---

[109] Walter Lippmann, "The State of Education in this Troubled Age," *Vital Speeches*, Vol. 7, No. 7 (January 15, 1941); also *The Public Philosophy*, pp. 160–161.
[110] *The Public Philosophy*, p. 162.

impulses, even to their own will to live. Unless the citizens would govern themselves with such authority, the Athenian city would be ungovernable. If they followed their first natures, Athens would be trampled down in the stampede.[111]

This is the image of the man who, according to Lippmann, has become fit to rule, and this is the kind of man who should conduct the business of the state today. Needless to say, this is an image which one sees only infrequently. Government by men who are the twentieth-century counterparts of Socrates can only mean rule by public-spirited elites. But Lippmann's elite does not resemble Pareto's elite, whose relation with the masses is only one of coercing and manipulating them. Nor is he the totalitarian "god," acting as the agent of history and the bearer of a mission. Rather, he resembles the Stoic humanitarian and approaches Plato's "guardian" or "philosopher-king"; the essential difference being that he is open to criticism and dismissal by the electors. He can propose a measure to the people, but he cannot impose it on them. If he cannot do his duty, because his policy is unpopular with those who must finance its execution, he should resign his office.[112]

Government by philosopher-kings may be desirable. But where do we find our Socrates? His like are not born every day. And even if we did find him, would he be able to govern? He is a "new man," "led of the spirit," regenerated and transformed so that, as Confucius said, he may follow his heart's desire without transgressing what is right. He appeals to experience which men have not yet had, he deals in things which are beyond their immediate reach. He speaks a

[111] Ibid., p. 139.

[112] Lippmann has often criticized the popular notion that a presidential election in the United States can take place only once in every four years. The resignation of a President, if it is in the public interest, is neither morally nor legally outlawed. See "Should the President Resign," Senior Scholastic, Vol. 49 (December 2, 1946), p. 12.

language which is too subtle and obscure for the common man. Will he be able to rule the old Adam? Will he be able to demonstrate that his policies are the product of right reason? It may take generations, as C. S. Peirce has said, to find the answer of reason to a given question. Socrates will have drunk his cup of poison long before the Athenians find, if ever they do, that he was right and they were wrong. Lippmann is not unmindful of these difficulties. Indeed, he concedes that Socrates cannot rule. Commenting on the assassination of Mr. M. K. Gandhi, who was allegedly an apostle of non-violence, he observed:

[Gandhi] posed the perennial question of how the insight of the seers and saints is related to the work of legislators, rulers and statesmen. That they are in conflict is only too plain, and yet it is impossible to admit . . . that the conflict can never be resolved. For it is necessary to govern mankind and it is necessary to transform men. . . . The ideals of human life which the seers teach— nonresistance, humility, and poverty and chastity—have never been and can never be the laws of a secular society. Obviously, the greatest seers knew this. . . . At the summit of their wisdom they teach not how to behave [in the practical details of everyday life] but to what ultimate values [men] should give their allegiance.[113]

Socrates, then, cannot rule a modern state. But those who do rule must have him as their model and must try to approximate his devotion to the law of reason.

But do thieves and burglars not also apply the principle of rational and disinterested inquiry in discovering and perfecting the art of housebreaking? If so, then what is the difference between their commitment to the law of reason and that of rulers and statesmen? How do we ensure that even when they are devoted to the principle of rational

[113] T and T, February 3, 1948. See also *The Public Philosophy*, pp. 147–152.

determination, governors will govern unselfishly and justly? Lippmann would remind us that the law of reason is not merely another name for the so-called scientific method. It is also a norm of conduct. It has a spiritual and moral content which guides and directs the reasoning faculty of man. But what is the source of the spiritual and the moral in a rational being? Are they born of the reason itself? Is the moral being at once the creature and the ruler of the reasoning being? It would not do to say that to reason is to reason morally, for that would merely beg the question.

There are two possible answers to the question we pose. One is that the ability to reason morally is acquired. By personal experience, by trial and error, by reflecting on the course of human affairs in the past and in the present, men arrive at the principles of a good life. The faculty of reasoning, which in some rudimentary form we all possess, constantly feeds itself on its discoveries, grows, and is transformed. Finally, it reaches the stage where it has imbibed the principles of the moral order of the universe to such an extent that its possessor cannot but reason morally. He has become the Socrates who will not, because he cannot, employ reason to discover the best way of escape from prison. This is the answer which Aristotle would give.[114]

But this is not the answer of the Stoics, with whom the beginnings of the doctrine of natural law are traditionally associated. For them the law of nature was the law of reason because nature was synonymous with reason and reason with God.[115] Similarly with Thomas Aquinas. The faculty of reason was divine in origin. It was a gift of God. It dis-

---

[114] See Ernest Barker's Introduction to Otto von Gierke's *Natural Law and the Theory of Society* (Barker's translation) 1934, p. xxxv. Lippmann draws upon this source repeatedly in *The Public Philosophy*, especially in his discussion of the natural law.
[115] *Ibid.*, p. xxxv.

covered the law of nature "as it sought to apprehend the purpose of God's Will and the rule of His Reason."[116]

Now shall our governors obey the law of nature in its Aristotelian conception or according to the meaning which the Stoics and Thomas Aquinas gave it? We may recall that Lippmann cites the loss of the public philosophy as a principal cause of the decline of the West. What is it that the men of the West have lost? Is it the capacity to believe in the efficacy of reason, or is it the capacity to believe in the supremacy of God? Lippmann is equivocal on this point. He seems to incline to the Aristotelian view when he says that the public philosophy is "the wisdom of a great society over the generations."[117] It is significant that while he mentions the Stoics and Thomas Aquinas in his discussion of the natural law, he does not quote their definitions which relate it to God. On the other hand, he does tell us about the Roman jurists who believed that there was in theory a natural law, which was "the law imposed on mankind *by common human nature, that is, by reason in response to human needs and instincts.*"[118] [Italics mine.] It will be noticed that this definition bears a marked resemblance to Aristotle's view as noted above.

Yet at times Lippmann does seem to say that the capacity to believe in the sovereignty of God is an integral part of the public philosophy, that its weakening has engendered a terrible feeling of loneliness and isolation among modern men and has contributed to the decline of the West. In 1941 he wrote that the system of education in the United States had committed the "greatest crime" against American youth in that it had deprived them of their classical heritage. The institutions of the West, he said, were the product of a culture which

[116] *Ibid.,* p. xxxviii.
[117] *The Public Philosophy,* p. 99.
[118] *Ibid.,* p. 107.

is essentially the culture of Greece, inherited from the Greeks by the Romans, *transfused by the Fathers of the Church with the religious teachings of Christianity,* and progressively enlarged by a countless number of artists . . . and philosophers from the beginnings of the Middle Ages up to the first third of the nineteenth century.[119] [Italics mine.]

In *The Public Philosophy* he criticizes the rigid separation of church and state which is characteristic of several modern democracies. He laments the contemporary view that the temporal power has no jurisdiction over the ideas, principles, moral and spiritual values of the individual, which are his private concern so long as they do not pose a "clear and present" threat to public order. Freedom has acquired a meaning which is foreign to the traditions of civility.

Originally it was founded on the postulate that there was a universal order on which all reasonable men were agreed; within that public agreement on the fundamentals and on the ultimates, it was safe to permit and it would be desirable to encourage, dissent and dispute. But with the disappearance of the public philosophy —and of a consensus on the first and last things—there was opened up a great vacuum in the public mind, yawning to be filled.[120]

In the public philosophy, the realm of the spirit and the realm of material existence, of ideas and of "overt" action, are disparate yet inseparable. "Church and state need to be separate, autonomous and secure. But they must also meet on all the issues of good and evil."[121]

One may ask whether the church and the state are joined in a common purpose, whether they mingle with each other, whether they are mutually related. If so, what is the nature of their relationship? Lippmann does not explicitly answer our

[119] "The State of Education," *Vital Speeches* (January 15, 1941), p. 201.
[120] *The Public Philosophy,* p. 100.
[121] *The Public Philosophy,* p. 155.

question. But we would venture to submit that his answer is implicit in the statements quoted above. It is that the men who rule the state must be deeply religious. This interpretation can be further substantiated. He tells us time and again that the men who founded the institutions of liberal democracy were steeped in the public philosophy.

The men of the seventeenth and eighteenth centuries who established these great salutory rules . . . were themselves the adherents of a public philosophy—of the doctrine of natural law, which held that there was law "above the ruler and the sovereign people . . . above the whole community of mortals."[122]

These men, he says, were the leaders of English political and intellectual life during this period. Let us briefly inquire into their philosophy.

In the first place, we should clear up an ambiguity which arises from Lippmann's interpretation of the English liberal tradition in terms of natural law. The concept of natural law, says Barker, is not completely foreign to English thought. It was invoked by Judge Hobart, who declared in 1614 that an act of Parliament against "natural equity" was null and void. There is some emphasis on it in Hobbes and Locke. Even in the eighteenth century the "ghost of the idea" comes occasionally to "haunt English thought." Yet it is not an important part of the English tradition.

The English thinkers and lawyers of the eighteenth century have little regard for natural law and natural rights. Indeed, it may be said that *natural law is generally repugnant to the genius of English legal thought, generally busied with a common law, which however common, is still peculiar, and anyhow is sufficiently actual, sufficiently practical, sufficiently definite, to suit the English temper.* [Italics mine.] To Burke any speech of natural law and natural rights is metaphysics, and not politics. To Blackstone

[122] *Ibid.*, p. 97.

[though he is inconsistent] . . . the law of nature is not a concern of English courts, and may therefore be treated, for their purposes, as non-existent.[123]

If the British statesmen of the seventeenth and eighteenth centuries did not believe in the natural law, then what was the hallmark of their tradition? Once again we turn to Barker, who enlightens us on the subject in an essay entitled "British Statesmen." Two of the characteristics he ascribes to them seem to be particularly relevant to our enquiry. An overwhelming majority of them, he tells us, had had a university education, which imbued them with a liberal tradition of philosophy and "humane letters." They carried this influence to the larger world of government and politics.

If you take English political thought and action from Pitt and Fox onwards, it seems to me that you will always find present . . . strands of feeling which are due—of course among many other causes—to this germination of Greek influence.[124]

The Pitts and Fox, Canning and Peel, Gladstone and Asquith were all immersed in the classics. Burke, in his Dublin days, had drunk deep at the fountain of Aristotle. Here then is one of the things—the classical heritage—with which the older liberals were so richly endowed and which Lippmann finds so conspicuously lacking in the education of contemporary American youth.

Another salient characteristic of the majority of British statesmen was that they followed the way of religion. Barker notes:

Without any hypocrisy (a charge readily brought by the facile mind against those who introduce thoughts of eternity into tem-

[123] Ernest Barker, "Natural Law and the American Revolution," in his *Traditions of Civility* (Cambridge University Press, 1948), p. 317.

[124] Ernest Barker, "British Statesmen," in his *Essays on Government*, p. 24. Our frequent recourse to Barker may be justified on the ground that in *The Public Philosophy* Lippmann himself refers to him repeatedly.

poral affairs, but a charge which a reflective mind will no less readily repel), they accepted the primacy of religion and the ultimacy of obedience to its guidance. "Sir," said Cromwell, "you see the work is done by a Divine leading." "We know," wrote Burke, "and it is our pride to know, that man is by his constitution a religious animal . . . *all persons possessing any portion of power ought to be strongly and awfully impressed with an idea that they act in trust, and that they are to account for their conduct in that trust to the one great Master, Author, and Founder of society.*" [Italics mine.] The same conception of a religious order of the world, and of the duty incumbent on states and statesmen to observe that order, inspired the policy of Gladstone, as it also inspired the policy of Salisbury.[125]

We may then conclude that in the formative period of the public philosophy neither statesmen, nor men of letters, nor the general public set great store by the natural law. This should not be taken to mean that they did not believe in the efficacy of reason. They did. But unlike the Greeks, they made the reason of man subservient to the Reason of God. Burke provided an illustration of how faith and reason might intermingle and become inseparably bound in a single whole personality. He believed that in a Christian commonwealth, the church and the state were two different but integral parts of the same whole. And he believed that the "sovereign reason of the world" must not be subjected to the will of a majority.[126] It is interesting to note that even though he dismissed the natural law as metaphysics, and did not accord absolute sovereignty to human reason, he arrived at precisely the same conclusion with respect to ideal human behavior as Lippmann did. In his "Reflections on the Revolution in France," Edmund Burke wrote a passage which

[125] *Ibid.*, pp. 32–33.
[126] Ernest Barker, "Burke on the French Revolution," in his *Essays on Government*, pp. 228–233.

would make an excellent summary of the political philosophy of Walter Lippmann.

Certainly the people at large . . . *should not be suffered to imagine that their will, any more than that of kings, is the standard of right and wrong.* They ought to be persuaded that they are full as little entitled, and far less qualified, with safety to themselves, *to use any arbitrary power whatsoever.* . . . When the people have emptied themselves of all the lust of selfish will, *which without religion is utterly impossible they ever should,* when they are conscious that they exercise . . . the power, which to be legitimate must be according to that eternal, immutable law, *in which will and reason are the same,* they will be more careful how they place power in base and incapable hands. In their nomination to office, they will not appoint to the exercise of authority, as to a pitiful job, *but as to a holy function;* not according to their sordid, selfish interest, nor to their wanton caprice, nor to their arbitrary will; *but they will confer that power on those only, in whom they may discern that predominant proportion of active virtue and wisdom,* taken together and fitted to the charge, such, as in the great and inevitable mixed mass of human imperfections and infirmities, is to be found.[127] [Italics mine.]

The foregoing should suggest that Lippmann accepts the Aristotelian, without rejecting the Stoic, interpretation of the natural law. If there is a paradox here, it is more apparent than real. For while like Burke he bears the imprint of Aristotle's thought, like him he also believes that those who wield the power of the state must be deeply religious. The two—reason and faith—are reconciled in his thought by virtue of the fact that in his view "there can be, indeed there is, great faith and deep religion without any concrete image of God."[128] But it should be added that he has no quarrel with those who must adhere to organized religion in order to be religious.

[127] Burke, *Works,* Vol. II, pp. 365–366.
[128] *The Public Philosophy,* p. 176.

Lippmann's theory of the independent executive rests on the assumption that men can be found who are wise and virtuous to the extent that they may follow the desires of their hearts without transgressing what is right—men who, in other words, can do no wrong. For evidently he cannot invoke the sovereignty of reason to annul the right of the masses to rule the state and, at the same time, countenance rulers whose reason, like that of the masses, is imperfect. Yet he must concede that his assumption is impossible of fulfillment in the world of mortal, imperfect men. We may then say that his theory, like the "insight of the sages," enunciates an ideal, rather than a practical formula, which men in government and politics should try to approximate. Aristotle, we may recall here, was referring to the ideal state when he advocated that the people should elect the rulers but not rule. Lippmann nostalgically refers to the seventeenth and eighteenth centuries as the period when the institutions of liberal democracy were shaped. But it is not the political practice but the ideals which a handful of men enunciated during this period that commend it to our attention. In many ways the practice was gruesome.

VIII

Conclusion

Lippmann's Theory of International Politics

WALTER LIPPMANN HAS A VIEW OF HUMAN NATURE WHICH dominates his thinking on domestic and international politics. Men, he believes, are inherently neither good and innocent nor wicked and evil. But for the most part they are foolish and obstinate. They fail to reason and to subdue their lusts and impulses. Attached to their habits and customs, they abhor the "intolerable disease of thought." Not all men are alike. Nor does any one man adhere to a uniform pattern of thought and action throughout his life. Human nature should, therefore, be viewed as developing behavior. The final stage in the development of human personality is maturity or the civilization of desire. The mature man is he whose reason rules his lusts and impulses—his first nature. He understands the reality of things around him, and he knows what he can possess and hold and what he cannot. There is a harmonious relation between his desire and its objects. He seeks nothing that is impossible or improper for him to have. In his knowledge and in his virtue he is happy and he is contented. He is the "new man," the "regenerated man," not the old Adam.

CONCLUSION 327

Although the door to maturity is not closed and although those who seek to build the good society must never give up the effort to lead men through it, the fact remains that only a few do actually enter it. The vast majority of men are uncivilized—foolish and ever refractory against reason—or only partially civilized. They will remain so, for the passage to civilization is long and difficult regardless of the road one may choose. The way of artistic creativeness, of intuition and of the will, is no less difficult than the way of reason and of knowledge.

A low estimate of the intellectual and moral qualities of the common man is fundamental with Lippmann. Even when he viewed man as a willful rather than a rational being, he rejected the premise that all men were equally fit to discover and pursue their true interests. He looked to the "creative genius" and the "dynamic purpose" of the artist, not to the "uncivilized desire" of the average "willful being," for realizing the goal of human endeavor—the creation of harmony and beauty in social relations as well as in the inward life of the individual.

The immature and undisciplined desires of men conflict with one another. Each man is in some measure a battleground of rival impulses, and society is the arena where the desires of individuals act and interact upon one another, producing patterns of cooperation and conflict. It is society which creates organizations and institutions to keep this process of interaction from becoming anarchic or violent. In the modern world these societies are national.

Lippmann traces the feeling of nationality to the loves and hates, associations and prejudices of our first nature. Since men have been barbaric much longer than they have been civilized, and since most of them are even today only partially civilized, this expression of their first cultures, this appeal to their primitive natures is a powerful factor in human affairs.

It gives men self-confidence and a sense of belonging to a higher and greater entity than their own individual personalities. It defines them against the background of the world. But by the same token, it plants in their minds the notion that they are sovereign and therefore entitled to live as they like, that in some way they are superior to the rest of the human race, that they have the right to realize their vital interests and their "destiny" on their own terms. Nationalism poses men living in states other than our own as potential enemies of our national individuality. It engenders distrust and, often, hate of the foreigner. In emphasizing the separateness and sovereignty of nations, it interdicts the civilized ideal of a state in which diverse peoples find liberty and justice under a system of equal laws. It points to autarchy as the symbol of national independence, and calls for a regimentation of national life which ultimately leads to totalitarianism. It accentuates our aggressive and defensive reactions to the foreigner, and increases the possibility of war. And finally, by disparaging international cooperation, which is so essential to improving the lot of man on earth, it impedes the establishment of the good society. The division of the world into sovereign nation-states is to be deplored. Yet it is a fact given and unalterable in the foreseeable future. The operative unit in world affairs, even in building the good society, is the nation-state. World politics is international politics.

Therefore, the pursuit of the national interest must be the guiding principle of a nation's foreign policy. Lippmann concedes that it is difficult to define the national interest in concrete and precise terms. At any given time, several interests may present themselves as possible objectives of foreign policy. They must be accepted or rejected, and assigned positions on a schedule of priorities, according to their bearing on national survival, which is the first and foremost interest of a state. Another criterion of judgment in this respect is attainability; the objectives chosen may not be the best that could be desired, but they must be such as can be realized without committing the whole wealth or the power of the nation. The policy-maker must maintain a balance between the ends sought and the means available to attain and defend them.

Lippmann does not conceive the national interest in purely material terms. He defines survival—the supreme national interest—as continued physical existence and the preservation of a nation's way of life, its moral codes, its value systems, its religious, social and political institutions. He would endorse a nation's attempt to promote its way of life abroad and its desire to live in an environment which is friendly to its ideals. Indeed, he goes so far as to say that a people which does not advance its faith has already begun to abandon it. But he cautions that ideals, as such, do not make good objectives of policy. They must be translated into concrete terms in order to be realized. Governments must also take account of the valid interests of other states in determining their own vital interests. In the anarchic world of nation-states, this is idealism par excellence.

The ensuring of national survival and the protection of lesser interests presuppose the ability to defend them against foreign encroachment. The instrument of defense as well as of aggression is power, which is one's ability to persuade others to do one's will. The conflict of interests between nation-states being essentially anarchic, national power ultimately means military power. Since power is the master-key to the problems of defense as well as of conquest, its pursuit becomes a major interest of all states. And since it is a relative quality, nations seek to be more powerful than their rivals. They realize this objective by increasing their own power and/or by diminishing the power of their potential enemies or intended victims. The conflict of interests

between states thus becomes a struggle for power: armaments lead to counter-armaments, alliances to counter-
alliances, and issues tend to be judged and determined not
on their individual merit but in view of the ups and downs
of relative power positions. A nation may disapprove of this
struggle for power, but it cannot escape it. Nor can it ignore
it except at the cost of its vital interests, for failure to back
up interests with necessary power is to leave them unde-
fended and to invite their capture by foreign states.

Nations have to depend on their own military might in
order to protect their vital interests, because there is no common higher authority to judge and decide international disputes. The existing machinery of international law can
settle only such disputes as do not touch upon the vital
interests of states. Moreover, international disputes do not
relate to questions of right and wrong or to interpretations of
law. Nations, says Lippmann, fight to decide whose word
will be supreme in world affairs. One way to end the brutal
struggle for power would be to abolish the operative unit in
the struggle, the nation-state, and to create a world state.
Since the supreme authority in human affairs is the universal
law of nature, men, as the Stoics held, should not live their
lives in so many "civic republics" separated from one another
by different systems of justice; they should all be fellow
citizens in "one life and one order" under one joint law. The
constitution of a world state must then be the ultimate objective of all thinking men who wish to see a more peaceful and
progressive world. But desirable though it is, the objective is
not immediately attainable because at the present moment
there is no world community to form the basis of a world
patriotism. Most men—who are, incidentally, not "thinking
men"—and especially organized groups and interests in
national societies, do not favor the dissolution of the sovereign
nation-state and its substitution by a world state. It will take

decades of experience in international cooperation before the psychological obstacles to the creation of a world state can be surmounted. However, there is no prospect that a world democracy based on adult suffrage can be established even in the remote future. The rich and powerful states, which alone could foot the bills of a world state, would not agree to take orders from a Parliament of Man in which they were hopelessly outnumbered by "underdeveloped" peoples. At any rate, the world must have peace, a longish peace, in order that habits of cooperation may take root and lay the groundwork for the construction of a world order.

The peace we seek cannot be had by organizing a system of collective security. The maintenance of peace and order is a typically governmental function, and no agency can perform it unless it has governmental powers. The theory of collective security wrongly assumes that nations are willing to fight and bleed anywhere and everywhere in the world to punish aggression. It ignores the fact that nations are more interested in their own peace and security than in "world peace," and that quite often they want a change in the status quo much more passionately than they want peace. Nor does every state have the means to participate in wars of collective security. Only the united action of the great military states, which alone have the power to enforce peace, can maintain world peace. But it is rare that they unite in such a venture, for they are the great rivals in the struggle for power. And, of course, when they fight one another no one can police them. Finally, the principle of collective security works, if and when it does work, as the guardian of the status quo. It seeks to prevent war, but does not touch the conditions that lead to war.

Though it is the seedbed of a future world state, an international organization such as the United Nations should not act as if it were already a world government. It should not take up the problems of international peace and security. Nor should it arrogate to itself the right to examine and judge the conduct of member states. It should eschew issues which bear upon the vital interests of states, with the possible exception of those on which the great powers are willing to cooperate. As a rule, it should operate as a meeting place of diplomats who confer on matters of mutual interest. As a body, it should deal with relatively harmless and unexciting matters: it should promote cultural and scientific exchanges between the member states and encourage international cooperation in the solution of economic, social and educational problems facing mankind, especially in underdeveloped areas. In short, it should devote itself to the "arts of peace" and try to solve the problems of individual rather than national security. As the prestige of the organization rises, the habit of cooperation formed in these "unexciting" ventures may one day begin to bear upon the solution of political issues—the issues of war and peace and security.

In the meantime, the nation-state must rely on its military power to defend its independence and vital interests. It must make alliances with states which share its interests, for the power of a reliable ally is one's own power. That alliances are a necessary instrument of policy does not mean that one should have as many of them as possible. The value of an alliance varies in direct proportion to the identity of interests, especially the strategic interests, which exists among its members. A nation that shares our political ideals, our cultural traditions, our economic philosophy and, above all, our strategic interests is our natural ally. A great power should therefore not rely too heavily on alliances with feeble, immature and far-flung states. Such alliances are expensive and cumbersome in that they call for constant intervention in the internal affairs of the ally. Moreover, they can be easily disorganized by the state against which they are directed. Allies should be distinguished from satellites. Since alliances are a factor of power, their formation provokes counter-alliances into being. Their provocativeness increases all the more when they are made with a state in the strategic neighborhood of a great rival power.

It is not possible to abolish the rivalry of nations and establish a universal identity of interest in world peace. Nor is it possible to create a pool of power to end the struggle for power. But it is possible to mitigate the lawlessness and the brutality of the struggle. The way to do it is to confront power with power, to check and to balance it. Lippmann believes that nations, like individuals, tend to restrain their ambitions and to see the light of reason when they know that their ability to get what they want is limited, checked and balanced—that force will be met by force. The existence of a global balance of power may help maintain world peace. But, essentially, the balance of power is not an instrument for the maintenance of peace. Rather, it is the best available means by which a nation can safeguard its independence and by which a group of nations can prevent a dynamic and aggressive power from establishing its hegemony over them.

Lippmann holds that since the impossibility of success is the only effective deterrent to aggression, a state which seeks to preserve its independence must maintain a favorable, rather than an even, balance of power vis-à-vis its enemies. But simple balances in which two states or two coalitions face each other to the exclusion of third parties are inherently unstable. They are liable, sooner or later, to break down. The existence of third states, ready to throw their weight on the weaker side in the balance, not only adds to the stability of the system of the balance of power but also exercises a restraining influence on would-be conquerors. The larger the number of great powers which can act as balancers, the greater the chance that the system will endure and that the independence of the member states will be preserved. However, in order that great powers may be able to play this important role, it is essential that they should be securely settled in their strategic neighborhoods or spheres of influence, unencumbered by local balances. For if they have to contend with hostile coalitions in their own neighborhoods, they will fail to exert much influence on the global balance. Lippmann recognizes that complex balances of power also break down. Moreover, they do not give the world a sense of stability and security even when they successfully guard the independence of states. In the ideal state of affairs, a supremely powerful, disinterested and liberal nation or coalition presides over a global balance of power. It regulates the rivalries of the member states without seeking self-aggrandizement. For all practical purposes it rules the world, albeit in the interest of mankind. In the hands of such a ruler, the balance of power becomes the structural principle of public order in the good society.

Lippmann's Theory of Government

Walter Lippmann views society as a corporate entity which lives on while new members are born into it and the old pass out of it. It is a partnership between the living and the dead and the unborn. It is here, in society, that the interests and desires of individuals come into contact and find accommodation and adjustments. It is essential to the goodness of society that these adjustments be made not in an arbitrary manner but according to law. In the final analysis, they must be made according to the law of reason, which is also the "Law of Nature and of Nature's God," and which is higher than the letter of particular laws, higher than even the will of the people. Society is then a partnership in good and virtuous living, not a device to find the means of expression for the primitive instincts of man.

The function of civil society—accommodating the conflicting desires of individuals—is then at once judicial and spiritual in nature. It cannot be performed by the majorities of voters, who are by hypothesis unregenerate and immature. The art of government, which is essentially the art of judging between competing interests, requires an insight that comes only from an objective and discerning knowledge of facts and a high degree of disinterestedness. The voters possess neither the skill nor the information nor the disinterestedness needed for wise and just governance. They cannot govern, and their wishes cannot be accepted as propositions in public policy or as the standards of right and wrong in public affairs. Nor do they have the right to make decisions for the corporate community. Lippmann maintains that the rights of the individual are not inherent or immutable but merely the creatures of law. Moreover, he argues, governance is not a right; it is a sacred duty, which must be performed by those who are fit to perform it. The only right of men which no law may change is the right not to be dealt with arbitrarily, the right to be governed according to laws which are in conformity with the "higher law."

If there is a law higher than the will of the people, then the people cannot be sovereign. Rather, sovereignty must reside in the source of the higher law—in reason. And then also, the theory which ascribes sovereignty to the people must be deemed a heresy. That it is indeed a heresy is evidenced by the evil consequences which its operation has wrought in our times. Lippmann finds that acting on the theory of popular sovereignty, the people have arbitrarily established themselves as the highest tribunal for the judgment, approval and disapproval of public policy. Since they are manifestly unable actually to govern, their seizure of executive power has created a vacuum of authority in government. Men who supposedly rule the democracies are intimidated and tyrannized by popular assemblies. They lack the will and the power to deal resolutely and effectively with the grave issues that confront the Western world in the mid-twentieth century. The paralysis of government, resulting from the usurpation of the executive power by the representative assemblies, threatens to uproot the institutions of liberal democracy and to pave the way for totalitarianism. For while it is possible to govern without giving men adequate representation, it is not possible to go on for long without a government that can effectively govern.

Lippmann contends that in order to turn back the rising tide of totalitarian barbarity, and in order also to produce men who are fit to rule their fellow men rationally and disinterestedly, the people in the democracies must unlearn the theory of popular sovereignty. They must also relearn the public philosophy which gave birth to the liberal democratic tradition. In the traditions of the "public philosophy," the people do not rule, they elect the rulers. And they elect to public office men who are disinterested, virtuous and wise, men who comprehend the moral order of the universe and their own duty to it as the holders of public office.

Theory and Policy

In recent years, Lippmann has been alarmed by the rising influence of Congress on the formulation and execution of policy, especially in the realm of foreign affairs. Contrary to the letter and the spirit of the Constitution, the feeling has grown on Capitol Hill that the executive is the servant of Congress, which represents the sovereign people. The readiness of Congress to usurp the powers and the prerogatives of the executive, and thus to derange and disrupt the balance of the Constitution, stems from an imperious denial that there is a will higher than its own will.

The maintenance of peace and order in the community requires the making as well as the enforcement of laws. Lippmann believes that except perhaps in small rural societies, laws cannot be enforced by the legislative body; they must be enforced by the executive. Nor will they be enforced justly and effectively if the sword of Damocles, in the form of congressional harassment, constantly hangs over the heads of those who are charged with their enforcement. It follows that any increment in the power and prestige of Congress which is realized at the expense of the executive hurts the vital interests of the United States.

The executive, which is the repository of vital facts on which all policy must be based, is much better situated than Congress to define the American national interest at any given time, and the means to achieve it. Therefore, the initiative in policy-making as well as in law-making must come from the executive. The executive should lead Congress and not be led by it. Yet the American system of government does not always permit executive leadership in the management of public affairs. Often enough, a President has to contend with a hostile Congress, which far from being led by him, insists on mutilating his legislative program and obstructing the implementation of his policies. Sometimes he finds himself in the anomalous position where his oath of office compels him to enforce a law which he deems to be detrimental to public interest. While the Presidential system can and does create stalemates between the President and Congress, it does not provide the machinery to end stalemates, to force a showdown such as a vote of confidence or a new general election to both Congress and the Presidency. Lippmann rules out the possibility in the near future of extensive constitutional revision to ameliorate the situation. But he does not consider this to mean that all roads to improvement are blocked. He points out that there is nothing in the Constitution to prevent a more frequent Presidential election than once every four years. A President who does not command the loyalty and the support of the majority of Congress and who cannot, therefore, carry out his program should, together with the Vice President and the Cabinet, resign his office. A measure of this kind would arouse the American people to the need of returning such men to Capitol Hill as will cooperate with the man they choose to occupy the White House. It would also mark the beginning of new traditions in American government and politics.

We are living in the midst of a fierce conflict in the arena of world politics. On one side of the fence stands the Soviet Union, whose ultimate aim is nothing less than the establishment of a world empire and the conversion of mankind to its way of life—by propaganda if possible, by force if necessary. On the other side are arrayed the nations of the Western world, determined to yield neither faith nor freedom to the men of the Kremlin. The United States, being the richest, as well the greatest military power on earth, should lead the Western democracies in their struggle for self-preservation. The mechanism of their defense is the balance of power. Lippmann argues that however the Soviets may rate their obective of world conquest and communization, they will not want to jeopardize their very survival in trying to achieve it. It is therefore imperative for the United States to leave no doubt that she will answer a Soviet invasion of Western Europe with an all-out attack on Russia. In order to convince the Kremlin that the threat is not a bluff, she must maintain a favorable balance of power vis-à-vis the Soviet Union. She should keep her nuclear power, which is the chief deterrent to Soviet expansionism, ahead of Soviet nuclear power. Moreover, she should promote the internal strength and stability as well as the external unity of her allies.

Toward the Good Society

The conflicts of interest and the rivalries between individuals, factions, localities and nation-states are facts which must be reckoned with. But the adjustment and accommodation of these conflicts—actual cooperation between individuals, groups and even nation-states, and likewise the natural as well as the contrived identity of certain interests between them—are also facts which support the hope that a better world order can be created. The ultimate ideal of civilized men must be the establishment of a world state where the blessings of God's earth are the common property of all mankind, and where men, in spite of their diversities, find liberty and justice under equal laws. It may take generations, indeed centuries, to establish such a Commonwealth of Man. But men must move in the general direction of a universal order if they are ever to realize it. Two concrete steps may be usefully taken. Lippmann points to the fact that the vast majority of men in the world groan under the crushing weight of poverty, disease and ignorance. Their lot cannot be improved by the existing nation-states, many of which are poor, weak and immature, and all of which spend a large percentage of their resources on defending their so-called sovereignty. The sovereign nation-state, especially where it is small, weak and helpless, must, therefore, give way to larger regional communities.

In this world of regional communities, as also in the world of nation-states, the West has an important part to play. However the world is organized, the Western states would together constitute the richest and the most powerful part of it. It is all for the good of mankind that they are rich and powerful, for they are also humane and liberal. The United States and Great Britain—the two powers which form the core of the Atlantic Community—acting with or without

Europe, should develop and maintain a position of such preponderance in the world as to rise above the rivalry of nations and the struggle for power. Having gained such power, they should use it to serve the cause of peace, freedom and justice, to promote the rule of liberty under law. They should help and guide the underdeveloped peoples in their pursuit of the good things of life. In short, they should take the world under their wing. While Anglo-America, backed by irrestibile force, regulates the rivalries of nations, maintains peace and order in the world and shapes its destiny, the illiberal powers would play the role of an opposition party in the "empire." The opposition, ready to exploit discontent and eager to unseat the ruling aristocracy, would serve to keep the latter on the path of liberalism and disinterestedness. A benevolent Anglo-Saxon—that is to say, Anglo-American —dictatorship over the whole or the greater part of the world is, next to a genuinely democratic world state, the best thing that could happen to mankind.

In the view of Walter Lippmann, such is the course of man's journey toward the good society.

Idealism versus Realism

The preceding pages should suggest that Lippmann is neither a Machiavellian realist nor a Wilsonian idealist. What is he? A superficial reader of his works would tend to agree with some of his harsh critics that far from being "The Great Elucidator," he is an "Obfuscator de Luxe" and an equivocator who can be "quoted on either side of almost any question." Let us place in close juxtaposition his statements on some of the controversial issues in the theory and practice of international politics:

The man who rebels against the "dumb affections" which constitute his sense of nationality becomes a restless, homeless wanderer, an interloper. Yet, we are told, he should rebel against them, for they represent his first and uncivilized nature.

The principle of national self-determination is barbaric. The nation-state is not only an anachronism but also a perversion of the natural and ideal order of things; men should all live in one commonwealth and not in separate "civic republics." At the same time, we learn that the continued survival of this same nation-state is the first and foremost concern of national governments.

The rivalry of nations and the struggle for power between them are "criminal." They must be abolished. They cannot be abolished, and it is the moral duty of every state to participate actively in the international struggle for power.

Americans rightly distrust power politics. They rightly believe that security and serenity require a universal order of equal laws, and can never be had in a mere equilibrium of sovereign states. It is the major error of American thinking on foreign affairs that a nation can ignore or escape power politics. In the interest of their own security and serenity, and to defend the survival and independence of their allies, Americans must establish and maintain a global equilibrium of power vis-à-vis the Soviet Union.

These propositions have all come from the pen of Walter Lippmann. On the face of it, they do seem to contradict each other. Yet when we consider them closely we cannot but discover that their incompatibility is more apparent than real. It will be noticed, for instance, that the statements under review fall into two distinct groups, based on two major propositions about the nature of man—one normative and the other positive. The ethical goal for the development of human personality is maturity, which is the stage where man's reason governs his conduct. Reason is the supreme authority in the ideal state of human affairs. Since the dictates of reason are universally identical and valid, its authority must be coextensive with mankind. The creation of a world state which is ruled according to the law of reason —or, in other words, the Law of Nature and of Nature's God—must then be the ultimate ideal of all rational men. It is in the context of this ideal that nationalism is barbaric, the rivalries of nations are criminal, and the balance of power is the structural principle of public order in the good society.

But we cannot move toward the cherished goal unless we manage also to keep alive, for dead men walk only in ghost stories. The makers of policy should not lose sight of the ultimate ideal. But their policies will not contribute to its achievement if they are not workable. They will not be workable if they ignore the immediate reality. When we look at the immediate reality we find that the majority of men are immature, that they do not reason, that the desires of individuals and groups conflict with the desires of other individuals and other groups, and that often they seek to realize their desires by the use of force. Since survival is a prerequisite of progress toward the ideal, a policy which imperils survival, and with it the prospect of progress toward the ideal, is not only inexpedient and unwise but also immoral. We must not, as T. H. Green would say, risk social chaos and wreck the existing system of law and order for the sake of adding a new element to it. In the context of human nature as it is, in a world where rivalry and strife are a fact, survival cannot be ensured unless power is confronted with power, unless it is checked and balanced.

Realism in international politics entails more than making alliances and maintaining a favorable balance of power against the adversary. It refers also to that state of intellectual maturity which persuades us to give up that which is valueless to hold and that which cannot be held. During the post-World War II period, Lippmann, calculating that the West is not powerful enough to compel the unconditional surrender of the communist world, has urged settlement of outstanding issues through negotiation, compromise, give and take. At various times, he has proposed: withdrawal of all foreign troops from Germany; Western withdrawal from West Berlin so that it may become a "free city" under international protection; American withdrawal from Europe so that Europeans may direct their own destiny; American withdrawal from Formosa, Laos, and South Vietnam. He has urged that a greater part of Europe, Africa and Asia should become neutral in the cold war. He has advised the United States government not to attempt to overthrow the communist, anti-United States regime of Fidel Castro. He has suggested not only that Latin America can no longer be a sphere of influence of the United States but that Europe should be involved in Latin America so as to make it the "three-legged stool" that it was during the nineteenth century when the British navy actually supported the Monroe Doctrine. He is even somewhat apologetic for his country being far more rich and powerful than other countries are. All this adds up to a long list of recommended withdrawals.

Is Lippmann afraid of his nation's own power, uncomfortable at the prospect that it may be used in a fight? Probably not, but he is cautious. Concerned with maintaining a balance between ends and means, he has repeatedly criticized the "containment policy" of the United States as an extravagant over-extension of this nation's foreign commitments. We have seen that Lippmann is especially averse to American commitments in Asia. He seems to think that the problems of freedom, stability and security in Asia are beyond American resources in military power, material wealth and knowledge. Moreover, Americans are not the arbiters of human destiny all over the world. Helping Asia and Africa should be a joint Western enterprise.

Apparently, Lippmann is not entirely unaware that recommendations of retreat are subject to criticism. Not long ago, he invited those "who shout 'Munich'" at every proposal of withdrawal to read the following paragraph in Winston Churchill's book, *The Gathering Storm*:

Those . . . who are ready to fight whenever some challenge comes from a foreign power have not always been right. On the other hand, those whose inclination is to bow their heads, to seek patiently and faithfully for peaceful compromise, are not always wrong. On the contrary, in the majority of instances they may be right not only morally but from a practical standpoint. How many wars have been averted by patience and persistent goodwill! Religion and virtue alike lend their sanction to meekness and humility, not only between men but between nations. How many wars have been precipitated by firebrands! How many misunderstandings which led to wars could have been removed by temporizing! How often have countries fought cruel wars and then after a few years of peace found themselves not only friends but allies!

We should note also that in Lippmann's theory of the balance of power one must concede that there may be at least a modicum of reason in the position of the adversary. One's own side does not necessarily have a monopoly of truth and justice.

The Principle of Aristocratic Government

We can view the issue of idealism versus realism with reference to Lippmann from another angle too. It will be seen that while his psychology and his political policy are generally grounded in realism, his political philosophy has an unmistakably idealistic base. If the war of conflicting impulses within the individual is not checked, it will paralyze him. To do anything, and especially to do good, he must bring his "irascible and concupiscible powers" under the "royal and politic rule" of reason. If the ability and the propensity of unreasoning men to realize their desires by the use of force are not restrained, the world would become the scene of a perpetual war of every man against every other man. The need to prevent such a war arises from the moral necessity to protect each man's right to live a good life. The protecting agency is the state. But the rulers of the state cannot protect the aforementioned right unless they understand the nature and the principles of the good life, unless they comprehend the moral order of the universe—unless, in other words, they are able to reason rightly. Government is then a duty which devolves upon men who can reason. The majority of men cannot reason, and therefore majorities cannot claim to have an inherent or immutable right to rule. Only a few in society are able to reason, and it follows that these few should rule the state.

Lippmann thus arrives at a principle of government which is aristocratic rather than democratic. Here again there is a mingling of idealistic and realistic premises. The principle of aristocratic government is based on the assumption, taken from psychology, that the majority of men do not reason, and on the premises, borrowed from moral philosophy, that freedom means the freedom to do good and that the rights of man are all reducible to the right to live a good life. The principle under discussion holds good for the government of a world state as well as for the government of the nation-state.

Gradualism

Lippmann's procedure is typically British. He is a conservative and a gradualist. His advice on some of the major problems in the fields of theory and policy bears out this conclusion. Here are a few instances: The United Nations should devote itself to the "arts of peace" and educate the member states in the virtues of cooperation before it handles the issues of international peace and security; the emergence of a world community and a world patriotism must precede the creation of a world state; the sense of unity and of a common destiny must be sharpened before Europe may unite.

Lippmann also shares with the British their proverbial distaste for plain, clear-cut, unequivocal and binding arrangements. The Atlantic states constitute a community for war and peace. They must have a common strategy and a common diplomacy. But "organic consultation" and a "habitual exchange of views" are all they need have to ensure the formulation of common military and foreign policies. Lippmann takes the design of the Commonwealth as the model for the Atlantic Community. No wonder then that neither of them is an operative force in international affairs. Despite Lippmann's flattering references to it as a "great power," the Commonwealth is, in the power-political sense, a nonentity. The ties between the Dominions and the "mother country" are gradually breaking: the former look to the United States rather than to Great Britain for their defense in a future conflict. One cannot but think that the Commonwealth would be a powerful influence in world politics today if instead of being a loose and informal connection it were an organically united entity, if it were, let us say, a federation. That informality, looseness and ambiguity do havoc to the Atlantic Community as conceived by Walter Lippmann is evidenced by the fact that in that conception its membership sometimes consists of forty-two states—the entire Western world —and sometimes of only two—Great Britain and the United States.

Lippmann's "united Europe" is not far different from his Atlantic Community. Its hallmarks are looseness and vagueness. Sometimes it is a federation of the whole of Europe, at other times it is a federation of Western Europe, and still at other times it is anything but a federation. More often than not, it means merely the end of the present division of Europe at the Elbe. Lippmann has written countless articles advocating the creation of a "European system"—a phrase that could hardly be called self-explanatory. After months of research his reader discovers that the phrase "European system" means merely the withdrawal of foreign troops from Europe and leaving the problem of European unity to France and Germany. Again, Lippmann's reader knows that the fate of Europe depends on Franco-German reconciliation. But he does not know what would be most likely to promote it. The only enlightenment he receives from Lippmann on the subject is that the rest of the world, especially the United States, should leave France and Germany alone to discover for themselves how best they can become friends and partners in the business of Europe. The net result of this noncommittal and ambiguous approach to the problem of European unity is that in the writings of Walter Lippmann Europe hardly ever seems to unite.

Lippmann and the Classics

It should be apparent that the hue and color, the tone and temper of Lippmann's political philosophy are distinctly classical. His assumptions about human nature, his premises concerning the moral end of human existence, his view of the state as a partnership in virtue, his definition of statesmanship in terms of judicial disinterestedness, his concept of freedom as the freedom to do good, his distrust of popular democracy, his principle of aristocratic government, are all Greek concepts—Platonic and Aristotelian, to be more precise. From among the modern political thinkers, the influence of Burke on Lippmann is clearly visible. Burke's philosophy, in turn, is also classical.

Lippmann's contribution to contemporary political thought lies essentially in his attempt to revive a tradition which is going out of vogue in the modern world and especially in the United States. It lies in his criticism of some of the questionable premises of popular democracy, in his reassertion of the supremacy of reason and of the principle of aristocratic government in individual, national and international affairs, and in his call for a restoration of the vital connection between faith and reason.

Lippmann's theory of international politics is predominantly British. The influence of Hobbes and Hume is apparent in his discourses on the "realities" of international relations—the conflict of interests, the rivalries of nations, the struggle for power, and the mechanism of the balance. His emphasis on the ultimate identity of human interests, the need for a universal order of equal laws, the desirability of establishing a Commonwealth of Man bears the imprint of English idealists such as T. H. Green, as well as of Kant, the Fathers of the Church and the Stoics. We should look for Lippmann's contribution to the study and understanding of international politics in his attempt to rehabilitate a time-honored but lately unpopular approach to international relations. He has tried to give his idealistically inclined readers a needed dose of political realism. He has sought to awaken them to a consciousness of what the world of sovereign states actually is, and in so doing he may have awakened some of them to a consciousness of what it should be.

Writings of Walter Lippmann

Select Bibliography[1]

Books

Lippmann, Walter. *American Inquisitors.* New York: Macmillan Co., 1928.
———. *The Cold War.* New York: Harper and Bros., 1947.
———. *The Coming Tests with Russia.* Boston: Little, Brown and Company, 1961.
———. *The Communist World and Ours.* Boston: Little, Brown and Company, 1958.
———. *Drift and Mastery.* New York: Henry Holt and Co., 1914.
———. *Essays in the Public Philosophy.* Boston: Little, Brown and Co., 1955.
———. *The Good Society.* Boston: Little, Brown and Co., 1937.
———. *Interpretations 1931-1932.* Allan Nevins (ed.). New York: Macmillan Co., 1932.
———. *Interpretations 1933-1935.* Allan Nevins (ed.). New York: Macmillan Co., 1936.
———. *Isolations and Alliances.* Boston: Little, Brown and Co., 1952.
———. *Liberty and the News.* New York: Harcourt, Brace and Howe, 1920.
———. *Men of Destiny.* New York: Macmillan Co., 1927.
———. *The Method of Freedom.* New York: Macmillan Co., 1934.
———. *The New Imperative.* New York: Macmillan Co., 1935.
———. *The Phantom Public.* New York: Harcourt, Brace and Co., 1925.

[1] Exclusive of Walter Lippmann's column "Today and Tomorrow" in the New York *Herald Tribune* from 1931 to 1963.

349

———. *The Political Scene.* New York: Henry Holt and Co., 1919.

———. *A Preface to Morals.* New York: Macmillan Co., 1929.

———. *A Preface to Politics.* New York: Mitchell Kennerley, 1913.

———. *Public Opinion.* New York: Macmillan Co., 1922.

———. *The Stakes of Diplomacy.* New York: Henry Holt and Co., 1915.

———. *U.S. Foreign Policy: Shield of the Republic.* Boston: Little, Brown and Co., 1943.

———. *U.S. War Aims.* Boston: Little, Brown and Co., 1944.

———. *Western Unity and the Common Market.* Boston: Little, Brown and Company, 1962.

Articles

Lippmann, Walter. "Acquisition of the British Naval Bases," *Congressional Digest,* Vol. 20 (January, 1941).

———. "Albert the Male," *New Republic,* Vol. 7 (July 22, 1916).

———. "America and the World," *Life,* Vol. 8 (June 3, 1940).

———. "The American Destiny," *Life,* Vol. 6 (June 5, 1939).

———. "America's Great Mistake," *Life,* Vol. 11 (July 21, 1941).

———. "The Anglo-American Job," *Life,* Vol. 34 (March, 1953).

———. "Assuming We Join," *New Republic,* Vol. 7 (September 3, 1919).

———. "The Atlantic and America," *Life,* Vol. 10 (April 7, 1941).

———. "Awareness of the Danger," *Time,* Vol. 37 (April 28, 1941).

———. "Big Businessmen of Tomorrow," *American Magazine,* Vol. 117 (April, 1934).

———. "Big Four and World Peace," *Newsweek,* Vol. 24 (August 21, 1944).

———. "Break-up of the Two-Power World," *Atlantic,* Vol. 185 (April, 1950).

———. "Britain and America," *Foreign Affairs,* Vol. 13 (April, 1935).

———. "The Case for a Smaller Army," *Readers Digest,* Vol. 39 (November, 1941).

———. "The Case for Wilson," *New Republic*, Vol. 8 (October 14, 1916).

———. "The Deepest Issue of Our Time," *Vital Speeches*, Vol. 11 (July 1, 1936).

———. "Defects in the Presidential Succession System," *Congressional Digest*, Vol. 26 (January, 1947).

———. "The Defense of the Atlantic World," *New Republic*, Vol. 10 (February 17, 1917).

———. "The Economic Consequences of a German Victory," *Life*, Vol. 9 (July 22, 1940).

———. "For a Department of State," *New Republic*, Vol. 20 (September 17, 1919).

———. "The Four Policemen," *Vital Speeches*, Vol. 10 (December 15, 1943).

———. "How to Enforce International Agreements," *Readers Digest*, Vol. 48 (April, 1946).

———. "The Indispensable Opposition," *Atlantic* (August, 1939).

———. "Integrated America," *New Republic*, Vol. 6 (February 19, 1916).

———. "Issues of 1916," *New Republic*, Vol. 7 (June 3, 1916).

———. "Liberty and the News," *Atlantic*, Vol. 124 (December, 1919).

———. "The London Naval Conference," *Foreign Affairs*, Vol. 8 (July, 1930).

———. "Man's Image of Man," *Commonweal*, Vol. 35 (February 13, 1942).

———. "Mare Nostrum," *Forum*, Vol. 106 (July, 1946).

———. "Moral Test in North Africa," *Time*, Vol. 41 (January 4, 1943).

———. "The Most Dangerous Man in the World," *Saturday Review* (August 23, 1947).

———. "Mr. Kahn Would Like to Know," *New Republic*, Vol. 35 (July 4, 1923).

———. "Needed: A Joint Plan," *Forum*, Vol. 105 (February, 1946).

———. "One World of Diversity," *Vital Speeches*, Vol. 13 (December 15, 1946).

———. "The Outlawry of War," *Atlantic*, Vol. 132 (August, 1923).

------. "Pacification for Peace," *Atlantic*, Vol. 174 (December, 1944).

------. "The Peace Conference," *Yale Review*, Vol. 8 (July, 1919).

------. "The Point of No Return," *Readers Digest*, Vol. 53 (May, 1951).

------. "The Problem of Germany," *Current History*, Vol. 4 (June, 1943).

------. "The Permanent New Deal," *Yale Review*, Vol. 24 (June, 1935).

------. "Philosophy and United States Foreign Policy," *Vital Speeches*, Vol. 14 (February 1, 1948).

------. "The Providential State," *Atlantic*, Vol. 158 (October, 1936).

------. "Reckoning: Twelve Years of Republican Rule," *Yale Review*, Vol. 21 (June, 1932).

------. "Rise of Personal Government in the United States," *Vital Speeches*, Vol. 3 (May 1, 1937).

------. "The Rivalry of Nations," *Atlantic*, Vol. 181 (February, 1948).

------. "Rough-Hew Them How We Will," *Foreign Affairs*, Vol. 15 (July, 1937).

------. "Scholar in a Troubled World," *Atlantic*, Vol. 150, (August, 1932).

------. "Security," *American Magazine*, Vol. 119 (May, 1935).

------. "Should the President Resign," *Senior Scholastic*, Vol. 49 (December 2, 1946).

------. "The State of Education in this Troubled Age," *Vital Speeches*, Vol. 7 (January 15, 1941).

------. "Two Conventions in Perspective," *Vital Speeches*, Vol. 2 (July 15, 1936).

------. "Uneasy America," *New Republic*, Vol. 5 (December 25, 1915).

------. "Unrest," *New Republic*, Vol. 20 (November 12, 1919).

------. "Vested Rights and Nationalism in Latin America," *Foreign Affairs*, Vol. 5 (April, 1927).

------. "Waging World Peace," *Vital Speeches*, Vol. 13 (June 15, 1947).

------. "Wake up America," *Readers Digest*, Vol. 37 (July, 1940).

———. "War or Measures Short of War," *Readers Digest*, Vol. 38 (January, 1941).

———. "Washington Notes," *New Republic*, Vol. 5 (January 29, 1916).

———. "The Weapon of Freedom," *Life*, Vol. 9 (October 28, 1940).

———. "What Modern Liberty Means," *Atlantic*, Vol. 124 (November, 1919).

———. "What Program Shall the United States Stand for in International Relations?", *Annals of the American Academy of Political and Social Science*, Vol. 66 (July, 1916).

———. "The White Passion," *New Republic*, Vol. 8 (October 21, 1916).

———. "Why the Voice of America Should be Abolished," *Readers Digest*, Vol. 63 (August, 1953).

———. "Why Should the Majority Rule?", *Harpers*, Vol. 152 (March, 1926).

———. "The World Conflict in its Relation to American Democracy," *Annals of the American Academy of Political and Social Science*, Vol. 72 (July, 1917).

———. "A Year of Peacemaking," *Atlantic*, Vol. 178 (December, 1946).

Index